Disenchantment

the Guardian and Israel

Disenchantment

the Guardian and Israel

Daphna Baram

**Guardian
Books**

First published in 2004 by Guardian Books
Guardian Books in an imprint of Guardian Newspapers Ltd

Copyright © Daphna Baram

The right of Daphna Baram to be identified as author of this work has been
asserted in accordance with section 77 of the Copyright, Designs and Patents
Act, 1988.

The Guardian is a registered trademark of the
Guardian Media Groups Plc and Guardian Newspapers Ltd

A CIP record for this book is available from the
British Library

ISBN 1 84275 119 0

Distributed by Politico's Publishing, an imprint of Methuen Publishing Ltd,
215 Vauxhall Bridge Road, London SW1V 1EJ

Printed in Great Britain by Cambridge University Press

Cover Design: Two Associates
Text Design: www.carrstudio.co.uk

Contents

In memory of Inbal Perlson, Yohanan Lorwin and Elias Garesi, a secular Israeli, a Hassidic Jew and a socialist Palestinian, who were swept away by a flood when travelling together in a Judaea desert wadi in January 1999. Their lives, and their death, symbolised all we could have been but never came to be. The flood that took them away seemed to have taken with it every shred of reason and decency from our home.

Foreword

THE publication of this book could not be more timely. The breakdown of the Oslo peace process in the summer of 2000, the outbreak of the al-Aqsa intifada, the violence, and the bloodshed have all combined to keep the Israeli-Palestinian conflict constantly in the headlines. Following the rise to power of a hard-line Likud government under the leadership of Ariel Sharon, more and more of the blame for this dismal state of affairs has been laid at Israel's door. At the same time there has been an upsurge of anti-semitism in Europe, giving rise to a new debate as to whether anti-Zionism can be distinguished from anti-semitism. The Guardian, with its extensive coverage of the Middle East conflict, has been at the centre of this debate. Official Israeli spokesmen and Israel's friends in Britain have repeatedly accused the Guardian of an anti-Zionist and in some cases even of an anti-semitic bias in its reporting and comment on the conflict. These are very grave charges.

The book in front of us is an admirable achievement, combining extensive research with searching analysis. The scope of the inquiry is extremely broad, covering the period from the first world war to the present. Moreover, in a field that is pervaded by partisanship and polemics, the author remains strikingly objective and fair-minded. The result is a book that is not only detailed and highly informative but also one that displays consistent intellectual integrity. In addition, the book is written with a keen sense of drama which helps to turn it into a gripping story about the Guardian's involvement in the Zionist saga and about the trials and tribulations of covering the Israeli-Palestinian conflict.

Daphna Baram is eminently well-qualified to undertake this difficult task. She is an Israeli journalist with extensive experience as a news editor. She came to Oxford in 2002 as a Reuters Foundation Fellow and produced an excellent paper on the Guardian's coverage of the battle of Jenin, a particularly contentious episode in Israel's reoccupation of the West Bank

9

in the spring of that year. A year as a Senior Associate Member of St Antony's College enabled Ms Baram to develop this case-study into a full-scale book. In the book she uses a wide range of sources to very good effect. The sources include the Guardian's archive and numerous interviews with journalists involved in covering the Middle East for the paper.

One of the great merits of this book is that it is not confined to current controversies but traces the evolution of the Guardian's position on the conflict over a whole century. Special attention is paid to the role played by successive editors and the general picture that emerges is one of deep and consistent support for the Jews in their struggle to achieve independence and to consolidate it. There are fascinating accounts of CP Scott, who was instrumental in securing the Balfour Declaration, of WP Crozier, who turned the paper into a tool of Zionist advocacy in the 1930s and early 1940s, and of Alastair Hetherington (1956-1975), who translated his personal support for Israel into a strong editorial line. Other editors were less partial to Israel; none of them was hostile.

The great watershed was the June 1967 war which enabled Israel, for the first time in its history, to trade land for peace. It gradually emerged, however, that Israel was more interested in land than in peace. The Guardian continued to show understanding of Israel's security dilemma but at the same time kept emphasising that a peaceful resolution of the conflict with the Arabs would be in Israel's best long-term interest. As Israel failed to heed this advice and persisted in the policy of creeping annexation of the Palestinian territories, disenchantment set in. The main landmarks in this process were the invasion of Lebanon in 1982, the first intifada, the second intifada, and the rise to power of Ariel Sharon.

Disenchantment with Israel is not unique to the Guardian. It is widely shared by liberals and leftists in Britain and Europe who shifted from a sympathetic and supportive attitude towards Israel to a highly critical one. Nor should disenchantment with the hard-line policies of specific Israeli governments be taken to imply the questioning of the country's basic legitimacy. One can fully accept Israel's legitimacy within the pre-1967 borders while opposing its colonial project beyond the green line. That is my position, and that is probably the Guardian's collective position if one can talk of a collective position in so democratic and pluralistic a newspaper.

The main purpose of this book is to trace the evolution of the Guardian's attitude towards the Zionist movement and the state of Israel. The book is the story of the liberal newspaper's predicament. Inevitably, the conflict with the Palestinians features very prominently in this story but the focus is on Israel. Ms Baram's style is direct and forthright and she does not avoid even the most sensitive of issues. She recognises at the outset that some readers would expect this book to clarify the question of whether the Guardian is an anti-semitic newspaper. Her answer to this question could not be more categorical: it is not. A more interesting question is whether the Guardian has become an anti-Zionist newspaper in recent years. This question is explored with a wealth of material and with great insight in the final chapter of the book.

The Israeli-Palestinian conflict is one of the most intense, bitter, and protracted international conflicts of modern times. Anyone who writes about it runs the risk of getting caught in the cross-fire between the two warring sides. The Guardian is no exception. People on both sides of the Israeli-Palestinian divide have accused the Guardian of hostility, misrepresentation, and malice. Accusations of bias and distortion from the Israeli side have grown steadily more vehement and vitriolic in recent years. Ms Baram subjected these accusations to critical scrutiny in the light of all the available evidence and found them to be largely baseless. What struck her most in the course of her research is the inordinate time and effort devoted by the staff of the newspaper to ensure accuracy, balanced reporting, and fairness to both sides. Given that this is only one issue out of a wide range of domestic and international issues which the paper has to cover on a daily basis, this level of thoroughness and responsibility is all the more impressive. No less impressive are the paper's openness and responsiveness to its readers. Ms Baram is to be congratulated on having produced a remarkable book about a remarkable newspaper.

Avi Shlaim
St Antony's College, Oxford
June 2004

Preface

IN October 2002 I came to Oxford as a fellow of the Reuters foundation programme at Green College to write a paper about the Guardian's coverage of the second intifada and battle of Jenin. I didn't know much about the newspaper. Echoes of a vociferous internet campaign against the Guardian were heard in Israel, and the director of the Israeli government press office was interviewed by my paper, Kol Haír, and launched a brutal attack on the Guardian's Jerusalem correspondent, Suzanne Goldenberg. Vain as only a Jerusalemite news editor can be, I assumed that the Guardian, while probably not anti-semitic, must have been a bit lazy about the facts. This, I thought, combined with the paper's critical position, was the formula that enraged Israeli officials.

But even before I came to Oxford I discovered that none of the Guardian's opponents in Israel had any grievance over the factual content of the paper. "They just don't like us," was the common description by would-be experts.

A couple of months later, while I was sitting talking to the editor of the Guardian, Alan Rusbridger, in his office, he told me that the Guardian had always supported Zionism. "I'm sure you know of the story of CP Scott, Chaim Weizmann and the Balfour Declaration," he said. I nodded knowledgably, and, grateful for my inability to scribble in English, wrote in my notepad, in Hebrew, "find out who CP Scott is. Urgent". Rusbridger, it seems, assumed that every Israeli knew that Scott was the person to whom Zionists are indebted for the Balfour Declaration.

This conversation set me on a fascinating journey starting at the Firs in Manchester, where Scott, the legendary editor and proprietor of the Manchester Guardian, entertained Zionist leaders and prominent politicians in the early years of the 20th century. My path led me through the close cooperation between a later editor, WP Crozier, and the Jewish

Agency during the 1930s, the courageous conduct of Guardian correspondents in Europe during the Holocaust, the pained disillusionment of Alastair Hetherington, the paper's editor from 1956 until 1975, over the fading dream of peace in the Middle East, and the angry and bitter disappointment of the paper with Israel during the invasion of Lebanon in 1982 and the first intifada of 1987.

This process was not unique to the Guardian. The liberal left in Britain and all over Europe had made similar journeys of disenchantment over Israel. Developments in the Guardian were nearly identical to those in the British Labour party, which shifted from unequivocal enthusiasm for Israel, "the great socialist experiment", in the 1940s, to a split on the question of Zionism after the 1967 war, and a grave, almost uniform, sense of disgust during the 1980s. These changes are often viewed as an outcome of changes in the nature of Israel itself after its occupation of the West Bank and Gaza in 1967, but they are also deeply connected to a revision of Zionist history and a re-evaluation of the moral implications of the Jewish national project in Palestine.

This book could be read as the tale of the left and Israel, but the Guardian has its special traits and rights. With a combination of almost colonial white-man's-burden commitment and deep-rooted liberal values, its staff still regard the Balfour Declaration as a guideline. They strive to find the right place between the promise for a "national home for the Jews in Palestine", and the obligation that the rights of the "other religious groups" should not be prejudiced. Colin Schindler of London University wrote that the Guardian mirrored faithfully the "confusion on the British left", but in my opinion the paper had actually gone a few steps ahead, and pioneered new notions about Israel and the Middle East conflict over the years, as I hope this book demonstrates.

After Green College I took up an associate membership at St Antony's College, and while I absorbed myself in the adventures of past Guardian journalists in my homeland, the world was in turmoil. The initial campaign of accusations against the Guardian had relaxed only to be surpassed by a fresh combination of the charge of anti-semitism against all critics of Israel including the Guardian, and a real concern among Jews worried by signs of a growing hatred in Europe towards Israel which sometimes went beyond politics and was manifested by hostility towards Jews as collective representatives of Israel's policies. The implications of this new situation, deeply related to the era of the "global war on terrorism", the invasion of Iraq, Ariel Sharon's policies on Palestine and a sense of alarm within the Jewish community, are discussed in chapter 11.

Methodologically, this is not a "media" book. There are no charts in it, and it is outrageously free of concepts such as "focus groups". It is a book by a journalist who loves newspapers, and is addicted to politics and preoccupied with the pain of her homeland. The parts of it I like best border on a Fleet Street novel, and the personalities and tensions of the Guardian supply many such moments, in the past as well as in the present.

Since much of the book discusses bias, or allegations of bias, I feel obliged to acknowledge my own biases, which are numerous, hoping that while probably not cancelling one another out, they may have helped me develop a complex outlook on the questions I have examined. First, this is a book about the Guardian commissioned and published by Guardian Books. Readers would be right to bear this in mind, while hopefully judging it on its merits. I believe that letting an Israeli journalist into the paper, exposing its people, documents and internal debates to her and letting her poke her crude sabra fingers into the painful wound of the Guardian's relations with Israel and the Jewish community, was a courageous act. Nobody in the Guardian interfered in my writing or tried to confine my steps. This is only to be expected from a newspaper with the Guardian's tradition, and still the frankness, the willingness to engage in hard questions and soul-searching demonstrated by all in the Guardian, impressed me deeply.

Another bias derives from my perspective as an Israeli. I came to Oxford from Jerusalem where I had lived all my life, following three hard years as a weekly magazine news editor in this hurt, bleeding and beloved city. Day in and day out I had to send young reporters to the killing fields that used to be our city centre. Week after week I had to push important municipal or political stories into the inside pages to make space for an atrocity that hit a crowded restaurant, a wedding party, a bus, or the very café I was hoping to go to for a relaxed drink once the paper was put to print.

And yet, many Israelis and Zionist Jews would question my love of my home. I have been a supporter of the Palestinian struggle against oppression and occupation ever since I can recall, and have striven to promote turning Israel into a state of all its citizens, Jews and Palestinians alike. My torn and tortured community includes Jewish Israeli friends and neighbours who leave work every afternoon to convey their children directly home from school, protecting them from using the bus; Palestinian friends and neighbours of Israeli citizenship, who can't decide what scares them more when they go to the shopping mall, a bombing, or a brutally offensive security check combined with racist comments from passers-by; and Palestinian friends and neighbours of the West Bank, now behind the monstrous wall, half a mile away from my house, who struggle to feed their children under constant curfew, and do not feel safe in their own beds, fearing an air raid at any moment.

Some readers may expect this book to clarify the question of whether the Guardian is an anti-semitic newspaper. I can unburden you from any further reading by saying straight away: it is not. The allegation is offensive and lacks any basis. A more interesting question is whether it is an anti-Zionist newspaper, and again, and somewhat to my surprise, I discovered that it is most certainly not. It is a paper that clung in the very early days of the Zionist movement to the doveish tendency of the Israeli Labour party and refused to let go, even years after that tendency had vanished, and after the Labour party itself had dwindled into a phantom institution in Israeli politics. The Guardian has always been obsessed with the question of Israel-Palestine, carries a burden of guilt and responsibility for its part in its creation, and constantly seeks ways to get it right. This book is the story of its predicament.

The major part of chapter 10 has been re-edited from my paper on Jenin; and the appendix on Jenin consists of a section of that paper.

I owe a debt of gratitude to so many people, without whom this book could have never been written. I cannot possibly mention them all here, but there's no harm in trying.

Professor Avi Shlaim who invited me to St Antony's College, supervised me voluntarily, listened to me patiently, pushed me back on track whenever I meandered, read all my chapters with his hawk eye, and treated me with the utmost kindness.

Alan Rusbridger, who kindly endorsed this project and let me roam around 119 Farringdon Road and harass him and his staff with endless queries.

My editor, Michael McNay, for knowing just what it takes to bring an exhausted and anxious writer back to life, and for struggling with my eccentric turn of phrase.

The people of the Guardian, who were generous with their time and frank with their thoughts, Seumas Milne, Ewen MacAskill, Simon Tisdall, Ian Mayes, Ian Katz, Brian Whitaker, Martin Woollacott, Chris McGreal, Suzanne Goldenberg, Ian Black, Harriet Sherwood and Linda Grant. Special thanks to Jonathan Freedland, whose great help and engagement turned him into "the reader in my head". Our conversations and debates were in my mind throughout writing.

Michael Adams, for sharing his story and his archive with me.

Lisa Darnell of Guardian Books who carried this project through.

The people of the Guardian Newsroom archive, Luke Dodd, Gavin McGuffie and Sian Wynn-Jones, who went out of their way to help my research.

James Peters from the John Rylands Library at Manchester University and Dr Bill Williams of the University of Manchester.

Brian Klug of St Bennet's Hall, Oxford, for enjoyable brainstorming sessions.

The Reuters Foundation programme and its staff in Oxford, Jenny Darnley and Paddy Coulter, who took great care of me at the early stages of this adventure, and made me feel at home in Oxford long after I ceased being a Reuters fellow. Special thanks to all the Reuters fellows of 2002-03 year.

My special readers, my father Haim Baram and my friend Diego Crenzel, who read everything I wrote with care and thoughtfulness and contributed helpful comments and endless encouragement.

Mimi Baram, for her friendship and generous contribution.

Oz Shelach and oznik.com, for technical, emotional and intellectual support.

To all my friends in Oxford, London, Jerusalem, Tel Aviv and around the world, who fed me to cheer me up, poured drinks into me to cheer me up further, introduced me to new places and people, answered the phone at 3am, had me over for weekends, let me crash out in their houses, posted me wonderful presents, put up with passive smoking and endless lecturing about the Guardian and Israel, fixed my treacherous computer, brought me cheap cigarettes from Ben Gurion airport, suffered in silence my fits of sulking and mess in the living room, and were the sweetest group of people on earth. Those who say that writing books is a solitary job know not what they are talking about.

And to my mother, Shula Baram. She knows what for.

Daphna Baram
Oxford
May 2004

CHAPTER ONE

Making Righteousness Readable

Introduction to the Guardian

T HE Manchester Guardian, as it was called until 1959, was established as a radical paper on May 5, 1821, and it takes a pride in its radicalism to this day. Its founder, John Edward Taylor, the son of a Presbyterian minister who became a Quaker after the French revolution, was a political reformer who freelanced for various Manchester newspapers. Two years before he first published his own paper he had achieved some fame for his coverage of what was to be known ironically as Peterloo after the triumph of arms by Wellington over Napoleon only three years before.

The year 1819 had seen growing political agitation over the under-representation in Parliament of the rapidly growing industrial heartlands of the midlands and the northern districts of England. Industrial interests, not least the cotton manufacture of the north-west, demanded free trade, cheap imported corn to feed the workforce and to keep labour costs low, and also to enable the corn exporting nations to import Manchester cotton. The interests of the rising middle-classes and of the working classes were broadly similar; but the interest of the English landowning classes was in protected trade and high corn prices; and the landowning classes not only held parliamentary power but wielded it in their own interest. More than half the boroughs returning MPs to the House of Commons were in rural Wiltshire. One of them, Old Sarum, was not even a village. Radical activists in Leeds, Birmingham, and Manchester initiated meetings for the election of "shadow MPs" to represent the manufacturing towns. These protests passed off peacefully in Birmingham and Leeds, but on August 16, 1819, the Manchester meeting in St Peter's Fields ended catastrophically. The organisers had invited the popular orator Henry Hunt to speak. The magistrates panicked and called out the special constables with the armed regular cavalry and the yeomanry, largely manned by Tory youngsters, also armed, some hot-headed, to arrest Hunt. The troops found themselves hemmed in by the crowd of up to 60,000, drew their sabres, killed 11 unarmed demonstrators and injured around 400, including 100 women. John Tyas, the reporter for the London Times, was arrested and Taylor, anxious to get the story into the London papers, sent a report to the Times from which the leader writer drew the facts for his column before Tyas was released and able to file his own report; the Times's coverage turned Peterloo overnight from a negligible occurrence in the north into a national scandal.[1]

During the subsequent autumn and winter Taylor thoroughly researched and wrote a close analysis of Peterloo in a pamphlet called Notes and Observations. In it, he insisted on using a dry and factual narrative, and only at the end was moved by the triumphalist behaviour of the yeomanry into an overtly passionate statement: "That waving of swords I saw, those cheers I heard, and the sight and sound smote heavy on my heart." The Guardian's first historian, David Ayerst, recognised the manner of the pamphlet, a "combination of much cool, deprecating observation with occasional, vehement protest", as a characteristic of the future Guardian.[2]

The success of the report and Taylor's growing enthusiasm for moderate reform, together with Parliament's repressive Six Acts outlawing further public demonstrations of more than 50 people, prompted his friends to put together a loan of £1,050 to found a new local weekly newspaper. And so, in the Manchester Guardian's first edition, Taylor's leader outlined a mission statement for the new publication: "For ourselves, we are the enemies of scurrility and slander [...] we hope so to deliver them [pointed animadversions on public questions — Ayerst's paraphrase] that even our political opponents shall admit the propriety of the spirit in which they are written, however fundamentally they may differ from their own principles and views."[3] The new paper, in line with its middle-class liberalism, sought readers "among the classes to whom, more especially, advertisements are generally addressed."[4] So that hasn't changed.

Despite its rebellious origins at Peterloo, the Manchester Guardian was to be, for the first 50 years of its existence, a moderate and pragmatic publication. To survive in a market in which there were already six other well-established Manchester weeklies Taylor needed to make his paper different. Four of the six were Tory papers, so that was no problem, but two were, like the upstart Manchester Guardian, liberal and in favour of parliamentary reform. Taylor knew that the population of Manchester was growing fast. "We were formerly a community of manufacturers," he wrote; "we have now [...] become also a community of merchants," and it was to this new merchant class that Taylor aimed to sell his paper, proposing support for whichever political party at any time produced the measures to forward the causes of reform without violence and liberty, civil and religious.[5]

By the time Taylor died in 1844 his marketing hunch had paid off (nearly a century and a half later the Guardian's financial pages still published the daily Manchester cotton prices). He was succeeded by his printer, business manager and reporter Jeremiah Garnett and, on Garnett's retirement in 1861, by Taylor's son, (John) Edward Taylor. But the young Taylor was heavily involved in an ultimately successful battle with the postal and telegraph services to win lower costs for the special needs of the press, which involved spending most of his time in London. So he looked for someone to take over the editorship in Manchester. He picked his young cousin, Charles Prestwich Scott, fresh out of Oxford, for the job. In 1872, at the age of 25, CP Scott became the editor of the Manchester Guardian, and was to keep this position for the next 57 years, in the process turning a local newspaper into a journal of international renown. From the very beginning Scott was the patriarch of the Guardian, and his piercing eyes under thick eyebrows still watch everybody who enters the Guardian building in London from Epstein's bronze bust in the glass-fronted archive opposite. After Edward Taylor's death in 1904, Scott bought the Manchester Guardian, and became proprietor as well as editor; under him it rediscovered its radical roots.

His editing style was autocratic. "There is but one God, and Mohammed is his prophet. CP's idea of an editor was that he had both functions,"[6] wrote the great labour historian and Guardian leader writer JL Hammond. At the Guardian's centenary dinner, Lord Robert Cecil described CP Scott's work as "making righteousness readable".[7] Scott took the Guardian from a political position on the right of the Whigs and moved steadily to the left. Between 1895 and 1905 he was a Liberal Member of Parliament, a position that gained him invaluable political influence and connections for years to come. David Lloyd George, who was to become prime minister, was Scott's close friend and confidant.

Scott saw the role of a newspaper as "a public organ servicing the community as directly as a department of the civil service and under a sense of responsibility equally strong".[8] Scott's reporters spent nights in the slums with sick children, and the paper exposed social deprivation; politically it supported independence for Ireland and women's suffrage.

But it was the Manchester Guardian's stance on the Boer war that made the paper hugely controversial at the turn of the 20th century, and set the benchmark, professionally and morally, for generations to come. In April 1899, six months before the war broke out, the Guardian dedicated numerous articles to warning that the diamond-rich imperialist Cecil Rhodes and his business partners were trying to drag Britain into a war in the service of their capitalist and expansionist ambitions in Africa, in direct confrontation with the Boer farmers, who had already been forced into retreat beyond Natal. The Guardian warned its readers that in the war that might erupt, the army and politicians would turn into "troopers of Mr Rhodes".[9]

Rhodes had purchased control of most of the British South African press, and during the war the Manchester Guardian relentlessly opposed what it considered the warmongering newspapers in South Africa and in Britain — Alfred Harmsworth's new-born ha'penny Daily Mail ("All the news for half the price") was already into its flag-waving jingoistic stride — as well as attacking the British government and antagonising a broad swath of public opinion. The Guardian's effort to disclose to its readers the realities of South Africa was invaluable. Its coverage culminated in Emily Hobhouse's exposure of the devastating conditions in British concentration camps for Boers. Hobhouse was deported from South Africa and returned to England under military guard, but continued to break the news with stories obtained from local informants.[10]

The Guardian was swamped by furious letters imbued with the patriotic spirit of a country at war. Readers protested at what they saw as the paper's defeatism and its insults to the British fighting man. Many declared that they would stop taking the paper. But simultaneously, letters poured into the Manchester Guardian's Cross Street offices from London, where liberal readers were looking in vain for an anti-war paper. Those London readers either demanded the Manchester Guardian in the capital, or begged for the launch of a London edition. "You are the only Liberal newspaper left in Britain,"[11] wrote one reader. This phenomenon, of a protest-motivated decline in Manchester readership, followed by an increase in London-based readership, was to repeat itself years later, when the Manchester Guardian took a similarly unpopular stance over the Suez war in 1956.[12]

CP Scott retired from the editorship in 1929. In the period after the deaths in 1932 of both Scott and his son Ted, who had succeeded him, his surviving heirs became concerned for the future of the Guardian. Takeover would have ruined its aims as a newspaper (Lord Beaverbrook, the proprietor of the Daily Express and cheerleader for the British empire, was interested in buying); ruinous death duties could have killed it. And so in 1936 John Scott, CP's surviving son and managing director of the Guardian, divested himself of the ownership of the paper and set up the Scott Trust as sole proprietor,[13] "as a device to ensure the continuity and editorial independence of the Guardian newspaper in the spirit imposed on the paper by its founder".[14] The trust itself went on record in 1992 with a statement of its purpose, which was "to secure the financial and editorial independence of the Guardian in perpetuity; as a quality national newspaper without party affiliation; remaining faithful to its liberal tradition; as a profit-seeking enterprise managed in an efficient and cost-effective manner".[15] In pursuance of this the trust appoints the company chairman and the Guardian editor. The only instruction ever given to the editor is to carry on the paper "in the same spirit as heretofore".[16]

A chain of editors, whom Ayerst refers to as "the guardians", each had to deliver his own interpretation to the spirit of those resonant yet laconic words, "the same spirit as heretofore". During the 1930s the Guardian exposed the first violent attacks on German Jews by the Nazis, and later described the conditions in the concentration camps. Its stance was vehemently anti-Nazi, and it ardently opposed Neville Chamberlain's appeasement policy towards Adolf Hitler. In 1953, at the coronation of Queen Elizabeth II, the newspaper enraged many of its readers by publishing David Low's cartoon mocking the extravagance of the event while Britain was only just emerging from wartime food rationing and so many of its people were impoverished.

In 1959 the Manchester Guardian dropped Manchester from its title, and in 1961 it started printing in London as well as in Manchester. In 1964, Alastair Hetherington (editor 1956-75), moved to the London offices, thus finally shifting the paper's centre of operation to the capital, though it retains a strong connection with its native city, and the northern editions are printed in Manchester.

The Guardian's radical liberal tradition became so strongly entrenched, and the empowerment of writers in the paper was so forceful, that it survived even under a mainstream editor like Hetherington. During the 1960s staff vehemently opposed his decision to switch editorial policy to supporting the American war in Vietnam. They protested again in the 1970s over editorial support for the internment of suspects in Northern Ireland.[17] The never-ending internal debate over the paper's position on Israel is merely part of a long-lasting tradition: staff members have been as often as not involved in internal rifts, out of their commitment to what they regard as Guardian ideology.

The current editor, Alan Rusbridger, takes pride in this historical continuity. "The paper that once campaigned against the British concentration camps in the Boer war exposed the Serbian detention camps in Bosnia a century later. The same paper that revealed the slave wages paid by British firms in South Africa under apartheid led the international campaign for debt relief in the 1990s."[18] Rusbridger explains how the instruction "to carry on in the spirit as heretofore" materialises: "In recent times, this has involved giving a voice to republicans, to dissidents, to public servants and to prisoners, among others. After the calamity of September 11, 2001, it opened its pages to Muslims, rabbis, Afghans, poets, warmongers and peaceniks."[19] The mission of "giving a voice to the voiceless" received a fascinating interpretation when the Guardian published an article by a convicted paedophile, on the basis, strongly defended by Rusbridger (see chapter 11) that society needs to understand even such taboo subjects as this to engage with them.

The columnist Madeleine Bunting has outlined the principles of liberal journalism and how they are practised in the Guardian.[20] The first responsibility of a liberal newspaper, she wrote, should be to challenge and bring to account those exercising power. "The most striking and dramatic instance of this principle in the last decade," she continued, "was the paper's series of court cases over allegations of sleaze."[21] The Guardian exposed 10 MPs who were paid to raise parliamentary questions,[22] and deciphered the relationship between personal business interests and national politics in bringing to light the Jonathan Aitken affair, which culminated in imprisonment for perjury of the former chief secretary to the Treasury and defence procurement minister after his libel action against the Guardian and Channel 4 television spectacularly imploded.[23] The paper did not hesitate to probe the New Labour government with similar zeal, exposing the Peter Mandelson scandal, in which the architect of New Labour resigned over a loan of £373,000 from his fellow minister, Geoffrey Robinson, to purchase his Notting Hill home.[24] In addition, said Bunting, "the Guardian's traditional remit to challenge over power no longer solely lies in Westminster but increasingly in the company boardroom".[25] The Guardian conducts an annual survey of directors' pay,[26] and, unlike newspapers which are addicted to publishing admiring lists of the richest people in the nation, it provides a "giving list",[27] which examines how a range of large companies tackles philanthropic and social responsibility programmes. The paper also advocates electoral and constitutional reform, and calls for the abolition of the monarchy.

The second liberal principle Bunting outlines is giving a voice to "those who are often excluded or marginalised in public debate";[28] and the third principle involves promoting public debate, manifested, for example, in extensive examinations of such issues as genetically modified food, gene patenting and the growth of the internet. Other examples are the paper's backing for the participation of Sinn Fein in peace negotiations, and the post-September 11, 2001, debate on America and Islam.[29]

Beyond the daily practice of liberal principles, Bunting argues, the Guardian also has its own political agenda, at the heart of which is a commitment to social justice.[30] Issues of social deprivation receive major allocations of space, whether it is inner-city violence or the campaign for debt relief to developing countries or the running sore of the Israeli-Palestinian conflict.

And yet, adhering to liberal values, or being regarded as a liberal, seem to mean different things at different times. Some of the more left-leaning Guardian readers were dismayed in 2003 to discover that their paper was hesitant over the war against Iraq. Soul-searching in the leader column — the unsigned opinion of the paper — and attempts to stress the importance of achieving UN support for any move against Iraq, replaced the single-mindedness and ideological coherence of the anti Boer war and anti-Suez campaigns. Although columnists who opposed the war were published in the opinion pages, some disappointed readers found refuge with the Independent, which opposed the war vehemently. Rusbridger explained that the Guardian's policy on the Iraq war was influenced mainly by the government's declared conviction, allegedly relying on intelligence sources, that Iraq might indeed have possessed weapons of mass destruction.[31]

Throughout these travails of the 90s and into the new century the Guardian has maintained, with occasional wobbles, a circulation of around 400,000 copies of the print edition (there is also a website with an international readership running into millions). The newspaper and its readers have developed an intimate relationship over the years, unique even in Britain, where a person is often defined by choice of a newspaper. "A Guardian reader" has become a social definition, describing an educated, liberal with a small l, middle-class consumer.

"The traditional Guardian readers see any contemporary editorial board as a mere custodian of their paper," explained Ian Mayes, the Guardian readers' editor, or ombudsman.[32] "A newspaper without a proprietor," wrote Alan Rusbridger, "has only one relationship that matters — with its readers. Any journalist working for the Guardian soon realises that those who buy and read the paper have a strong sense that they are its true owners. The bond is one of trust based on broadly shared values."[33]

The interaction between the readers and their paper takes various forms. In addition to the traditional format of letters to the editor, Mayes was the first readers' editor on a British newspaper to whom readers turn with complaints about the content of the Guardian. "When they argue with the paper, even when they are extremely angry with it, they are still arguing within the spirit of the paper," says Mayes about the readers of the print edition.[34] Mayes runs a daily item on the leader page called Corrections and clarifications, and he writes a weekly column, in which he addresses some of the more complex issues, running from the nature of caricatures to even minor questions of political correctness, such as whether people in their 60s should be described as elderly. He presents the debate and reaches a conclusion, sometimes agreeing with the complainant, sometimes disagreeing, and occasionally leaving the question open.

Sometimes Mayes acts as the reader's "agent" in the paper, though he would disagree with this definition. One of his columns was dedicated to a detailed account of a staff meeting in which the paper's policy on the looming war with Iraq was discussed.[35] "The editor never intervenes in the content of my column, even when it is not convenient for the paper. I don't regard myself as representing the readers in front of the paper, or the other way around. It is my job to listen to the readers and relate to their complaints."[36] Mayes answers most of them personally.

The paper also reaches out to readers through lectures, public meetings, debates and discussion forums in which Guardian staff and contributors often take part. The creation in 2002 of the Newsroom, the archive and visitor centre of the Guardian and its sister Sunday paper, the Observer, with free entry to its exhibitions, lectures and online historical material, has opened another door between the paper and the public, not least schoolchildren, who can among other things gather news and make up newspaper pages on screen in special workshops organised for them in a dedicated schoolroom.

The Guardian's readership has grown immensely since the launching of the website, Guardian Unlimited, in April 1999. According to Adam Freeman, head of commercial development, Guardian Unlimited has approximately 6 million users a month.[37] But the huge new readership does not necessarily share the old unwritten convention which exists between the Guardian and its print readers. "The internet totally changed the rules of the game," says Mayes. "For nearly 200 years this paper had a very defined readership, constructed of liberals. The internet has added into our readers' circle millions of people. Some of them are foreign to the Guardian and to the traditions of the British media."[38]

Many of the new readers are American, who are used to a totally different journalistic tradition. They often complain that the newspaper is not "objective", a term that, as will be shown in the next chapters, has different connotations in Britain. Foreign readers seldom share the British tradition of subtlety when addressing newspapers in writing: the language of some of the emails filling the mailbox of the readers' editor is appalling. The Guardian has been introduced to the phenomenon of internet campaigns, which unleashes orchestrated attacks over issues such as its treatment of Israel. "This is a new reality that we have to get used to, and it is developing very fast," says Mayes, "I think nobody has all the answers for how to deal with it yet."[39]

CHAPTER TWO

Early Days

CP Scott and the Balfour Declaration

CP Scott, Jacob Epstein, 1926

W HEN Chaim Weizmann encountered CP Scott, at a charity party in Manchester in the autumn of 1914, he had no idea who the old man with the impressive beard and blue, penetrating eyes could be. Weizmann, master of small talk and diplomacy, discovered that the stranger was intrigued by his Zionist ideas and the zeal with which he expressed them. Scott invited Weizmann to his office the next day; it was the beginning of a fruitful friendship, at least for Weizmann and the Zionists.

Weizmann, who was to become the first president of the state of Israel, was born in the village of Motol in Russia in 1874. He had studied chemistry in Switzerland at the universities of Fribourg, where he obtained his doctorate, and Geneva. He came to England from Switzerland in 1903, tired and frustrated by the split in the Zionist movement between those known as Ugandists, who favoured a home for the Jews in the British protectorate of Uganda, and the Zionists of

Zion, who insisted that only a charter to go to Palestine could solve the Jewish predicament. The so-called Ugandists were horrified by the pogroms against the Russian Jews and were seeking an immediate solution, relying on the support of the British and reinforced by the active support of Theodore Herzl, the legendary founder and president of the Zionist movement. Weizmann himself was convinced that there was no alternative to Palestine, since in his opinion it was impossible to recruit Jews to join the Zionist movement unless it led them to the promised land, the cradle of their cultural and religious tradition.

Palestine, ruled at the time by what Scott would later describe in a leader as "the vast Ottoman tyranny", seemed almost unreachable, so the Ugandists were willing to opt for second best in Africa. After the split, Weizmann felt that there was nothing left for the time being to do in the Zionist movement, and he moved to Manchester with his future wife Vera to continue his research in chemistry at the university until circumstances became favourable to engage in Zionist politics once again.

But he could not stay away from politics for long. His reputation as a Zionist went before him and a lively group of ardent Manchester Zionists welcomed him with admiration. There were between 10,000 and 15,000 Jews in Manchester by the beginning of the 20th century, leading a vibrant social, political and cultural life. The Zionists were not yet a majority among them, but they were energetic and determined, and they regarded Weizmann, who had been a delegate to all Zionist congresses after the second in 1898, as their mentor.

The initial meetings between Scott and Weizmann left them mutually impressed. Scott concluded that Weizmann commanded the two essentials of genuine statesmanship, a "rare combination of the idealistic and the severely practical". What struck him, he wrote, was first the perfectly clear conception of Jewish nationalism — an intense and burning sense of a Jew as a Jew; just as strong, perhaps more so, as that of the German as a German or the Englishman as Englishman — and, secondly, arising out of that, necessary for its satisfaction and development, his demand for a homeland, which for him, and for anyone sharing his views of Jewish nationality, could only be the ancient home of his race.[1]

Weizmann found Scott, "so unaffected, so open, so charming that I simply could not help pouring out my heart to him. I told him of my hatred for Russia, of the internal conflicts of the Jews, of our universal tragedy, of our hopes and aspirations for Palestine, of the little we had already done there, and of our almost messianic dreams — such as they appeared then — of the future".[2] Following that meeting, Weizmann wrote gratefully to Dear Mr Scott, as he always addressed him:

> In conclusion allow me to thank you heartily for the kindness you
> have shown to me and for the patience with which you have
> listened to my perhaps somewhat voluminous talk. It is the first
> time in my life I have 'spoken out' to a non-Jew all the intimate
> thoughts and desiderata, you scarcely realise what a world of
> good you did to me in allowing me to talk out freely. In this cold
> world we 'the fanatics' are solitary onlookers, more especially
> now. I shall never see the realisation of my dream — 'the 100 per
> cent Jew' — but perhaps my son will see it. You gave me courage
> and please please forgive my brutal frankness. If I would have
> spoken to a man I value less, I would have been very diplomatic.[3]

The Guardian's historian David Ayerst noted that Scott responded with surprise to Weizmann's Zionist ideas, strangely at first sight, since many of them had been espoused in his own newspaper for years by members of the local Zionist group, among them the Manchester Guardian reporters, Harry Sacher and Henry Sidebotham, and the news editor, William Crozier. Sacher was Jewish, and an ardent Zionist. In 1907 he was dispatched, alongside Weizmann himself, to cover the seventh Zionist congress for the Guardian. Sidebotham, a military correspondent and a zealous imperialist, was convinced that a Jewish entity in Palestine would serve the British interest in the Middle East. Other influential members of Weizmann's circle, also known to Scott, were the young Jewish businessmen Israel Sieff and Simon Marks, who took Marks & Spencer from small beginnings to high street success.[4]

Journalists, however, might find Scott's Zionist revelation less intriguing. It is not uncommon that one's editor incidentally meets "a source" and discovers some great truth that has seemed to escape him beforehand, no matter how often it has been mentioned in his own paper. Whatever the case, the Zionists on the Manchester Guardian's staff found no reason to complain about the new interest their editor and proprietor took in their cause.

The Guardian's interest in the Jewish community preceded Zionism. The paper had welcomed the wave of new immigrants, mainly from Russia, who settled in Manchester during the 1870s and 1880s. It seems that it consciously took on the mission of introducing the Jewish community to local readers, while incorporating the new arrivals into its circulation. During 1881, for example, the Guardian published 11 articles on the persecution of Jews in Russia (out of 40 articles about Jewish affairs in general). The subject remained a main theme in the Jewish coverage of the Manchester Guardian in the late 19th century and early 20th century. It was accompanied by reports covering the lives of Jews in other parts of Europe, mainly Germany, and a number of stories exploring the lives of Jews in Morocco. The paper took to describing Jewish holidays and festivals,[5] following the construction of new synagogues and Jewish schools in Manchester[6] and informing the readers of political and cultural events within the crystallising community.[7]

Zionism and Zionist activity were covered favourably from the very early days. In 1880, which is widely considered to be the birth of Zionism, marked by the publication of YL Pinsker's book, *Autoemancipation*, the Manchester Guardian published a piece about Palestine, in which it noted a Jewish aspiration to reclaim it.[8] In 1891 it was already reporting Jewish settlements in Palestine.[9] Zionist congresses were reported from the first, in Basel in 1897, and coverage grew in the years following. In 1900 nine articles were dedicated to the Zionist congress in London and its implications.[10] The Manchester Guardian followed the creation of the Jewish Colonial Trust,[11] Zionist fundraising events[12] and the break between the Ugandists and the Zionists of Zion.[13]

Coverage of Zionism was concentrated in the news pages; a first leader column on the subject appeared only in 1907 and for some time remained a rare event. In 1913 Sacher's report from the Zionist congress emphasised the takeover of the movement by the "practical Zionists" (Herzl's opponents, including Weizmann and Sacher himself).[14] He devoted a few paragraphs to the discussions about the construction of a Hebrew university in Jerusalem (an old vision of Weizmann's). In presenting the argument between the advocates of German as the language of study (German Zionists) and the supporters of Hebrew (mainly Russian Zionists), Sacher stated: "Hebrew is the language of Palestine."[15] Thus, by the time Scott himself became involved with Zionism, his newspaper was supporting this movement, mostly by the comprehensive coverage of its activities, but also through the interest of staff Zionists implicitly taking sides in the quarrels between Weizmann and his opponents in the movement.

Weizmann's and Scott's mutual enchantment was soon to be translated into more practical terms. Weizmann noted: "Scott carries great weight and he may be useful".[16] Scott placed all his impressive political contacts at Weizmann's disposal: "I would like to do something for you. I would like to put you in touch with the chancellor of the exchequer, Lloyd George," he wrote, and added: "You know, you have a Jew in the government, Mr Herbert Samuel." Weizmann was keen on meeting Lloyd George, but much less so on making the acquaintance of Samuel, who had been chancellor of the duchy of Lancaster and postmaster general, and would become home secretary and, from 1920-25, high commissioner for Palestine. To Scott's suggestion Weizmann reacted, by his own account, almost rudely: "'For God's sake, Mr Scott, let's have nothing to do with this man.' I thought, on general grounds, that Herbert Samuel was the type of Jew who by his very nature was opposed to us. It will be seen that I was mistaken."[17]

Whenever Scott came up to London on the night train from Manchester, Weizmann would meet him at Euston for breakfast. Weizmann reported that Scott's usual greeting to him would be, "Now, Dr Weizmann, tell me what do you want me to do for you." But on the morning of December 3, 1914, Scott simply announced: "We're going to have breakfast at nine o'clock with Mr Lloyd George."[18]

Weizmann felt the time was right to start negotiating with the British government. The way the world war was developing indicated that the colonies of the collapsing Ottoman empire, including those in the Middle East, were likely to fall, at least in part, into the hands of Britain and France. The new rulers, Weizmann guessed, might view the idea of a Jewish charter to Palestine more favourably. He described his intentions clearly in a letter to Scott:

> Don't you think that the chance for the Jewish people is now within the limits of discussion at least? I realise of course, that we cannot 'claim' anything, we are much too atomised for it, but we can reasonably say, that should Palestine fall within the sphere of British influence and should Britain encourage a Jewish settlement there, as a British dependency, we could have in 25-30 years about a million of Jews out there, perhaps more; they would develop the country, bring back civilisation to it, and form a very effective guard of the Suez canal and — perhaps be a valuable protection against an aggression from Constantinople. I need not dwell upon all the possibilities. I have only put down the minimum, Palestine can easily become an Asiatic Belgium in the hands of the Jews.[19]

This breakfast meeting went well, far beyond Weizmann's expectations, in spite of the bewilderment caused by his ignorance of English understatement. "I was very very serious-minded," he reminisced 35 years later, "did not quite appreciate English humour, and did not understand at first that behind this seeming flippancy there was a deadly seriousness."[20] Lloyd George was there, as well as Samuel Wedgwood, a Liberal MP and grandson of Josiah Wedgwood, the famous 18th century Staffordshire pottery proprietor. By 1924 he had joined Labour and was to distinguish himself as the first guilty party in a divorce action to become a member of the cabinet. Weizmann discovered that they all viewed Zionism favourably. He had what he called "the surprise of my life", when he heard that Samuel had adopted his ideas. "Messianic times have really come," he reported about his conversation with Samuel to his wife Vera. "The first thing 'we' shall build, he said, is a Jewish university. He told me that his programme is more ambitious than mine."[21] Lloyd George was highly impressed with Weizmann. "When you and I are forgotten," he told Samuel later, "this man will have a monument to him in Palestine."[22]

Lloyd George suggested that Weizmann should meet Arthur Balfour, who had been Conservative prime minister from 1902 until 1905. "Weizmann needs no introduction, I still remember our conversation in 1906," was Balfour's response to the idea of a meeting. The 1906 encounter, while Balfour was visiting Manchester, generated a couple of Weizmann's most memorable lines. He was trying to explain to Balfour why so many Zionists rejected the Uganda proposal. "Suppose I was to offer you Paris instead of London, would you take it?" he asked. "But Dr Weizmann, we have London," retorted Balfour. "That is true," said Weizmann, "but we had Jerusalem when London was a marsh."[23] Weizmann purported to be speaking on behalf of millions of Jews. Balfour argued that the Jews he met were quite different. "Mr Balfour, you meet the wrong kind of Jews,"[24] said Weizmann. Their second meeting in 1914 led to a friendship which, in 1917, when Balfour was foreign secretary in the Lloyd George wartime coalition government, reached a climax with the Balfour Declaration promising the Jews a national home in Palestine. But the political road to that coveted charter was still tortuous.

Scott took his role as Weizmann's political and personal sponsor seriously. He kept introducing him to leading politicians, bringing him along to breakfasts at Whitehall, and opening for him doors he could never have hoped to enter without the assistance of his patron. Scott's political effort to invoke a declaration of support by the British government to Zionist aspirations in Palestine lasted all through the first world war, and became more and more vigorous towards its end, as General Allenby's troops were marching towards the promised land.

Scott, reputed to be a man of shrewd political instincts, was extremely careful not to overuse the Manchester Guardian as a tool in this campaign, though Zionist matters leapt from time to time from the news pages to the leader column. In 1915, shortly after his first encounter with Weizmann, Scott wrote a long leader that was clearly influenced by his new friend. Scott described the plight of the Jews, scattered among nations, and reacted enthusiastically to Zionism, which he portrayed as "an effort of the Jewish spirit to establish a firm ground for its own continuance and development in a changed world".[25] Regular articles in support of Zionism appeared in the Manchester Guardian between 1915 and 1917, but Scott's policy was to keep advocacy of Zionism low-keyed, to avoid embarrassing the government.

The Zionists on the Guardian staff found an outlet for their ideological commitment in the pages of *Palestine*, a weekly magazine published by the British Palestine committee, an organisation founded by Sidebotham and Sacher. *Palestine* aimed to rally influential public opinion behind Zionism.[26] As a Guardian staff member, Sidebotham asked Scott's permission to run the committee. It seems he felt that strong persuasion was needed. Sidebotham explained that he would attend to his duties as the committee's director in his free time, and that it would not engage him more than any other hobby he might take on. He stressed that his activity was not only compatible with the Guardian's editorial line, but was in full agreement with it.[27] Scott yielded. He even joined the Palestine committee. But unlike his successor Crozier, Scott made it clear that his personal and political support did not mean that Zionists could regard the Manchester Guardian as their own private backyard. The journalistic duties of staff members had to come before their political activity. Once he politely but firmly declined Weizmann's request to grant Sacher leave from the Manchester Guardian to attend a Zionist conference.

Palestine incorporated the young Zionist group of Manchester. Sidebotham chaired the committee and wrote most of the articles, Sacher was the editor and an occasional contributor, Sieff and Marks, the successful businessmen, wrote and provided funds. The group members were young and passionate, even fanatical. Maximalist in their demands, they sometimes spelt trouble for Weizmann. The issue of *Palestine* of February 15, 1917, opened with an article called The Boundaries of Palestine, which delineated the borders of the desired Jewish homeland in a way that even the most radical 21st century Israeli rightwinger wouldn't dare dream of. It started north of Sidon, moved conveniently eastwards to include Damascus, Hauran, and farther territory on the eastern side of Jordan river, and ended somewhere north of Aqaba.

All hell broke loose. Weizmann and Nahum Sokolov, a journalist and Zionist activist, were negotiating at the time with a foreign office senior official, Sir Mark Sykes. The article infuriated Sykes. He explained to Sokolov that too much public emphasis on the idea of British control of Palestine could do harm by intensifying French opposition. Neither Weizmann nor Sokolov were aware of the secret agreement signed by Sykes and the French negotiator, François Georges Picot, carving up the Middle East between Britain and France. According to the agreement, later to be altered, the northern parts of Palestine were to be under French influence. Hence Sykes's angry reaction.[28]

Weizmann did his best to mollify Sykes and called his Manchester soldiers to order, only to discover that the young zealots were out of control and rebelling against the voice of political caution. Weizmann discovered that the initial article was written by Semuel Tolkowsky, who was now fuming over the additions made to his proposed boundaries by Sidebotham. Sidebotham admitted to allowing his geographical imagination to run wild. Sieff, in response to Weizmann's letter of inquiry, answered that he was convinced that Sykes was more interested in his courtship of the Arabs than in Zionist aspirations in Palestine. Therefore, however much Sykes might object to articles in *Palestine* there could be no question of giving way, since it was the British Palestine committee's "holy duty to combat an Arab Palestine". Adding insult to injury, Sieff defiantly advised Weizmann to hint diplomatically "that you are not responsible for the hot-headed youth of the BPC", and that objections should be addressed directly to the committee. Weizmann and Sokolov attended a meeting of the committee, attempting to clarify their grievances. Sidebotham admitted that including Damascus might have been provocative. Sacher alone refused to yield, and eventually it was agreed that Sidebotham and Tolkowsky should seek an interview with Sykes to clarify matters.[29] Scott never intervened in this affair, nor in the contents of *Palestine* in general. As long as Sidebotham and Sacher were kept under control in their writings for the Manchester Guardian, he was content.

Apart from introducing Weizmann to the corridors of power and acting as his advocate for Zionism in private to statesmen, Scott was deeply engaged in making high-ranking politicians view Weizmann and his ideas favourably. In 1915 Weizmann, who had maintained his work in chemistry, discovered bacillus BY, a way of producing large quantities of acetone in a short time. Acetone was a vital component in the British munitions industry and was increasingly needed for the war effort. Conveniently enough, Lloyd George was appointed minister of munitions in 1915 and Balfour became first lord of the Admiralty. Scott had no problem marketing the bacillus BY to those two friendly cabinet members, and Weizmann moved to London and took charge of the technical work.

Whitehall civil servants treated him with great suspicion. To them, he was a foreign scientist, jealously guarding his work from prying eyes "as though a conspiracy were afoot to steal his secrets".[30] Scott soon discovered that taking care of Weizmann's scientific ventures involved more than he had bargained for. Weizmann swamped him with letters complaining about ill-treatment. Scott, ever loyal, never failed to address Lloyd George, who swiftly intervened on Weizmann's behalf. After severe clashes between Weizmann and Lord Moulton, the director general of explosives supplies in the Ministry of Munitions, Lloyd George, once again prompted by Scott, clamped down firmly on Moulton. Moulton had actually prevented Weizmann from going to a conference on munitions in Paris by refusing to arrange a visa, and then even refusing to return the passport.

Lloyd George told Scott and Weizmann of his dealings with Moulton over breakfast. Scott confided to his diary: "Lloyd George gave an amusing account of his encounter with Lord Moulton and his chief assistant, Sir F. Nathan, being also present. He had been furious about the withholding of Dr Weizmann's passport which he had handed to them to be visa'd and which they then refused to return, told them it was monstrous to treat a distinguished scientific man who was giving his best service to the country in that way and ended up by saying 'if you offer me your resignation I shall accept it', but they didn't offer it."

Scott was touched by Lloyd George's emotional response to Weizmann's plight. "What evidently had enraged him particularly was that they should treat Weizmann, as a Jew and a foreigner, in a way they would not venture to treat a man in a different position. That is the generous side of Lloyd George."[31] Scott wrote of Moulton, "I was surprised to find such small a man (so he appeared to me) in so great a position".[32] As for Weizmann, he seemed to take the intervention for granted: "Once more you settled a point and it was high time that you should settle it, as the importance of it cannot be underrated," he wrote to Scott.[33]

Weizmann kept grumbling. He regretted his earlier promise to give up any payment from the government for his contribution until the end of the war. He started demanding money, and could find no responsive ear but Scott's. The historian Tom Segev remarks, "While Weizmann was sending Scott to intervene on his behalf with the empire's ministers, these men, responsible for more than 400 million subjects, had in excess of 8 million soldiers at the front."[34] Scott continued to badger Lloyd George, Arthur Balfour and anybody else involved, and managed to get the government to pay Weizmann £50,000 for his work.

If Scott was disturbed by Weizmann's endless complaints and demands, he never revealed it, at least not in writing, and Scott was more than capable of expressing discontent when he was moved to. More of his correspondence with Weizmann of that period concerns Weizmann's problems with the Ministry of Munitions than the Zionist political struggle, but nothing was too much trouble for Scott. Ayerst explains: "Scott felt that Weizmann had performed a notable service for the country, and he felt that his personal honour was at stake in having advised Weizmann to trust implicitly in the honour of the British government."[35] This is possible, of course, but it seems to go farther than that. Weizmann and his friends touched a soft spot in Scott's heart. Scott, often referred to by Weizmann as "the old man in Manchester", was in his 60s when he became involved with Zionism. Weizmann was in his early 40s, Sacher in his 30s, Sieff and Marks in their 20s. Scott was a father figure to them all.

When Weizmann was struggling with a committed opposition in the Zionist movement Scott was there to console him. "You are the only statesman among them",[36] he wrote. Other members of the Zionist group also benefited from Scott's attention to their personal matters. In the 1920s Sacher moved to Palestine for a few years, and ran a law practice there. His Zionist enthusiasm did not go so far as to let his own child be educated by the pioneering system of Hebrew education. In a letter to Scott he asked for help to gain his young son entry into Rugby school, to which Scott had sent his own son (and successor as editor), Ted. CP Scott wrote to the head master of the school, and was able to inform Sacher that his son would be welcomed there. Sacher thanked him warmly, and wondered whether he might agree to do the same favour for Simon Marks's son. Scott did.[37]

In April 1917 Scott was informed by a French colleague of the Sykes-Picot agreement broadly allocating the previous Turkish holdings of Syria to France and Mesopotamia to Britain. He immediately leaked the information to Weizmann. Weizmann was stunned. It became sharply clear to him what was holding back his own negotiations with Sykes, although, unlike many of his comrades, he didn't feel cheated by Sykes. "He was, in effect, modifying his stand in our favour, seeking to revise the agreement so that our claims in Palestine might be given room," wrote Weizmann, who had no doubt that Sykes was bound to secrecy on this matter by his government.[38] But the revelation, as the end of the war approached, made it clear that time had come for the Zionists to increase their political efforts if they were to seize the historic moment. Arab interests in the Middle East began to be heard, though still faintly. Sykes himself was a great supporter of Arab independence as well as a committed Zionist. He did not think that Arab claims clashed with the Zionist goals, but Weizmann was suspicious on this point. "I cannot help feeling that he considers the Zionist scheme as an appendage to the bigger scheme with which he is dealing, the Arab scheme," he wrote to Scott.

The Zionists rejected any notion of French control over Palestine, though Weizmann found the idea of combined British and American rule possible. He made it clear to Sykes and his assistant, Sir Robert Cecil, that he was aware of the Sykes-Picot agreement, and resented it. An energetic round of discussions with Lloyd George, Balfour, Samuel and other Zionist-friendly ministers insured that the cabinet supported a British commitment to a Jewish entity in Palestine. On November 2, 1917, when General Allenby, commander-in-chief of the expeditionary force against Turkey, had yet to reach Jerusalem, the Jews in Palestine constituted less than 10 per cent of its population. Sykes emerged from the cabinet session and handed a document to Weizmann, who was pacing nervously back and forth in the corridor. "Dr. Weizmann, it's a boy," he announced.

The declaration, as was previously agreed between Balfour and Weizmann, was sent in the form of a letter to Lord Rothschild, as spokesman for the Zionist movement:

> His Majesty's government view with favour the establishment in Palestine of a national home for the Jewish people, and will use their best endeavours to facilitate the achievement of this object, it being clearly understood that nothing shall be done which may prejudice the civil and religious rights of the existing non-Jewish communities in Palestine, or the rights and political status enjoyed by Jews in any other country.[39]

The Balfour Declaration (though it also veiled the British purpose of keeping the French at a distance from the Suez canal) was the greatest Zionist diplomatic achievement. It paved the way, though not without difficulties, to the United Nations resolution on the partition of Palestine 30 years later, and the founding of Israel. For the first time in history, Zionist ambitions were recognised by an international colonial superpower, and the organised immigration of Jews to Palestine was promised protection. The British government had thereby committed itself to support the colonisation of Palestine by Jews.

The loopholes in the declaration were to haunt the British government for years to come. Every sentence in it contains ambiguities. The Zionists were unhappy with the vague expression "a national home", and with this home being designated as "in Palestine", rather than the whole of Palestine designated as the national home. They were also far from happy to have the non-Jewish communities mentioned in "their" declaration.

The Arabs, as more than 90 per cent of the population, naturally hated the declaration, which acknowledged their civil and religious rights but blithely ignored their political right. The declaration also ran counter to the promise made by a British negotiator, Sir Henry McMahon, of Arab statehood as a reward for their participation in the war against the Turks. The Arabs claimed that Palestine was included in that future Arab state. The British government disputed this interpretation.

A minority in the cabinet opposed the declaration. Prominent among them was the only Jewish cabinet minister at the time, Edwin Montagu, who feared that a Jewish nation would compromise the rights of Jews in their countries of residence. He considered Zionism to be a "mischievous political creed, untenable by any patriotic citizen of the United Kingdom". Anti-Zionists like Montagu were by no means a minority. Lord Curzon, the colonial secretary, was troubled by the declaration's implications for the Arab population. "How was it proposed to get rid of the existing majority of Mussulman inhabitants and to introduce the Jews in their place?" he asked in cabinet.[40]

Curzon's question was precisely that which both the Zionists and the British government were trying to obfuscate. Not so much because they had a plan, but rather because each of these organisations separately wanted to delay the answer for as long as possible. Most Zionists believed that the Arabs of Palestine could be bought out and persuaded to leave. They underestimated Arab commitment to the land, but the Balfour Declaration had prompted the creation of the Palestinian national movement, and violent resistance to Zionism was soon to follow. In 1922 the League of Nations awarded Britain the dubious honour of operating a Palestine mandate and during the years until 1948 when Britain quit Palestine, successive governments managed as a matter of convenience to shift between even-handed dealing with the Jews and Arabs of Palestine and towards a more pro-Zionist position. The intentional ambiguity of the Balfour Declaration enabled such shifts, but the dual commitment proved irreconcilable.

"Well — I didn't like the boy at first. He was not the one I expected," Weizmann wrote about the infant handed to him by Sykes, "but I knew that this was a great event." He telephoned his wife but Scott, it seems, received neither a telephone call on this day, nor a courtesy visit. Weizmann's vast correspondence does not include a cordial letter of thanks to his patron dated from the days or weeks following the declaration. This did not prevent Scott from openly rejoicing in the great achievement of the Zionists. On November 9, 1917, when the declaration was made public, it was proudly carried on the main news page of the Manchester Guardian. Scott wrote a long leader, Palestine and the Jews, which expressed his deepest feelings in ringing tones. "It is at once the fulfilment of an aspiration, the signpost of a destiny," he wrote. He argued that without a national home the Jews would never have security. "The example of Armenia and the wiping out of a population fiftyfold that of the Jewish colonies in Palestine was a terrible warning of what might at any time be in store for these." Of the Arabs, Scott wrote only: "The existing Arab population in Palestine is small and at a low stage of civilisation. It contains within itself none of the elements of progress, but it has its rights, and these must be carefully respected."[42]

After years of caution, Scott now felt that the Manchester Guardian could push forward its Zionist agenda as openly as he wished, and it did. 1917 was a turning point: from this year on the Guardian's coverage of Jewish affairs in general declined, while the coverage of Palestine consistently increased. This was partly because Palestine was soon to be subjected to the British mandate, but it is apparent also that Scott had developed a blind eye to Jews who were not Zionists. Maybe, as Weizmann told Balfour years before, for him they were "the wrong kind of Jews".

Scott's leader on the Balfour Declaration was dismissive towards the Arabs of Palestine. To the 21st century reader it seems bluntly racist. Not until 1921 did the Manchester Guardian air the point of view of the Arabs of Palestine, when an Arab delegation came to London to explain their predicament to government officials.[43] The Arab agenda was straightforwardly and fairly presented in the Guardian through the medium of an interview with Jamal Shibly, one of the delegates, but the paper still did not take up Arab claims in its leader column, or in opinion pieces. It would be a while yet before that became unavoidable.

Late 20th century historians have wondered about Scott's affiliation to Zionism. Over the last years of the century it became difficult to see it as an obvious liberal cause. Liberals increasingly tended to support the

Palestinians, who were perceived as being on the receiving end of nearly a century of conflict that was born with the Balfour Declaration. Weizmann's biographer Norman Rose noted:

> In some ways Zionism, particularly a Jewish national home under British auspices, was an unlikely cause for Scott to champion. A Liberal anti-imperialist, he had in the past strongly opposed 'forward' foreign policies. Weizmann was not always certain whether he could rely on Scott to press the case for a British commitment to Palestine, but he need not have worried. Weizmann clearly struck the right chord with his account of Jewish suffering, of the messianic dream of Zionism, of the vision of a tiny, persecuted people re-establishing their nationhood after 2,000 years. [44]

Rose may have exaggerated when he depicted Scott as an anti-imperialist. Indeed, the Manchester Guardian did oppose aggressive imperialist ventures such as the Boer war, but that hardly meant that Scott advocated folding down the empire.

Weizmann was the most brilliant propagandist Zionism ever had, and he was shrewd enough to emphasise those components of his plan that his listener would most respond to. When Balfour intimated to him, in 1914, that he favoured certain anti-Jewish ideas, Weizmann, without flinching, answered that Zionists shared some of the cultural anti-semitism of the Germans, and believed that the Jew would only become productive when living on his own land. To Sykes he explained the great strategic advantages that a Jewish presence in Palestine would carry for the empire. He utterly convinced Lloyd George that world Jewry was an immense power, attending Weizmann's command. Weizmann often talked about "our American friends", or "our people in Russia". His discovery of the Sykes-Picot agreement seemed an indication of his access to secret intelligence information. Many in the British elite believed that the Jews were behind the Soviet revolution, and thought that only the fulfilment of their national aspirations in Palestine could stop them from spreading the revolution abroad.[45]

Weizmann knew how to use the anti-semitic prejudices, fears and stereotypes of his listeners for the benefit of his cause, but Scott was not an anti-Semite. Not even a latent one. Ayerst describes the narrative which recruited Scott to Zionism: "Anyone reading now the papers and the correspondence of those days before the Balfour Declaration must be struck, as Scott was struck, by one argument freely used by Weizmann and his friends, not least in the Guardian. It is the role which they saw for 'The Jews of Judaea' as a bridge between the cultures of the West and the Middle East, a repetition in our time of the part played by Jews in the Muslim civilisation of medieval Spain." Ayerst wondered, "In the light of all that has happened, and is still happening, this hope seems so remote and vain that one is tempted to wonder whether it was ever seriously entertained. Was it perhaps, just an argument to win converts? Or was it an integral part of the Zionist hope? In 1967 one of the few survivors of the 'Manchester Group' gave this answer. 'No,' he said, 'it was not just an argument. We often spoke of it among ourselves'."[46]

Be that as it may, Scott definitely had a vision of the "New Judaea", as he called it, which was quite consistent with the image of the golden age of the Jews and Muslims in Spain. It is evident from a letter he wrote to Weizmann at the latter's request, congratulating him for the opening of the Hebrew University in Jerusalem in 1925, and saying that the New Judaea, to achieve its destined task and rise to the high conception of its founders, had to be not merely a national home for the Jewish people, but also the link between the ideals and the culture of the western and the eastern people, "the high road it may be of a developing commerce of goods, but the channel no less of the greater commerce of ideas". It should render great service to the people of Palestine, whose interest it would be its primary purpose to promote, but would serve also as "a reconciling and awakening force among the neighbouring Arab peoples, themselves also, if they could but remember it, the inheritors of great cultural tradition".[47]

Weizmann did not share any of those romantic perceptions of the Arabs. "The Arab is primitive and believes what he is told," he wrote. He explained to British military officials that he refused to negotiate with the Arabs of Palestine because they were "a race of low morals".

He advised Balfour to watch the Arabs closely and beware of them because they were treacherous. "They are willing to sell their souls to the highest bidder,"[48] he wrote to Samuel. Adopting a high and mighty colonialist manner, Weizmann was willing to state: "We don't desire to turn out Mohammed in order to put in Mr Cohen as a large landowner." The Arab, notes Segev, is merely Mohammed; the Jew is Mr Cohen.[49] This was in 1918. By the late 1930s Weizmann was, together with David Ben-Gurion and inspired by a few British officials, toying with the idea of driving the Arabs from Palestine.[50] But by then, his friend Scott was dead.

Geoffrey Taylor's explanation of Scott's Zionism is simple, maybe even simplistic, but it is worth a thought. "For a man of Scott's instincts and persuasions [...] the powerful advocacy of Zionism in its benign form was an obvious course to take. Persecuted minority? Then protect them!"[51] The Guardian was covering the plight of the Jews in Russia and Scott witnessed with his own eyes Jewish refugees from Russia settling in his home town. He knew Jews and Zionists, and liked them; it is very likely that he had never set eyes on an Arab. The predicament of Arab peasants in Palestine, whose lands and homes were bought over their heads to enable Jewish settlement, reached neither his ears nor his heart. To a 19th and early 20th-century liberal gentleman from Manchester, the Jews, just like the Irish, the suffragists and the Boers, were visible, both by being physically present, and by being white. It took European liberals into the second half of the century to become aware of the suffering of the black Africans, the Asian peoples, the Arabs.

Scott died in 1932, just before the dark clouds of fascism blanketed Europe and his vision of the horrors awaiting Europe's Jews materialised in the most heinous form. The Zionist movement owes him a great debt of gratitude. There is not a single street in Israel named after him.

CHAPTER THREE

Waving a Zionist Flag

Crozier and the British Mandate on Palestine

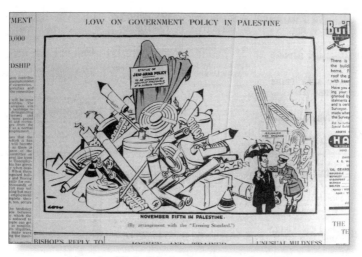

November fifth in Palestine, Low, 5 November, 1938

W P CROZIER, the first editor to work with the Scott Trust, had his hands full. His was the huge task of covering the years of Nazism and most of the second world war. He paid an enormous price for his endeavours, his health rapidly deteriorated, and in April 1944 he suddenly and prematurely died. From his early days on the Manchester Guardian as a young news editor, Crozier was a keen member of the Zionist group on the paper, and worked closely with Harry Sacher and Herbert Sidebotham. An agnostic son of a strict Methodist minister, he found in Zionism "a secular but profound fulfilment of his strongly scriptural imagination".[1]

Crozier's tenure as editor, from 1933 to 1944, was accompanied on the European stage by the systematic persecution and extermination of the Jews. From the Zionist angle these were the years of the Jewish Yishuv (settlement) in Palestine under the British mandate, marked by constant clashes with the Arab Palestinian population.

These two issues are naturally connected, but are not identical. The heavy emphasis given by the Guardian to the persecution of Jews did not necessarily derive solely or even mainly from Crozier's Zionist affiliation. The Guardian's robust opposition to the fascist Nazi regime, including its anti-semitism, was to be expected of a radically liberal newspaper reporting such atrocities as they occurred. But the long-lasting relationship with Manchester's Jewish community and the tradition of reporting the Jewish affairs around the world did influence the extent of coverage. Crozier's sources in the Zionist establishment gave him access to exclusive information.

Surprisingly enough, especially compared with the Guardian's approach earlier and later, its reporting of the first few days of the Nazi regime in Germany was hesitant. On January 15, 1933, Alexander Werth replaced Frederick Voigt, the veteran Guardian correspondent in Berlin, who was transferred to Paris. Werth lacked the adventurous spirit and moral certainty of his predecessor. "Much as I dislike Herr Hitler with his mad eyes," he wrote to Crozier, "it's going to be enormously interesting as a news centre; unfortunately, people like Hitler do not like papers like the MG […] Would you say that I should take full risks or only minimum risks? Curiously enough Ebbutt [the Times correspondent] showed me the article he wrote on Monday, and it was pretty violent; yet, at the London end, they cut out everything that was in the least likely to offend Hitler."[2]

Crozier's advice was "stick to the facts and avoid strong judgments. We, of course, may have to express the strong judgments and you may get put out for that, but I hope not".[3] Werth interpreted these guidelines timidly. On March 13, 1933, more than two weeks after the Reichstag was burnt down and as Hitler's forces were terrorising the streets of Berlin, he wrote: "There are rumours in Berlin about a sort of Nazi Cheka where terrible things are supposed to be happening, and while it is difficult to verify these stories, it is generally hoped that, whatever the government may wish to do to its enemies, all reprisals of whatever nature should receive the necessary publicity. Without such publicity rumours about abductions, torture and secret executions — which may be entirely untrue — are inevitable in the present state of nervous tension. That there is a great deal of illegality in the country may be seen from several cases reported in the press ... such acts are indeed being deplored by all law-abiding citizens — and no doubt by many Nazis, including Herr Hitler himself."[4]

David Ayerst explains that Werth was hoping for the readers to read between the lines, and that he was merely taken by the then popular view that some of Hitler's subordinates, including the SA commander Hermann Goering, were more extreme than their leader. (But he also describes how Werth, on the very day of this unfortunate publication, had prevented the publication of another story of his own, describing some atrocities that occurred in the Nazi headquarters — a story that could have corroborated the claims of Nazi terror.[5])

Back in Paris, Voigt read Werth's report and his blood boiled. In an angry letter to Crozier, he demanded the immediate removal of Werth from Berlin.

> What is the good of having a man in Berlin if he cannot establish the truth? [...] a Terror is an organised thing, organised from top to bottom. It is systematic, and while there are individual outrages too, it is a war and a particularly ferocious one, a war against everything the Guardian has ever stood for [...] It is not possible for Werth to write as a Berlin correspondent of the Guardian should be writing just now. How could he be expected to as a Jew? Even if he were to speak up, the argument — a dishonest one but none the less deadly — against him would be 'he is a Jew' [...] Every Jew who does not keep in the background is in danger of being beaten. I don't think it fair to expose Werth to this.
>
> The fact remains that on the German news the Guardian is being beaten hollow by the Times and the Telegraph whereas it should be the other way about.[6]

Werth lightly shook off Voigt's criticism. "I really do not think it's as bad as all that! The general atmosphere was distinctly unpleasant last week, but it seems to be calming down ... We shall probably, before long, have to recognise that they [the Nazis] are the government of Germany, and deal with them accordingly [...] The 'atrocity' side is, of course, a serious matter; but it is not the only thing; the historical process is enormously interesting, and should, I think, be given objective treatment."[7] As for his Jewishness, Werth thought it was too negligible to matter. "As I already told you, my mother is English; there is some Jewish blood on my father's side — and not a high proportion at that. I don't think even the greatest race purists among the Nazis could make a big case out of that!"[8] Obviously, Werth wasn't familiar with the details of Hitler's modern racist ideology and its implications, which were soon enough to be revealed in their atrocious entirety. For Hitler, Werth was as Jewish as any other "pure" Jew.

Voigt offered to take over the Berlin bureau himself, but Crozier decided that he no longer wanted to put his correspondents in jeopardy. He ordered Voigt to go to Berlin for two or three days, pull Werth out, and take him back to Paris with him. Crozier explained to Werth that he was concerned for his safety. "We must at all costs have a complete and unsparing account of the terror [...] and print what we like [...] without having to constantly fear the consequences to our Berlin correspondent [...] You have done the best that you could ... but both the Times and the Telegraph had a more adequate account of the terror than we have had."[9]

Although this episode concerns only a very short period of poor coverage in an era of robust and brave journalism in the Guardian about the Nazi regime, the Crozier-Werth-Voigt affair, in its intricacy, exposes a few significant themes and patterns that were to become characteristic of the Guardian's handling of controversial issues.

The first is the identification of staff reporters with the paper's ideology and traditions, and the importance they attributed to the content of the paper as a whole. Voigt insisted that the Guardian should keep upholding "all that we stand for". The fact that the editor might have been too distracted or lacked the information to intervene while Werth was failing to produce the goods prompted Voigt to intervene. It suggests that when a strong journalistic and ideological tradition exists, it takes more than a failure by one correspondent to compromise it. Later rivalries between reporters on the question of the desirable stance on Zionism derived from a similar sense of commitment.

Another important detail is that the complaints about Werth's inadequate reporting were made to Voigt by Norman Ebbutt of the Times and Darsie Gillie, the Morning Post's Berlin correspondent (later to be a great Paris correspondent for the Guardian). Voigt said that Gillie was prevented by his paper from speaking up "as he would wish to" and was therefore "begging me to do what I can to get something at least that tells the real story into the Guardian." Thus, the expectation that the Guardian would take a firm position also existed among its rivals and competitors.

Based in Paris, Voigt covered Germany, relying on his sources in Berlin, who risked their lives in their endeavour to send out information about the horrors of Nazism. The Guardian reported in detail the attacks on Jews in the streets of Berlin, the demolition of Jewish businesses and the arrests and torture of Jews and communists.[11] During 1933 the Guardian dedicated 170 stories and articles to the abuse of Jews in Germany. Wide coverage and editorial support were given to the boycott by British Jews of German products. The extensive coverage continued until the end of the war, naturally encompassing the persecution of Jews in countries under Nazi occupation.

The paper's attitude angered a few readers of German origin. "In my opinion all these lies are dictated by the infernal hatred which the German Jewish press has against all that is national in Germany," wrote the reader Heinz Bartsch. "[...] Of course, there is no planing without chips, but tell me, please, of a single Jew maltreated without being guilty of having supported the socialists and communists for the purpose of gaining a powerful influence upon political and administrative state affairs. There is not one. No, our national revolution is the most unbloody revolution the world has ever seen."[12] Another reader, who defined himself as an admirer of "the British spirit and way of living", claimed that the persecution in Germany was "very mild", and confessed that the rise of Nazism restored his sense of pride in his German homeland.[13]

On March 25, 1933, Voigt wrote: "The terror did not consist of sporadic excesses [...] it was not a series of disorders, it was not mob rule, it was systematic and an integral part of the counter-revolutionary offensive. For the terror as a whole the regime is responsible [...] A new terrorist period is drawing on — the period of the legal terror."[14] Within a few days, the Manchester Guardian was banned in Germany with only a few brief interludes when it was permitted.[15] In September the Guardian's correspondent Robert Dell managed to enter Berlin and write a few reports and commentary pieces from there, but he had to flee Germany two months later, after a German woman friend of his was arrested and told that she would not be released until he left the country. In Paris, Voigt was being followed by a new branch of the Gestapo, and had to be protected by three French detectives. Crozier decided to send Charles Lambert to Berlin as an above board correspondent with instructions to take minimal risks, as an addition to Voigt's special underground service. For his own safety, Lambert was prevented from knowing anything about Voigt's sources and activities.[16]

On January 1, 1934, Voigt exposed the truth behind Dachau concentration camp, which was presented by the Germans as a model institution where "politically misguided men are being trained to become good citizens". With details, numbers, names, and practices, the report gave a chilling description of life in the camp.

> Besides detention in the cells there is corporal punishment.
> This consists of a flogging with an ox-hide thong that has
> a strip of steel three to four millimetres wide running along
> its whole length (those thongs are made by the prisoners).
> The blows — the number varies from 25 to 75 according to
> the sentence — are counted by an SS man (Black Shirt). Two
> other SS men hold the prisoner down, one by the hands and
> one by the head, round which a sack is wrapped, so that the
> prisoner's cries are stifled [...] On September 2 one of the Nazi
> guards broke a prisoner's jaw with a blow of his fist [...] Some
> prisoners were beaten with lengths of rubber hosepipe. Some
> have been burnt with cigarette ends and some have been put
> to what the Americans call the 'water torture' [...] The total
> number of prisoners who have been killed or who have died
> of their injuries at Dachau cannot be far from 50.[17]

It is significant to note that neither the Nazi horrors nor their coverage in the Guardian focused only on the Jews; the German fascists also targeted communists, socialists, homosexuals, retarded people, the mentally ill and disabled, and other minority groups, and this was well reported in the paper.

In general, the Guardian, though sharing popular fears of a new world war, developed an increasingly belligerent attitude towards Nazi Germany during the 1930s, and rejected Neville Chamberlain's appeasement policy. It urged free Europe to arm itself against Hitler's aggression. "The only way to stop an aggressor is that the other countries should be as ready for war as he is," wrote Crozier in a leading article in 1936.[18] When Chamberlain returned from Munich in 1938 with the promise of "peace in our time", the Guardian commented: "Hitler will be able to advance again, when he chooses, with greatly increased power."[19]

The outbreak of war, and the spreading shadow of Nazi occupation over Europe, made it very difficult to obtain information about the fate of Europe's Jews, who were rounded up and led to death camps in the east. The Manchester Guardian, helped by sources created before the war and documents that were given directly to Crozier by Zionist activists, often managed to break the wall of silence. In September 1942 the Guardian reported the rounding up of Jews in Paris. "Not a single soul whom the police could lay hands on was allowed to go free [...] Children over three years old were separated from their mothers, about 5,000 of them being herded together in three school buildings, whither they were taken in lorries after their parents had been seized [...] The prisoners are half-starved and deprived of the most elementary comforts. There is no proper sanitation, no medical supplies, and no kitchen equipment."[20]

In December 1942 the Guardian reported that many hundreds of thousands of Jews had been massacred. "[...] of the 3.1 million Jews in Poland before the war over a third have perished in the last three years [...]" The article called for immediate and radical action by the allies. "The situation obviously calls for something more than a reaffirmation of principles or a condemnation of the indescribable deeds being done in fulfilment of a premeditated policy." The paper suggested that the United Nations, a proposed replacement for the ineffectual pre-war League of Nations, should assist countries that were still liable to receive an influx of Jewish refugees, and to make it clear to them that they would not have to carry the burden alone. "The German scheme for total extermination can only be combated by radical means," it said.[21]

No wonder that after the war, in a list found in the Gestapo archives naming British citizens who should be "taken care of" if Germany conquered Britain, a number of Guardian staff appeared. Among them were John Scott, the chairman of the Scott Trust, and Crozier. The Guardian published the list, in alphabetical order, without any editorial comment.[22] None was needed.

But while the extent of reporting and commentary dedicated to the organised slaughtering of Jews seems natural (and apparent, though to a lesser extent, in other British newspapers like the Times and the Telegraph), Crozier's engagement with every aspect of life in Palestine sometimes seemed excessive. Ayerst wrote that Zionism was threatening to become Crozier's King Charles's head. While CP Scott's involvement with Zionism was merely one of his political interests, Crozier was recruited into the service of Zionism. Unlike Scott's attempts to separate his political assistance to Chaim Weizmann and his group from day-to-day editorial work, Crozier turned the Manchester Guardian into a tool of Zionist advocacy. This inclination raises, in retrospect, more questions about Zionist influence on the paper's objectivity, since during Crozier's editorship the national Arab movement was already alive and kicking, which was not so during Scott's editorship. Arab "invisibility" was no longer the issue.

The depth and extent of Crozier's involvement with Zionism is demonstrated not only by the number of column inches dedicated to Palestine during his editorship (in 1936 alone 414 items in the Manchester Guardian concerned Palestine), but also by the scope of his correspondence and documentation about events in this tiny spot of the Middle East, while the rest of the world was being swept into the gory turmoil of the cruellest war in history.

By 1933 the British mandate in Palestine had to deal with growing Arab disquiet in face of the expanding Jewish settlement. The Nazi persecution led to a growing influx of Jewish immigrants to Palestine. The riots of 1929 ended in the killing of 116 Arabs and 133 Jews, 67 of whom were butchered in a massacre of the old Jewish community in Hebron. The British government, as always, responded with a committee of inquiry and a white paper, published by the colonial secretary, Lord Passfield, in 1930. The white paper posited that the Balfour Declaration laid a double and equal obligation on the British government to the Jews and the Arabs of Palestine alike. It stated that the quotas of Jewish immigration to Palestine should be defined not only by the economic capacity of the Jewish community in Palestine to absorb them, but also by the economic implications for the Arab inhabitants of the land. Weizmann, in a brilliant and sustained campaign, firing off letters and telegrams to rally influential supporters, harassing officials, lunching with the prime minister, Ramsay MacDonald, at the House of Commons, at last managed to reverse the government's decision. MacDonald wrote to Weizmann cancelling the proposed measures over Jewish immigration.[23]

On April 20, 1931, the Guardian published a long report, with a picture, of Weizmann's speech to a gathering of Manchester's elite as well as a leading article on the subject:

> Those who had lived and worked in Palestine were convinced that there was plenty of room for Jewish expansion without prejudice to Arab interests thanks to the possibilities of intensive agriculture. Unfortunately the various government experts who had recently visited Palestine for short periods were of a different opinion and had converted Lord Passfield to their point of view [... the government] may have been wrongly informed, and Mr MacDonald's letter to Dr Weizmann interpreting the white paper suggests that they are realising that this is in fact the case. At any rate the government now seem to take a more favourable view of the possibilities of Jewish colonisation, and Dr Weizmann last night expressed the hope that Zionism was now at the end of the very difficult period arising out of the white paper [...] Let's hope that he is right.[24]

The "Arab interests" thus passingly referred to in the leader were not otherwise mentioned in any part of this issue of the Guardian, and no Arab was asked to comment on MacDonald's letter. During the 1930s, in fact, the Arabs began to make their presence felt with a series of disturbances against the mandate authority and the Jewish immigrants, who were rapidly increasing in number as the Nazi terror took hold in Germany. On September 8, 1936, the Guardian leader column applauded the government decision to take "more rapid and effective action against the Arab revolt in Palestine: in other words, military reinforcement and martial law. The statement was accurate in substance and moderate in tone. It asserted that the Arabs refused to abandon either their strike or their terrorism 'until fundamental changes have been introduced by the British government in its policy.' The government could not concede these 'fundamental changes', which would betray alike British interests, the mandate, and the Jews, and which would incidentally make the Arabs, within and without Palestine, the masters of that country's future." The leader expressed the hope that the Arabs would "consent to meet the Jews, as the Jews are willing to meet them, and to work out a scheme by which the two peoples might live side by side on a footing of a constitutional equality."[25]

Two weeks later, the leader tone hardened further: the troops were urgently needed, the Guardian argued, "since we are summoned by bomb and gun to reverse our established policy, and apparently the Arab leaders up to the present think they have good prospects that we shall give them all they ask [...] The terrorist campaign must be ended: so much we owe to the Jews and to our self-respect as governors and trustees."

The article disparaged the Arab fear, expressed by "the wilder of their propagandists", that the Zionist aim was to gain control over the whole of Palestine by expelling the Arabs. "If the Jews are found willing to recognise that the Arabs have been rooted in Palestine for so many hundred years, have not the Arabs the imagination to realise what it means that, in Dr. Weizmann's historic illustration to Mr AJ Balfour, 'Jerusalem was ours when London was a marsh'?"[26]

The intensifying violence in Palestine led to another committee of inquiry, the Peel commission, which recommended for the first time a division of Palestine into two separate states, Jewish and Arab. The Guardian line on partition, as always in its policy on Zionism since Scott's day, was in line with the doveish section of the pragmatic Zionist labour movement; that is, it was Weizmann-inspired. The pragmatists believed that the Zionist movement should adopt any offer that might ensure Jewish statehood in Palestine, and then strive to improve on it, mainly in terms of territory. Hardliners among the Zionists and the Arab-Palestinian leadership rejected partition out of hand.

The Guardian dedicated endless pages to the debate, and the letters editor's desk was flooded with responses by Zionists of all affiliations. The paper wholeheartedly backed partition, but gradually accommodated its support to match Zionist demands; as a leader published on July 22, 1937, put it: "Having diminished the Jewish Palestine to the size of an English county, it presents to the Arabs the great, undeveloped Negev country, which will be useless to them but might be of priceless value to the Jews confined within a too strait Palestine."[27]

Another stated:

> It is strange that both the great Jewish commercial concerns, the potash works on the Dead Sea and the power station at Lake Tiberius (almost all of whose output is consumed by Jews), should be thrown into the Arab state [...] Even more serious on a long view is the proposal that the desert area between Gaza and Beersheba on the north and the Gulf of Akaba on the south should (except for a small piece) be given to the Arabs [...] There is, too, the question of Jerusalem, of Zion. By the new plan the whole city will come under permanent British mandate. But Jerusalem excites the deepest emotions in the Jewish race; it is so much the just object of their pride, their veneration, and their historic griefs that it seems impossible that we should not find a way to associate some parts of it directly with their new state.[28]

This sensitive understanding for the most subtle economic, territorial, emotional and national needs of the Jewish settlement in Palestine, which by now had increased to 30 per cent of the population, did not extend to Arab grievances over the partition plan.

> The chief Arab grievance, apart from the existence of the plan at all, will be that purely Arab parts of Galilee are given to the Jewish state. But Galilee is the region where from ancient times the Jews have maintained settlements; it is impracticable here to draw a line between the mixed communities. The Arabs should find their compensation in getting the best possible terms for the transference of Arabs from the new Jewish into the new Arab kingdom [...] and the Jewish state will be wise to use its funds generously — it will probably have a surplus if no other state has — in order to make this scheme work.[29]

In other words, had Jerusalem, parts of the Dead Sea, Tiberius and the whole Negev desert been added to the proposed Jewish state, the Manchester Guardian would have been happy with the partition plan of 1937. The Arabs, according to the Guardian, should have relinquished claims on Galilee (a part of Israel where they remain a majority to this day), and surrendered to a "voluntary" transfer away from the area, an idea that Weizmann and Ben-Gurion were toying with at the time.

Crozier's stance on Zionism did not alienate most of the Guardian's readership. Zionism was for many decades yet seen as a classic liberal cause, and the persecution of Jews by the Nazis made it seem even more so. But some readers evidently felt that the British government was victimising Palestinian Arabs, and expressed surprise that the Guardian should support such policies. In a letter to the editor of the New Statesman, Edward Thompson of Oxford, alarmed by the killing of Arab civilians by the British army in Palestine, protested:

> The Arabs are not people who seeped into Palestine since the Balfour Declaration. They and their ancestors have lived there from time immemorial, and have seen their country given away over their heads, and the Nazi and subsequent persecution in Europe have sent out a swirling river of misery which liberal

and Labour opinion seem to think can be crowded into the pint-pot of a country the size of East Anglia [...] The Jews have the press, and can ruin any paper or writer who takes up the Arab case. We read now of 6,000 cables to Downing Street from New York and 2,000 telegrams to our embassy in Washington [...] Only massacre and counter massacre (at present styled "firmness") can force the Jewish state on the Arabs [...] We have kept, and intend to keep indefinitely, one country in our empire without the beginning of representative institutions, which are to be established only when we have completely overturned the racial balance. And this is a course that the left support, and such papers as the Manchester Guardian supports.[30]

This correspondence between the Guardian editorial line and the political wishes of the Zionist leadership was not accidental. Crozier was a close friend of the eminent historian Lewis Namier, born a Polish Jew and educated at Balliol. Namier was a friend of TE Lawrence, popularly known as Lawrence of Arabia. But whereas Lawrence was drawn to Arab nationalism, Namier fell for the charms of Zionism and after his appointment in 1931 as professor of history at Manchester University, he became a passionate advocate, not least in his role as secretary of the World Zionist Organisation. The alliance between Crozier and Namier was to influence the content of the Manchester Guardian directly.

During the 1930s and 1940s Namier was the closest man to Weizmann in Britain. He virtually turned his London residence in Gloucester Road into a branch of the Jewish Agency and worked in full cooperation with Weizmann, striving to recruit prominent politicians and influential journalists to aiding Zionism. The campaign to reverse the white paper of 1930 was merely one of their efforts.

Namier was assisted by his close friend Baffy (Blanche) Dugdale, Lord Balfour's niece, the most fervent gentile Zionist of her time. Weizmann's biographer describes her: "Highly intelligent, a political animal to her last breath, she was related to some of the most powerful political clans in Britain: the Campbells, the Balfours, and the Cecils. Born into the British political elite, she knew everyone who mattered."[31] Weizmann and Namier made great use of the exclusive information which was accessible to Dugdale. She acted as Weizmann's confidante and as an informal channel of communication with the government.

Namier was a strange bird in Zionist politics. Although he was Weizmann's close ally, he detested almost all the other Zionists. They treated him with great suspicion, and resented Weizmann's tendency to entrust sensitive political tasks to him. His parents had converted to Roman Catholicism and this background was often used to question his credibility, but his loyalty to Weizmann was beyond doubt.

From 1937 until his death in 1944, Crozier exchanged letters and documents with Namier on a weekly basis, and the two men often met socially. Every letter from Namier was accompanied by a pile of documents, often highly secret. Army intelligence papers concerning the actions of Arabs throughout the Middle East, protocols of inner meetings of the highest ranking Zionist leadership, reports of meetings between the Zionist leader Moshe Shertok (later as Moshe Sharett to become prime minister of Israel) and the British high commissioner in Palestine, letters from Balfour describing his visit to Palestine, documentations of meetings between Zionist leaders and British cabinet ministers, and accounts of the fate of Jews in Europe, are examples.

On the face of it, it was astonishing that Namier should have revealed the contents of these documents to a newspaper editor, but he knew he could trust Crozier to keep the Zionists' secrets. In January 1938, for example, he sent him an intelligence document marked secret and headed "The Activities of the Mufti and his Associates in Syria."[32] The covering letter said: "I am sending you enclosed a very secret document on the activities of the Mufti etc. Even the parts which might possibly be printed, I think we had better keep secret, so as not to let the Arabs know how much is known to us about their activities. Copies of this document have been given by us to the authorities in Palestine, the colonial office and to the French. Further interesting documents are being copied in this office now, and I shall send them to you when ready."[33] In 1942 Namier wrote, "I can legitimately tell you everything I know about our affairs —

it is accepted in our political department that you are entitled to every piece of information we have."[34]

Crozier definitely earned this confidence. Namier kept him informed of Zionist agendas, and Crozier ensured that the message would appear loud and clear in the Guardian. In January 1938 Namier was concerned by information he received about the plans of the Arab prime minister of Iraq, Nuri Pasha as-Said, to hold political meetings in London aimed at changing British policy in Palestine in favour of the Arabs. Namier considered that Pasha might gain the support of the Foreign Office. He wrote to Crozier:

> The only way of spoiling this new little game would be by premature publicity, which might embarrass both Nuri Pasha and his friends in their heart-to-heart talks. Naturally, we had to make sure that such publicity would not interfere with anything we are doing from the Palestinian end; eg we know that Weizmann has written a letter to Ormsby-Gore direct on this subject. But having now their agreement, we would like to bring the matter into the open in a clear and yet discreet manner. Would you be prepared to do it in the MG? You are lunching with me on Thursday, but as the matter is urgent I send you these wires.[35]

Crozier understood perfectly what "clear and yet discreet" meant. Low down in the leader page a couple of days later the required column appeared:

> The government's methods with regard to Palestine invite increased Arab pressure, and the government is getting it [...] In London itself there is — or should one already say was? — the elusive Nuri Pasha, former premier of Iraq [...] And what, one wonders, is the aim of Nuri Pasha [...] about whose mysterious visit the Colonial Office and the Foreign Office will say nothing? [...] Nuri Pasha cannot hope to make the government abandon its partition plan outright [...] that would be too much, as yet, to

ask. But might he not desire the government to modify its 'firm' policy, to release the arrested leaders, to readmit the Mufti, and to re-establish the dissolved supreme committee, with the promise that they would then, like good citizens, give evidence before the new commission? It is, indeed, hard to think that such a fantastic 'deal' could be suggested, and certainly it could not even be discussed by the government. The meagre remnants of British prestige would vanish in a moment. The victory of the Arabs, gained by propaganda, threats, and violence, would be complete. They would think, and rightly think, they could eventually gain all that they desire.[36]

Beyond the swift compliance to Namier's needs, this article reveals the Guardian's polarised attitudes towards Arab and Zionist aspirations. While Weizmann would be praised for his success in reversing a governmental white paper by propaganda and discreet meetings with officials, Nuri Pasha would be regarded with suspicion for attempting (with far less success) a similar, though less ambitious, coup.

Again, Crozier and Namier orchestrated an attack on a government policy that followed the 1939 white paper restricting land acquisition by Jews in large parts of Palestine. Crozier condemned the policy in a leader. "The necessity, the justice, and the legality of the government's action are alike in question. Is not that a reason why this country should leave no doubt that it is doing everything possible to fulfil its international obligations?"[37]

The next day the Guardian published the Three Zones Map, which showed the division of Palestine into areas where Jews might or might not buy land, with a short explanation. Both the map and the explanation were sent to Crozier by Namier, but the piece was presented as something which came "from a correspondent".[38] Two days later the Guardian published a letter signed by Namier, congratulating the paper for publishing the map, while criticising the fact that parliament discussed the land issue without the benefit of a map.[39]

In another letter to the editor, published on March 15, Namier attacked a speech in parliament by prime minister MacDonald. But it was not a standard letter. Its accusation that MacDonald had distorted the facts ran to a column and a half of type. "Mr MacDonald achieved his Munich," Namier wrote, making the comparison to Neville Chamberlain's disgraceful accommodation with Hitler of 1938. "It would be ungracious, as it would be vain, to belittle Mr MacDonald's triumph. The speech was wonderful, like the leaning tower of Pisa." Namier continued by analysing MacDonald's rhetorical tricks and concluded: "With supreme skill he skimmed over the ice, rounding obstacles and drawing whatever figures he chose. The one thing which the figure skater cannot do is to walk straight."[40]

The practice of presenting materials as reports by correspondents though they originated with Namier developed at this time. The latest episode involved the Jewish brigade. The Zionists were pleading with the British government to form a Jewish force to fight against the Nazis within the British army. Negotiations started even before the war broke, but the government was biding its time, not quite sure how the Arabs might respond. In September 1940 Namier sent Crozier a memorandum, summing up a meeting between Weizmann and the foreign secretary, Anthony Eden, in which Eden agreed to the principle of the brigade. Namier explained that the news should be kept strictly secret for the time being, but, he added, "I look upon you as one of our best and most faithful friends, who has stood by us in the worst days, so I want to let you have the good news immediately. Once more, many thanks, if one can thank for all you have done for us."[41]

But by 1942, the mandate government was still dragging its feet over recruiting Jewish soldiers from Palestine. For the Zionists it was a matter of great importance. A Zionist force fighting shoulder to shoulder with British soldiers while the Arabs pinned their hopes on German victory would have an impressive political impact. There was also, naturally, a genuine moral motivation in the Yishuv to come to the rescue of Europe's Jews. Trying to avoid turning the issue into a political one (but succeeding in doing just that), the government was attempting to recruit equal numbers of Jews and Arabs. But as the Arabs, devastated by the suppression of their mutiny, did not show much inclination to fight for the army that had attacked their villages, the mandate authorities deemed it necessary to slow down the recruitment of Jews.

In January 1942 a report "from a special correspondent" appeared in the Guardian, detailing the obstacles which the mandate authorities had put in the way of recruiting the brigade. "This is not the normal British way. Behind it is, presumably, the desire to appease the Arab,"[42] wrote the special correspondent, who was none other than Namier. The article was complemented by a leader by Crozier which appeared on the same day. Sharp and ironic, Crozier mocked British recruitment policy:

The Jewish Agency had the idea that as more men were wanted by the services in the Middle East, it would be a good idea to have a recruiting campaign among the Jews. As an idea this is not wholly novel; other people also have thought that if you want men badly under a voluntary system it is reasonable to try to get them. But it will be agreed that the idea was at least sound. The Jews were not allowed to use Jewish national colours or import Jewish national sentiment into the recruiting leaflets. That, of course, is because the authorities desire to placate the Arabs, whose leaders — the Mufti of Jerusalem and Rashid Ali, the Iraqi rebel — are now in Berlin, plotting with Hitler for the happiness of the British empire. But that was not the truly comic, although highly serious, part of the performance. Our correspondent says that on the next day the Jewish papers appeared without a single word about the recruiting demonstrations. 'The censorship had intervened' [...] The Palestine censorship has done many strange things, and it is high time that it should be brought to light and examined, both by public opinion and by Parliament."[43]

The matter was indeed raised in Parliament. On February 19 the Guardian published two letters on the subject, one by the relentless Namier, and another by A. Creech Jones MP, presenting the unsatisfactory answers he had received to his questions on the subject of censorship.[44] The colonial under secretary, he wrote, denied any censorship, while the Jewish Agency informed him that their recruiting efforts were still suppressed by censorship. Crozier accompanied the letters with a leader, protesting once again against the censorship policy. "I thought the combination of my letter with that from Creech Jones yesterday, covered by your leader, very effective," wrote a grateful Namier.[45]

On November 2, 1942, Crozier's leader celebrated the 25th anniversary of the Balfour Declaration, "which this paper at the time called 'the signpost of a destiny'." Crozier protested against the policy laid out in the white paper, which limited Jewish immigration to Palestine. "The signpost still points, as in 1917, to a destiny, and the time will come when we must get back to the road from which we strayed in a moment of unworthy opportunism that presented a timorous government, but never the British people."[46]

Crozier saw himself, and his paper, as part of the Zionist effort, and never denied it. He was involved in the most intimate workings of the movement, including the personal rivalries and petty wars of prestige. In one of his routine letters, congratulating him on another very helpful leader column, Namier grumbled about the endless battles between Weizmann and Ben-Gurion. Ben-Gurion was not too bad, observed Namier, but he certainly suffered from an "anti-Weizmann complex".[47]

Answering a letter from Weizmann, who thanked him for a leading article condemning the British government for preventing Jewish refugees from disembarking in Palestine on the basis that they were "illegal immigrants",[48] Crozier wrote:

"You must never thank me for doing anything that I am able to do in that cause. My heart is in it and so is my head, and I shall go on using them both faithfully as long as I am here."[49]

Crozier died on April 16, 1944. On April 17, Baffy Dugdale wrote in her diary: "Back to Zionist office where helped Lewis finish a short article on Crozier of the Manchester Guardian, who died suddenly last night. A heavy blow to Zionism. That makes the fourth of the great non-Jewish friends lost in the past 12 months, just when they are needed most: Cazalet, Wedgwood, Wingate, Crozier."[50]

Crozier was the last editor of the Guardian who could afford, or even wanted, to be openly partisan over the developing conflict between Zionists and Arabs in Palestine. His position was determined by his personal and political commitment to Zionism, but gained public legitimacy because of the unprecedented persecution of Jews in Europe and the inability of the Arab national movement to attract the press to its own cause. The huge resources demanded for war coverage meant that the Guardian could not afford a reporter in Palestine, a situation that made Crozier depend heavily on his Jewish Agency sources. The Jews in Palestine had recruited their resources to the British war effort, but the Arabs were still remembered for their rebellion of 1936 to 1939. The end of the war was to bring about a violent Jewish resistance movement in Palestine, and with it a certain shift in public opinion. But dealing with these realities was a task for the next editor.

CHAPTER FOUR

Delightfully Impatient with Bores

Wadsworth Launches the State of Israel

There, Yesterday, Were We, Low, 23 March 1949

ONCE again, an editor of the Manchester Guardian began his
tenure at a crucial moment for the Zionist movement. AP
Wadsworth took over at the end of April 1944. The second world war
would soon be over, Europe was in ruins, and the horrified victors were
marching into Nazi extermination camps, liberating the few who had
survived through hell. Little more than skin and bones, survivors were
scattered in refugee camps all around Europe, without families and with
no homes to which to return. Fifty-five million people perished in the
war. Six million of them were Jews systematically murdered by the Nazis,
many in the gas chambers. One million of these were children.

In Palestine the Zionists, sensing the emergency of the moment and
the weakening of the British empire, turned against their patron, the
British mandate. For a few months, between November 1945 and June
1946, the struggle against the British common enemy led to military

67

cooperation between the three rival Zionist forces in Palestine: the mainstream Hagana, the radical Irgun, and the smaller and more radical Stern Gang. This united front, known as the Movement of the Hebrew Revolt, attacked British military targets, but was soon disbanded.[1] Hagana leaders felt that the terrorist operations carried out by Irgun and Stern Gang members were detrimental to diplomatic efforts, aimed at persuading the Anglo-American committee to recommend the founding of an independent Jewish state.

The formation of the Anglo-American committee marked the dissolution of the British empire and the start of the intensive involvement of the United States in the region and in the rest of the world. The British government, exhausted by the war and by the never-ending predicament of Palestine, sought American help for imposing a plan on the Jews and the Arabs of the region.

Wadsworth was very different, socially and politically, from his predecessors. He was Labour and trade unionist, and so the first editor of the Guardian who was not a member of the Liberal party. Although he had severed the affiliation between the paper and the party, he maintained its generally liberal spirit. During the election campaign of 1945, the Guardian urged the electorate to bring an end to Conservative rule (followed by Churchill's wartime Tory-majority coalition), but remained neutral between the Labour and Liberal parties.[2] By 1951 Wadsworth was telling his readers: "The Labour government has come to the end of its usefulness [...] Another spell of impotence and stumbling like that of the last 18 months might bring greater catastrophe and more lasting setback than Labour loss of office now." To his senior colleagues he is reported to have said: "Of course, I shall be voting Labour, as usual."[3]

Wadsworth was also reluctant to maintain the Guardian's classic "big causes". He strove to make the paper more up to date, more popular. "Making righteousness readable" wasn't on its own good enough any more. This tendency influenced the paper's position on Zionism, as on other matters. Wadsworth's deputy editor, John Pringle, later to make a career as editor of the Sydney Morning Telegraph, described the process:

He saved the Guardian by making it more lively, more entertaining, more realistic, and a far better *news*paper. He quickly dumped those causes, like pacifism, Zionism, internationalism and the official Liberal party, which however noble and idealistic they had once been, had become so many albatrosses slung around the Guardian's neck. He was splendidly impatient with bores.[4]

But as far as Zionism was concerned, Wadsworth's sentiments went beyond boredom. The Jewish violence in Palestine, culminating in the terrorist attacks committed by the Irgun and Stern Gang, angered him. Pringle said:

Another thing worth mentioning in the history of the paper was his marked cooling off towards Zionism. He [Wadsworth] was really very anti-Zionist but because of the tradition of the paper allowed me to carry on a moderate support for their cause.[5]

Wadsworth, it seems, thought that a pro-Zionist approach was part of the directive "to carry on the paper in the same spirit as heretofore". This obligation was strong enough to make Wadsworth allow his paper to be engaged in a fierce row with one of the politicians he admired most, his contemporary Ernest Bevin. Bevin, foreign secretary in Clement Attlee's cabinet, symbolised for the Zionists the "treachery" of Britain. Geopolitical realities were changing with the break-up of empire, the enfeeblement of Europe, and the emergence of the US and the Soviet Union as the two great powers; Arab oil was becoming an important feature of Middle Eastern and world politics and the Balfour Declaration, promising "the same thing to two peoples"[6] began to look to both Bevin and Attlee like a mistake. Bevin made his views obvious and the Zionists fought him on any possible front. Even the children who grew up in the Israel of the 1940s and 1950s would burn Bevin effigies in their Lag Ba'omer bonfires.[7] Bevin, inflexible and hardly diplomatic in his approach, did not concede. The increasing Guardian coolness towards Zionism noted by Pringle hardly showed in the paper's coverage of the violent Zionist struggle against the mandate, though it became more and more apparent towards the partition of Palestine and the founding of the state of Israel.

Wadsworth kept some contact with Lewis Namier, but the Zionist historian's influence was marginal compared to his spell on Crozier. Wadsworth also maintained Crozier's tradition of publishing leader columns by Harry Sacher, but Sacher was writing increasingly about general issues, and less on Zionism. The editor's famous impatience with bores and lack of sentiment to the paper's established icons is reflected in his correspondence with and about Israel Cohen. Cohen had covered early 20th-century Zionist conferences for Scott's Manchester Guardian, and felt free to keep sending long and not very intelligible letters containing ideas and advice to Scott's heirs. Wadsworth's replies were abrupt and impatient, though more or less polite.[8] In a letter to Norman Bentwich, the general prosecutor of Palestine and a Zionist Jew, he complained: "Really Israel Cohen is very trying. Is there any point in this letter of his I enclose? If there is not, I will tell him we can't publish it."[9]

Despite the mild cooling of the post-Crozier Guardian towards Zionism, there was a striking difference between the Guardian's gung-ho calls for suppressing the Arab rebellion during the 1930s, and its forgiving attitude towards the Jewish violence in Palestine in the late 1940s. On Saturday June 29, 1946, which was to be remembered in Zionist history as Black Sabbath, the British army raided dozens of Jewish settlements in Palestine. As many as 100,000 soldiers and policemen took part in the operation, named by the British Operation Agatha, and 3,000 Jews were arrested under suspicion of participation in the Movement of the Hebrew Revolt. Among them were senior members of the Jewish Agency. A big stockpile of weapons was exposed and confiscated in Kibbutz Yagur.[10] The Guardian's long leader reflected the paper's fury:

> The action which is now being taken against the Jewish
> National Home with the government's approval is clearly a
> grave development. We appear to have blundered into one of

those campaigns of suppression, all too common in our history, which are always abhorrent and nearly always unsuccessful, however natural they may seem to the British soldier with his passion for law and order. And our 'enemy' in this case are the very Jews whom we placed in Palestine to escape from persecution in Europe. So great a disaster demands more justification than was offered by Mr Attlee. Mr Attlee claimed that these operations 'are not directed against the Jewish community as a whole but solely against those who have taken an active part in the campaign of violence, and those responsible for instigating and directing it'. It is not likely to appear so to the Jewish people. The leaders of the Jewish Agency who were arrested on Saturday — the Jewish Sabbath — were the constitutional leaders of the Jews in Palestine. They may have condoned a movement which they could not stop, but it is difficult to believe they were guilty of terrorism [...] No doubt in the calm of the Cabinet room in Downing Street it sounds reasonable to say, 'First we must have order; let the Jews disarm and then we shall consider their case.' But it is only natural that the Jews should see it the other way round. They tend to reply, 'First, give us some indication that you will consider our case and then we will be ready to disarm' [...] Until then patience and forbearance, no matter how difficult, will pay us better than repression.[11]

Within four weeks Britain was to be shocked by the biggest terrorist attack in Palestine before or since. On July 22, 1946, Irgun members blew up the northern section of the King David hotel in Jerusalem, which housed the British government secretariat and British military headquarters. More than 90 people, including many Jewish and Arab civil servants and hotel employees were killed. The Guardian's headline, Palestine's worst outrage — 90 dead or missing in the ruins, reflected the horror, and a separate item described, "how the terrorists entered the building disguised as Bedouins 'delivering the milk'".[12] The paper also published the Jewish Agency's call for the community in Palestine to "rise up against these abominable outrages", in which the bombing was portrayed as a "dastardly crime perpetrated by a gang of desperados".[13] The leading article, however, expressed far-reaching understanding:

> The attack on the King David hotel in Jerusalem, in which so many British officers and men lost their lives, will be a shock to those who imagined that the government's firmness had put a stop to Jewish terrorism and had brought about an easier situation in Palestine. In fact, the opposite is the truth. The arrest of the Jewish leaders [...] merely meant that control passed more than ever into the hands of extremists, those desperate and daring men who believe that only by such means can the British government be forced to change its policy. Yesterday was their answer, and it would be foolish to hope that it will be the last. This brutal murder (for so in effect it was) will inevitably bring further repression upon the Jews, but that in turn will breed further terrorism and so on until the government can agree on a policy to break this vicious circle. And though we in this country think first of the victims, both men and women, few of whom had any responsibility for the present situation, we should be deceiving ourselves if we did not realise that many humane and moderate Jews in Palestine will think first with pride of the men who struck this blow at the headquarters of the administration. For such is the gulf which now divides the British and Jewish peoples in Palestine that what to us is a cruel and wanton murder is to them a brave and heroic action.
>
> To the British soldier in Palestine yesterday's outrage was unforgivable, to be answered by ruthless measures. But the government must take a wider view. If another division will help prevent such things in the future, let another division be sent. But even five more divisions (if we had them) will not solve the political problem of Palestine, as must surely be plain by now. The only answer to this is to hurry on the discussions which are now going on with the American mission in London

with a view of finding a just and final solution. So far nothing is known of these discussions, though there are many rumours. But perhaps the bombs which exploded so disastrously in the King David hotel will stress the need for speed.[14]

A year later Irgun members hijacked and hanged two British sergeants serving in Palestine as an act of revenge for the hanging of two of their comrades by the mandate authorities. The Guardian, although horrified by this crime even more than by the King David atrocity, held to its editorial line. Time to go was the leader heading:

> In the whole record of political terrorism there has been no worse crime than the brutal and cold-blooded murder of the two British sergeants. It is, as responsible Jews have already said, a greater blow to the Jewish nation than to the British government, and its effect on the British troops in Palestine can easily be imagined. Yet there must be no reprisals, official or unofficial. Events have swept British, Jews, and Arabs alike into a tangle of hatred and futility. There is now only one hope — that the United Nations will be able to find a clear-cut and final solution which will release us from our responsibility and give to both Jews and Arabs an opportunity to start afresh [...] It is time the government made up its mind to leave Palestine, not only because we have utterly failed to find a solution but because we cannot afford to stay there. Palestine is already a Jewish tragedy; it must not become also a British disaster [...] And if, as is possible, the United Nations can find no alternative, the Jews and Arabs must come to terms themselves without British troops to hold the ring. As we have just discovered in India, freedom and responsibility often go together.[15]

Crozier portrayed secret and illegal infiltration by war refugees into Palestine as heroic and just. Now, the same issue of the Guardian that carried the Time to go leader ran a story about 900 refugees, mostly children, on board three ships lying off the Mediterranean coast of

France: it indicated that French journalists at least were beginning to sniff cynical exploitation of the refugees by Hagana, the organisers in Jerusalem of the voyage. The hapless voyagers refused to disembark in France. The Guardian reported:

> Meanwhile, the French journalists have begun to ask themselves whether the Zionists are not taking upon themselves a very heavy responsibility by keeping women and children on board these uncomfortable and ill-equipped ships when they are at perfect liberty to come ashore. The same journalists who, two days ago in Paris Presse were writing of 'innocent galley slaves', now declare that 'if Zionist leaders continue to sacrifice innocent children to their cause, the popular masses of the French coast who trembled with indignation on first seeing the caged ships will rise in protest against an attitude they no longer understand'. The gradual growth of impatience with Zionist obstinacy, of which 900 small children are the victims, is naturally accompanied by a slight increase of comprehension of the problems with which the British government is faced.[16]

The story was accompanied by a cartoon by David Low, who was later to be the highest paid member of Guardian editorial, including Wadsworth himself, although in 1947, his work appeared by arrangement with the Evening Standard of London. The cartoon showed a stereotypical Jew pleading with a French journalist standing by the ship. "And anyway," says the Jew, "if it sinks and drowns 'em, think how you score over the British."[17]

By now the British government recognised that the mandate had failed and its decision to seek advice from the UN general assembly induced on November 29, 1947, UN resolution 181 for the partition of Palestine. Maybe CP Scott at this stage would have been spending time in UN corridors, and Crozier would have concocted with Namier the most useful ways to shift public opinion towards partition, but the times, and the editor, were different.

On December 1 the Manchester Guardian alloted a great part of its space to the partition resolution, forecasting that "Arabs will not accept a

UN decision on Palestine", and reporting "wild rejoicing by the Jews". The Guardian did not seem to share that joy. It pointed to two major problems with the plan: "The form of partition is absurdly complicated (the map of Palestine will look like a crossword puzzle), and no neutral force has been provided to impose it." Britain should not abandon its responsibilities in Palestine in spite of the understandable urge to do so, the leader continued. "Just as parents cannot disown their child just because the boy turns out badly or gets into trouble with the police, so we cannot disown Palestine." The leader's assumption was that the Jews needed to be protected from the Arabs. It didn't occur to its writer that it might be the Arabs who were about to need protection from the Jews.

Initially, their assumption seemed correct, because the next day Arab guerrillas attacked Jewish targets in preparation for the final phase in the struggle. The Guardian followed events closely, and the British mandate authorities, military and civilian, packed for their journey home, defeated. A new voice was heard in the Guardian leader column, still hesitant and ambivalent, but none the less a voice which expressed the fresh realisation that the Arabs might have a point in their objection to partition:

> Now the situation appears so menacing that it is a natural
> tendency to say that those who have long urged partition were
> wrong. And it is true that what could have been done easily in
> 1929 and with safety in 1945 is desperately difficult today. But it
> is a great mistake to imagine that any other solution could have
> prevented all trouble. If a unitary state had been set up giving
> the Arabs a major share in the government and limiting Jewish
> immigration, the Jews would have fought — and fought more
> fiercely than the Arabs. If no decision had been reached at all
> and we had just withdrawn as we threatened to do, the Jews
> would still have set up their state without waiting for authority,
> and would thereby have provoked the Arabs to far greater
> hostility. The situation is bad enough as it is and one can well
> sympathise with the Arabs' feelings, but it is, after all, largely a
> recognition of an accomplished fact. Those Arabs who at
> present rage against injustice should pause and consider how

they, with their meagre resources, could have stopped illegal immigration when a considerable part of the British army and navy could not stop it. Fortunately there are, both among the Arabs and the Jews, wise and moderate men who reject the heroics of the Mufti on the one side and the chauvinism of the Irgun and Stern Gang on the other. As soon as possible an attempt must be made to bring these more responsible leaders together. The Jewish leaders might start by banning illegal immigration until their state has been established. They might also publish a declaration of policy promising fair treatment and due representation to the large Arab minority. They might even — though no doubt it will seem painful — offer to make some concessions to the Arabs with regards to the boundaries of the new State, for the truth is that they could well afford to do so.[18]

The novelty of this article is that it indicates an about turn in the Guardian's editorial line on Palestine, and though the paper was soon to move back to a far more favourable view of the Jewish state, the leader includes some landmarks from which no turning back was possible. The Jewish national entity in Palestine was no longer being justified by historical rights or by the suffering of the Jewish people. It was presented as a given situation; its creation, and implicitly, the Balfour Declaration itself, might have wronged the Arabs, but there could be no going back. A very long time seemed to have passed between Crozier's leader calling for an expansion of the designated Jewish state, and this leader calling upon the Zionists to give up some of the land they had been granted by the UN. And still, as always, the Guardian expressed full trust in those "moderate" and "responsible" political leaders of Zionism — the Labour movement leaders — as the holders of the key to peace and prosperity. It rightly recognised that the Irgun and the Stern Gang, however radical, represented a marginal fraction of the population; but not for the first time it was wrong in assessing the true intentions of the mainstream Zionists who it embraced.

The state of Israel, once created, indeed stated in its declaration of independence an intention to treat its Arab citizens as equal, and immediately gave them the right to vote and be elected to Parliament.

But during the war of 1948, known as the war of independence by the Jews, and by the Palestinians as al-Naqba (the catastrophe), this same responsible leadership took care to turn the "large Arab minority" into a much smaller one. About 400,000 Arabs and 500,000 Jews were living within the boundaries of the proposed Jewish state in 1947.[19] By the end of the war, in January 1949, Israel had expanded its territory from the 55 per cent of the mandated territory of Palestine which was granted by the UN resolution to 79 per cent. Three-quarters of a million Palestinian Arabs were driven away from this territory. Some were expelled, some were "encouraged" to leave, others fled out of fear. The important fact is that the state of Israel prevented their return. Their property was confiscated and turned into state property. Their homes were invaded by new immigrants. The Palestinian problem was born. In the newly born state of Israel only 150,000 Palestinians remained. They were subjected to military government until 1965.

The British mandate in Palestine ended on May 14, 1948, and within minutes President Harry S. Truman announced US recognition for the new state of Israel. On the next day the last of the British army left Palestine. Arab military units from Iraq, Syria, Egypt and Transjordan invaded Palestine. The guerrilla fighting turned into a full-scale war. The Manchester Guardian welcomed the new-born state mainly by trying to estimate how history might view British policy on Palestine:

> The historian of the future, looking back on the history of the
> mandate, may decide that it perfectly expresses our national
> virtues and failings. He will see in Balfour's ready response to
> Zionism the idealism and sympathy of the British people when
> faced with human suffering. He will see in our simultaneous
> dealings with the Arabs and dubious attempts to safeguard our
> own interests in the Middle East something of that Anglo-
> Saxon hypocrisy which so annoys our neighbours and once
> gave us the name of 'Perfide Albion'. He will see in the Balfour
> Declaration a characteristic attempt to get out of our difficulties
> by taking refuge in vague and imprecise language which means
> different things to different people. The promise to favour 'the

establishment in Palestine of a National Home for the Jewish people' without prejudice to 'the civil and religious rights of existing non-Jewish communities in Palestine' led us straight to the terrible conflict which is now being settled by the blood of Jews and Arabs. Since we could never resolve the dilemma in our own minds we could not solve it in Palestine; knowing the knot must be cut, we lacked the will to cut it. The historian may wonder why no British government foresaw the rise of Arab nationalism, since Britain did so much to bring it about, but he will recognise that no one could have foretold the war in Europe and the terrible persecution of the Jews which turned Zionism from a creative movement into a passionate demand and from a disciplined march into a mad rush for safety. He will also note how easily our wish for 'fair play' may degenerate into helpless irresolution.[20]

As the war developed, the Guardian abandoned this melancholy soul-searching and returned to attacking the British government. Wadsworth had thought that Bevin was moving in the right general direction towards partition of Palestine, but doing it far too slowly. But on the issue of British military help for the kingdom of Transjordan in its war against Israel, Wadsworth, who rarely wrote about Palestine himself (most leaders on the subject were by Pringle, and after he left for the Times in 1948, by the editor-to-be, Alastair Hetherington) launched a very clear and typically strong attack, In the Wrong:

Our policy in Palestine is, there is reason to fear, Mr Bevin's personal policy, and Mr Bevin is an obstinate man. But our national credit matters more than Mr Bevin's obsessions and the Cabinet must act quickly to remove the reproach. To plead that we must help participants in the Palestine war with British gold and British officers because we are bound by treaty to a state we created is childish. Our business is either to help actively in bringing peace to Palestine or to keep absolutely clear of the war."[21]

By November 1948 the Guardian dispatched the writer Arthur Koestler to examine the nature of the new-born Israeli nation. His account makes fascinating reading. Koestler described the two strands of immigration to Israel: the "lost generation" of refugee-immigrants from Europe, many survivors of the concentration camps, and the expected arrival of Jewish immigrants from Arab countries, who would eventually outnumber the Jewish-European founders. He also engaged in a disturbing Darwinian analysis of the new generation of locally born Jews, the sabras. He was obviously impressed by the sabra male, who seemed to be "taller than his parents, robustly built, mostly blond or brown haired [...] he looks entirely unJewish". His conclusion sits well with the Zionist aspiration to create a "new Jew": "The whole phenomenon is a striking confirmation of the theory that environment has a greater formative influence than heredity and that what we commonly regard as Jewish characteristics are not racial features but a product of sustained social pressure and a specific way of life [...]"

Koestler noted: "The sabra's outlook on the world is rather provincial and hyper-chauvinistic. This could hardly be otherwise in a small and exposed pioneer community which had to defend its physical existence and build its State against almost impossible odds. One cannot create a nation without nationalism."

He wondered:

> What kind of a civilisation will Israel's be? Will it be a continuation of Western thought and art and values? Or the superficial veneer of Levantinism? Or will it go back to its ancient roots and develop out of them a modern but specifically Hebrew culture?
>
> For the time being the intellectual leaders of Israel are determined to choose the third alternative.

Like many of his contemporaries Koestler totally ignored the determining factor in the nature of Israel's existence: the 750,000 Palestinians who were driven from the new state. It was to be years before the world's media would turn its eye on the predicament both of them and of the Israelis. This was probably the reason for his hopelessly over-optimistic assessment, "no doubt this 'cultural claustrophilia' is also merely a passing phase".[22]

The Guardian did not ignore the refugees altogether; the news pages mentioned them from time to time. A sad Low cartoon from March 1949 showed Ben-Gurion and Moshe Shertok (later Sharett), looking back at a pitiful convoy of Palestinian refugees. "There, yesterday, were we," says the caption (see above, page 67), but the issue is absent from the editorial pages of the year. The Guardian, like the rest of the world, seemed tired of Palestine. There were more burning international issues to cover: the struggle between East and West, the rehabilitation of Europe in general and Britain in particular, the rise of communist China, and the Korean war. By the time the Middle East returned to the international agenda, it was to have changed beyond recognition, and the Manchester Guardian was to have a new and very different editor.

CHAPTER FIVE

Alastair Hetherington Goes to War

The Manchester Guardian and the Suez campaign

Petrol Prospects, Low, 23 November 1956

ALASTAIR Hetherington marched confidently into the editor's office on Wednesday October 31, 1956. AP Wadsworth was dying, and Hetherington was in charge though not yet editor. It was his 37th birthday, and the same day Britain and France bombed Egyptian airfields. Two days earlier Israeli paratroops had dropped into Mitla Pass, a narrow defile in the Sinai about forty miles east of the port of Suez but 150 miles inside Egyptian sovereign territory. Britain and France delivered an ultimatum to Israel and Egypt to stop fighting and withdraw 10 miles each side of the Suez canal. As anticipated, President Nasser of Egypt rejected the ultimatum and the British and French bombers went in. The next day Hetherington was finally appointed editor of the Manchester Guardian.

The tough Scotsman carried about him the uncompromising authority of the military man, forged by his experience in a tank regiment in the Normandy campaign and as a staff officer in Germany. After the war, followed by four years with the Glasgow Herald, he joined the Guardian in 1950 as a leader writer and defence correspondent, a role that he kept after being appointed foreign editor in 1953, and according to some staff members never really abandoned even when he became editor. He grew up in what he described as the academic household of the principal of Glasgow University, and graduated from Corpus Christi College, Oxford, before he went to war.

Wadsworth's relative disengagement from Middle Eastern affairs had meant that Hetherington filled the vacuum with regular leading articles. Unlike Wadsworth, Hetherington was a supporter of Zionism, but this did not save him from becoming the first editor of the Guardian to be attacked by Israel and its backers in Britain. Like his predecessor, Hetherington regarded with favour the growing power of the United States, judging it to be a great and positive force in the world.

He was also forced to take new circumstances into account. The grievances of the Arab states against Israel could no longer be ignored, especially in the light of Israel's growing belligerence towards them during the 1950s. Their alliances with other developing nations and the creation of the block of non-aligned states in the United Nations helped them to make their voice heard. On the fringes of history, a million Palestinian refugees drifted rootlessly around the Middle East. Soon, their time too was to come.

When the Suez crisis broke, in July 1956, Wadsworth, still formally editor, was already ill. Several meetings to assess the situation took place around his bed, and Hetherington was effectively in charge. On July 19, 1956, the Egyptian president, Gamal Abdel Nasser, had returned to Cairo from a triple conference with President Tito of Yugoslavia and Jawaharlal Nehru, the Indian prime minister. Upon his arrival he discovered that the American administration, followed by Britain and the World Bank, had withdrawn from their commitment to finance the construction of the Aswan High Dam. Nasser's reaction was swift. On July 26 he nationalised the Suez canal, from which British forces had withdrawn in June the same year. Egyptian soldiers now took over the canal company's offices and control centres. The canal remained open for shipping, and Nasser announced that its revenues would be used to fund the building of the dam.[1]

The British prime minister, Anthony Eden, was infuriated. Before an excited House of Commons the next day, he deplored the Egyptian action and said that the situation should be handled with "firmness and care". But his memoirs disclose that on the same day the chiefs of staff were told to prepare a plan and timetable to occupy and secure the canal. William Clark, Eden's press secretary, divulged years later that from the beginning Eden was determined to overthrow Nasser.[2]

The Manchester Guardian, unaware at this stage of Eden's real state of mind, responded with a level-headed leader on July 28:

> It would be a mistake either to lose our heads with vexation
> over Colonel Nasser's latest move or to underestimate its
> adroitness [...] The main interest of the Western countries in
> the Middle East is to be able to purchase and transport oil. The
> West can hardly use military power as a means of guaranteeing
> the oil supply. Any retaliatory measures which led to the closing
> of the canal would defeat the very end which Western policy
> should aim at securing.[3]

One of the ironies of the crisis was that during the action the canal was indeed closed by Egyptian block ships.

A few days later Hetherington received alarming information from the Guardian's Washington correspondent, Max Freedman. The US deputy under secretary of state, Robert Murphy, had been swiftly dispatched to London by President Dwight D Eisenhower to take the temperature after Nasser's action. Freedman classified his message to Hetherington as "strictly private and not for publication": he reported that Murphy had reported to the president that Britain was preparing for military action against Egypt; and that the Americans urged caution and negotiation. Hetherington was also disturbed by the leader in the Times of August 1. The editor, Sir William Haley, was believed to be close to Eden, and the Times's editorial line seemed to reflect the Prime Minister's state of mind. It likened Nasser's action with Hitler's march into the Rhineland in 1936, a favourite comparison of Eden's at the time. It urged the British government to take a belligerent approach, aiming to ensure that the canal would be in "friendly and trustworthy hands", unlike Nasser's.

Following this, an emergency meeting around Wadsworth's deathbed yielded Hetherington's leader of August 2, which was based on Freedman's information. It took issue with the Times, and thus with Eden:

> What Colonel Nasser has done may be awkward, commercially damaging to the West, and perhaps even part of a plan for creating a new Arab empire based on the Nile. But it is not ground for armed action — unless he closes the canal, or seizes the British maintenance bases there, or turns against his neighbours. We must be ready for action, but we must not launch it without cause.
> The Times argued yesterday that it 'would have been better to have had a foot in the door first' — which is a polite way of saying that our troops ought to be at Suez now — and that 'quibbling' about legal issues was unimportant. Such advice, if adopted, would destroy whatever claim Britain has to be an upholder of international law and morality. It would destroy the United Nations in a day, and it would land Britain in an appalling embroilment with at least three-fifths of the world ranged against her.[4]

As the days went by, it became clearer that the United States opposed a military intervention, and was making an effort to get all parties with an interest in the canal, including Britain, France and Egypt, around a negotiating table. But while Eden — pressed by the Americans on the one hand and by the hardliners in his government on the other — contemplated his next move, the two other conspirators to be, Israel and France, were advancing their own agendas.

Since the formation of his government in November 1955, David Ben-Gurion, who held the Israeli defence portfolio as well as the premiership, was striving to provoke Egypt into war, urged on by his maverick and belligerent chief of staff, Moshe Dayan. In spite of the fact that the chief of staff was supposed to be the mere implementer of government policies, Dayan took a leading role in formulating them as well. He believed that a war with Egypt was inevitable, and wanted it to start before the Egyptian army was ready. His tactic was to launch reprisal raids after relatively minor infiltrations from the Egyptian border, hoping to lure Egypt into a full-scale attack on Israel.[5]

The balancing element in the government was the foreign secretary, Moshe Sharett, who believed that war with Egypt was could and should be prevented. He opposed Dayan's massive reprisals, and considered them an obstacle to his efforts to purchase weapons from the United States. Sharett thought that in order to obtain arms from the West, mainly from the United States, Israel had to abide by international law, cooperate with the UN, and be seen as promoting peace efforts in the Middle East. Dayan, on the contrary, was convinced that if Israel was to make a nuisance of itself and behave as a vigilante, the West might arm it in order to allay its fears and keep it out of harm's way. Since the US allowed its allies to supply Israel with weapons only on the condition that it refrained from war, Dayan was seeking an alternative to Sharett's American orientation. The answer was France.[6]

France was disturbed by Nasser's growing influence in the Arab world. It believed (mainly on the basis of Israeli intelligence), that without Nasser's support the Algerian rebellion would die out. France offered arms to Israel in the hope of inducing it to fight Egypt. This fitted with Dayan's plans, and he joined the young general director of the defence ministry, Shimon Peres, in consolidating the French connection.[7] An initial relatively modest arms acquisition from France in 1955 laid the ground for the 1956 cooperation over Suez, and for the subsequent purchase of Israel's nuclear reactor from France.

On November 2, 1955, Ben-Gurion announced his confrontational policy towards Egypt to the Knesset, not without repeating his mantra about Israel's willingness to meet Arab leaders to discuss a settlement. That night a large Israel Defence Force brigade destroyed an Egyptian military post in Al Sabha in the Sinai, killing 50 Egyptian soldiers and capturing 50 others. It was the biggest Israeli military operation since the 1948 war, but it was soon to be overshadowed by another unprovoked attack, this time on Syria, on December 11, to be known as Operation

Kinneret. Sharett suspected that Operation Kinneret was intended mainly to undermine his arms negotiations with the Americans. It had certainly compromised the secret peace mission of the American envoy Robert Anderson, striving to initiate a dialogue between Ben-Gurion and Nasser. "Satan himself could not have chosen a worse timing," exclaimed Sharett in a cabinet meeting. In the spring of 1956 Ben-Gurion finally managed to push Sharett into resigning from the cabinet, and with his replacement by the hawkish Golda Meir, the road was paved for the warmongers, or "activists", as they were euphemistically referred to.[8]

At first, the Manchester Guardian had followed Israel's activities with little if any apparent concern. Its response to Israel's attack in El Auja seemed to support Dayan's assumption that Israel would be rewarded for its aggression. The Guardian leader concluded, "Exactly what has happened in the last 48 hours is not yet clear", but the solution to the situation seemed to be clear enough:

> [...] the measure which is immediately open to the West, and
> which might best improve the chances of peace, is the supply
> of arms, especially defensive arms, to Israel [...] and thus
> strengthen its government against those demanding preventive
> war as Israel's only hope of self-preservation. The American
> government seems a little nearer to coming round to this view
> in spite of contrary advice from some of its representatives
> in the Arab states. The present fighting may help it to move
> faster.[9]

This article treats the war advocates in Israel as though they were outside the government (that is, in the army), and the government itself as committed to preventing war, a description which fitted only Sharett. Years after Chaim Weizmann's death, and the departure of his personal friends from the paper, the Guardian remained loyal to its traditional line of supporting the moderate "Weizmanists", embodied by Sharett, against the Ben-Gurion activists. The Guardian had not forgotten Ben-Gurion's "anti-Weizmann complex". Yet, the paper was careful not to attack the Israeli government and its leader directly. At this stage the

Guardian had described Egypt as a warmonger trying to blackmail the West with its arms deals with the eastern block.[10]

Even after Operation Kinneret against Syria, although the Guardian admitted that Israel might have overreacted, the leader column supplied the necessary gloss on the action:

> There had been continuous, if minor, provocation by Syria.
> The Israelis retaliated in the end with disproportionate force.
> The Israelis make it no secret that this is the method by which
> they defend their very long frontier of 550 miles. They have not
> enough troops to guard everywhere against infiltration. But
> when infiltrations have reached a certain total they let fly with
> a single devastating blow [...] These tactics shock the bystander,
> and it is a mystery why the Israelis timed this last reprisal for
> the eve of the debate in the House of Commons on the Middle
> East. But whatever is thought, these incidents will continue to
> happen as long as the situation between Israel and the Arab
> states continues to be so electric.[11]

The article continued with an examination of possible deterrents against infiltration into Israel, on the assumption that the abolition of the problem would stop Israel from attacking its neighbours. From what is known today about Dayan's plans, this assumption appears naive.

This was how matters stood when Nasser made his announcement on July 26, 1956, to a huge and enthusiastic crowd in Alexandria of the Suez canal's nationalisation. The French government, led by Guy Mollet, was the most belligerent among the injured parties. While Eden, pressed by the Americans, apparently wanted to leave some leeway for negotiation, France was ready for war and was determined to topple Nasser. The French quickly suggested a triple alliance, France-Israel-Britain, against Egypt. Eden was reluctant to make a connection between the Suez crisis and the Israeli-Arab conflict. Ben-Gurion distrusted Eden, and feared British betrayal. The French put every possible effort into the seemingly impossible matchmaking between Israel and Britain. The true details of the plot remained confidential until the mid-1990s.

Eventually, a secret meeting was held at Sèvres, on the outskirts of Paris, between October 22 and 24,1956. The delegations of Israel and France were led by Ben-Gurion and Mollet; the foreign secretary Selwyn Lloyd with one senior official represented Britain, though it would be more than 20 years before the British admitted that any such meeting had taken place, let alone that there had been collusion in Musketeer, the plan to attack Egypt. On Ben-Gurion's insistence, the concordat was documented and signed by the parties. According to this, Israel was to launch Musketeer with a full-scale attack on the evening of October 29 aiming to reach the canal the following day. The French and British governments would then demand that the belligerents should stop fighting and each withdraw to a distance of 10 miles from the canal to protect shipping operations. This ultimatum was designed to make it impossible for Nasser to accept, since the canal was in their territory and would leave Israel within striking distance many miles inside the Egyptian border; it also included a demand that Egypt should agree to temporary occupation of key points on the canal by British and French forces. Once the Egyptians had declined the ultimatum, the British and French forces were to attack airfields in Sinai on the morning of October 31.[12]

The Guardian, like the rest of the world, was oblivious to this conspiracy. But during October it followed Israel's continuing raids on its neighbours with growing concern:

> The reprisal raids by Israel on Jordan are getting beyond the
> stage of two eyes for an eye and two teeth for a tooth. Admittedly
> the Israelis for long have suffered severe provocation. The Arab
> incursions go on ceaselessly — a painful and nagging trouble,
> even if each incident is small. But the reprisals are large and
> cruel, though less frequent. The latest, the Kalkilya raid, seems
> to have been one of the biggest military operations since the
> Palestine war. It has left 48 people dead on the Jordanian side,
> a police post and pumping station destroyed, and a village
> damaged. What good can it have done? It will not deter the
> irregulars and thugs who carry out the attacks from Jordan, nor
> will it bring a settlement nearer. On the contrary, it will give

Jordan all the better reason for seeking a military union with
Iraq — the kind of union against which the Israeli foreign
ministry protested yesterday. And the government of Israel
should bear in mind that the Tripartite Declaration, to which it
has so often looked for its own safety against a full attack, can
also be invoked against it.[13]

This, and a few other leaders in a similar spirit, provoked a debate on the
letters pages lasting several weeks between Zionists and Arabs. Among
the participants were Walid al Khalidi, an Oxford University lecturer in
Arabic (later to be known for his meticulous documentation of the
Palestinian villages which were destroyed during and after 1948), who did
his best to undermine the false Israeli claim that the raids were aimed
only against military targets; HM Woolf, who demanded that the
Guardian should present a solution to the cross-border raids on Israel
rather than simply criticise Israel's retaliation, and Jordanian and Israeli
officials.[14]

While Arab letter writers questioned Israel's version of the events,
Zionists engaged with the Guardian's leader writers, trying to alter the
paper's position. This phenomenon is intriguing, because it has persisted.
Rather than attack the paper, Arabs tended to confront Israel's
arguments directly in an apparent attempt to shift public opinion.
Zionists seemed keener on trying to change the Guardian's approach
than on disputing Arab claims.

On August 13 Hetherington was summoned by the defence minister,
Sir Walter Monckton, who told him that there was no decision to launch
any operation, and that he certainly wasn't a party to it. Hetherington
later noted that he was not aware that at the time Eden was operating
within an inner cabinet, excluding Monckton. A few days after meeting
Hetherington, Monckton himself, after an angry outburst about the war
plans in a meeting of the so-called Egypt committee, left the cabinet two
weeks before war broke out.

On August 14, another editorial meeting gathered around Wadsworth's
bed. The editor was worried by the number of readers' letters demanding
a harder line on Nasser. Lady Violet Bonham Carter, daughter of Herbert

Asquith and an old Liberal party friend of Winston Churchill, wrote to Wadsworth to say that the Guardian staff must be out of their minds if they thought that "dear Anthony" might launch a war.[15] Regardless, Wadsworth directed his team to continue the paper's line. On September 10 he wrote a leader that was to be his last for the Guardian, but his first about the Suez crisis. In it, he mocked those Sunday papers that had suggested that the government had been the victim of a wicked press campaign:

> With leading newspapers advocating the use of force, it is not
> surprising that people abroad thought the British were out of
> their minds [a phrase clearly borrowed from Lady Violet's letter
> …] The essence of the British position today, as most people
> understand it, is that we do not want to go to war unless a war
> is forced on us. We want above all things to avoid war in which
> the initiative is taken by us.[16]

A clear indication of the Guardian's political influence was the movement of Hugh Gaitskell, the Labour leader of the opposition, from an aggressive stance towards Egypt when the crisis broke, to a Guardian-like anti-war approach a few weeks before war was launched. This change of heart did not derive solely from his reading of the Guardian's leaders over breakfast, but also, it seems likely, from long talks with the paper's labour correspondent, Mark Arnold-Forster, who was sent on a mission to Gaitskell by Wadsworth.[17]

On October 29, according to plan, Israeli paratroops landed in the Mitla Pass and started driving towards the Suez canal; and the following day Britain and France presented the agreed ultimatum to Israel and Egypt. Israel accepted it, and withdrew its forces to a distance of 10 miles from the canal. Egypt declined. The British and French threatened to intervene militarily "in whatever strength may be necessary". The Guardian reacted to the ultimatum in its issue of October 31:

> The Anglo-French ultimatum to Egypt is an act of folly, without
> justification in any terms but brief expediency. It pours petrol
> on a growing fire. There is no knowing what kind of explosion

will follow [...] The Prime Minister sought to justify the ultimatum by saying that we must protect our shipping, our citizens, and 'vital international rights'. But what possible right have we to attack another country? The British and French military action threatened in the ultimatum, if carried out, will be flagrant aggression.

The leader concluded by arguing that the proper course would have been to call on Israel, through the UN security council, to withdraw its forces. At the same time both Israel and Egypt should have been reminded of the tripartite declaration of 1950 by which the US, France, and Britain undertook to prevent border violations.[18]

The Guardian opposition to the war was far more critical of the British and French governments than of Israel's actions. The same leader column gave Israel the benefit of doubt: "The Israeli operation has not yet turned into a full-scale campaign. There is evidence that it was conceived as a raid, very heavy and spectacular but with limited objectives."[19] Hetherington would probably have been stunned had he known that Ben-Gurion had gone to the meeting in Sèvres equipped with a plan he himself described as fantastic, and which included Israel's permanent occupation of the Sinai desert and the Tiran Straits, "cancelling" the state of Jordan and dividing its land between Israel and Iraq, and pushing Israel's northern frontier to the Litani river, at Lebanon's expense. The French and British had to push him back, politely but firmly, into the more limited scope of the original war plot.

However, the Guardian's editorial policy on Suez was enough, despite the leniency towards Israel, to turn Israel's supporters against the newspaper. Harold Lever, Labour MP for Manchester Cheetham, attacked the Guardian when addressing the Commons the same day:

If certain Arab aggressive intentions are not going to be moderated, than I am certainly not among those who would invite the Israelis to sit back quietly and be hacked to pieces, as their enemies mobilise on all sides ready to slay, bomb and ruin them, their consolation being to bathe their mortal wounds in the crocodile tears of the leader writers and cartoonists of the Manchester Guardian.

I, for one, could say many things in criticism of the sanctimonious humbug of those on the sidelines, who are rather like Othello […] who said of Desdemona that he would kill her first and love her after. I think the Manchester Guardian would sometimes like to do that with the Israeli people and the Israeli government; it is willing to admire and love them after they have lain down peacefully, qualifying under the rules of the best north-western Liberal school for a good conduct medal, but having sold the pass of their kingdom and sold the right of their people to live in peace, freedom and progress. Nobody on this side of the House need be ashamed of defending the rights of the Israeli people to exist.[20]

This intended confusion between Israel's right to exist and its alleged right to attack its neighbours at will was to become a permanent theme of Zionism's apologists. The Guardian, however, reported Lever's speech the next day, within its extensive coverage of the British-French attack on Egypt. The leader, headed "A disaster", left no room for mistake as to the paper's position on the military operation:

The world must be told clearly, as Mr Gaitskell said yesterday, that millions of British people are deeply shocked by the aggressive policy of the government. Its action in attacking Egypt is a disaster of the first magnitude. It is wrong on every count — moral, military and political. It is a severe blow to the Atlantic alliance, to the United Nations, and not least to Britain's prospects of material prosperity. To recover from the disaster will take years — if, indeed, it is ever possible.[21]

In spite of this fierce attack on a British government at war, Israel was still portrayed as nothing but a prospective victim of the British-French behaviour:

There is a further danger that, since a deplorable impression of collusion between Britain and Israel has been given (rightly or wrongly), the other Arab states will take the chance to attack Israel. Let us profoundly hope they do not.[22]

The next day the Guardian was flooded with readers' responses, some applauding the paper's vigorous line, some denouncing it as anti-patriotic. The philosopher Bertrand Russell, then 84 years old, wrote:

The criminal lunacy of the British and French governments' action against Egypt fills me with deep shame for my country. I endorse every word of Mr Gaitskell's indictment and of your leading article of November 1. Only one hope remains, that the United States will use its power to stop the fighting and to save us from the worst consequences of our government's insanity.[23]

The reader LG Minton of Cheshire felt as strongly, but in the opposite direction:

Your defeatist whine from the start and consistent failure to advocate a course of action — repeat, action — that anyone, however optimistic, had any reason to suppose would lead to a solution satisfactory to the British people can only have been of help to our enemies. Allowances can be made for politicians, who by reason of their 'calling' are invariably permitted extravagances, not to say a certain amount of licence, but the attitude of the world-renowned Manchester Guardian over Suez 1956 will undoubtedly go down in the history of journalism as its greatest disaster of all time.[24]

The Guardian was not alone in its objection to war. The Observer and, after a change of mind analogous to Gaitskell's, the Daily Mirror both opposed the Suez campaign. The Daily Telegraph, Daily Express and Daily Mail cheered for the government. The Times, in spite of its bellicosity during the crisis, withdrew at the beginning of the operation into a more detached position, and admitted that while boldness often paid there were grave risks in the government's course.[25]

At first it seemed that the Guardian would pay a heavy price for its stance on Suez. Circulation managers in the north of England were overwhelmed by the hostile response of formerly loyal readers. Norman Shaw, circulation representative in south-east Lancashire, said that for some readers to whom the Guardian had been essential, it became a dirty word. "It became the fashion to stop the thing. People used to say 'I'm never going to have it in the house'."[26] On November 10, Hetherington received a visit from the chairman and managing director Laurence Scott, who reported an alarming number of cancellations but, loyal to the family traditions, encouraged Hetherington to carry on with the paper's line. "Don't be put off," he said. "It may be economically painful for a time, but we shall have to live with it and you must not be influenced by it." Eventually, it turned out that the Guardian's circulation increased significantly during and after the war. What was lost in Lancashire and pointedly in Manchester, was gained in Sheffield, Leicester and London.[27]

Once the US had threatened to pull the plug on the British economy, the Suez campaign became a humiliating failure for Britain and France and settled their status as virtually defunct empires. Incidentally, it gave the Soviet Union the cover it needed to solve one of its own problems by invading Hungary knowing that the eyes of the world had been distracted by Suez. Israel had captured the whole Sinai peninsula by November 5, and Ben-Gurion hurried to make one of his most irresponsible speeches, declaring the occupied territory to be a part of the new Third Kingdom of Israel. Soon after, facing enormous pressure from the US and UN, and the explicit threat of a direct Soviet attack on Israel, Britain and France, Ben-Gurion had to recall his soldiers, to be replaced by UN forces in Sinai.[28]

Later in November, the Guardian reporter in Tel Aviv, James Morris, revealed that French pilots and Mystère aircraft took part in the Israeli attack on Egypt before the French-British intervention. Israeli censorship stopped him from sending his story and he had to fly to Cyprus to do so. Darsie Gillie, the Paris correspondent, gathered further evidence of the

French-Israeli collusion, published by the Guardian on November 20. The paper could find no proof of British involvement in the conspiracy, and Selwyn Lloyd denied outright any collusion between Israel and France when addressing the commons on October 31. He repeated this lie on November 24. Still, the Guardian expressed suspicion.

> Perhaps the denial is literally true. Perhaps the collusion was between France and Israel only. If so, were the British not informed in advance? Was the joint Anglo-French ultimatum to Egypt issued while the British were in ignorance of what the French had done? Is it likely that the joint operation to neutralise the Egyptian air force and seize the canal would have been launched so swiftly without prior knowledge of the Israeli plans? [29]

The combination of Israel's arrogant post-war behaviour, and the growing evidence that its government was deeply involved in the conspiracy to topple Nasser, no doubt prompted much more critical articles in the Guardian about it than before. Morris, for example, wrote from Tel Aviv:

> But the Israelis are perhaps optimistic if they suppose they can squeeze any concessions out of Egypt at all. Many of them think that by giving the Egyptian army a bloody nose they have strengthened their national position in the Middle East; they do not yet realise that in the eyes of most of the world it is they, not the Egyptians, who deserve to suffer sanctions. Indeed, though they complain of United Nations incompetence, their manner towards the representatives of that organisation is often insufferably arrogant.
>
> There can be little doubt that the powers now in the ascendant in the Arab world intend one day to obliterate Israel and are already doing their best towards that end. But the Israelis do not seem to know how to convince the world of that fact, or retain the international sympathies so easily commanded by the hideous agonies of recent Jewish history.[30]

Geoffrey Taylor observed in his volume of the Guardian history that Morris's piece encapsulated a great deal of Guardian sentiment at that time and since. The nature of this sentiment is complex. The Suez campaign marked a turning point in the attitude of the Guardian, and more so of some of its staff members, to the Middle East. If until 1956 Israel was seen by liberals around the western world as a state that could do no wrong — an inspiring socialist model, a democracy among dictatorships, a peace seeker among warmongers — it had now exposed some of its more belligerent tendencies. It was still very far from being denounced by the left or by the Guardian; but the general feeling was, and remained so for many years to come, that Israel's leaders might be moved by external threats to behave in a way contrary to their country's interests, but they were merely misguided. Israel's aggression was not to be presented as a threat to its neighbours and to the region's peace, but rather as a threat to its own chances of survival. Any criticism the Guardian might make of Israel was to be delicate and understanding. The paper still regarded the interest of Israel as paramount in the Middle East.

But on a deeper level, other elements were at work. Nasser's alliance with the developing world, and his policies of nationalisation and Arab unity, made an impact on parts of the socialist left, as did, to a lesser extent, the Ba'ath regimes which were rising in Syria and Iraq. It was no longer pure "socialist" Israel versus corrupt Arab royals. On the Guardian itself, the correspondents who covered the Suez campaign were still there for the next war, gathering new impressions and convictions regarding Middle East realities, which were sometimes very far from Hetherington's benevolence towards Israel. They were to have a great impact on the paper's position on Israel in years to come, as the climactic war of 1967 approached.

CHAPTER SIX

Watershed

The Guardian in the Strife of 1967

That's the trouble with the Arabs – they won't integrate, Abu, 25 July 1967

NAVIGATING the Guardian through the 1960s was not to be an easy undertaking for Alastair Hetherington. Dropping Manchester from the paper's title was the first change and was followed in 1961 by the addition of London printing to the Manchester operation. The Manchester Guardian had been well established as a newspaper with an international reputation long before CP Scott's ownership, but to be a national paper with a full reach across the country it needed to sort out its problems of distribution. Opening full operations in the south took care of that. When the editor himself moved to the London office in 1964 the Guardian became, de facto, a London-based newspaper, though no announcement in those terms was ever made.

The international political arena was dominated by the cold war and its regional manifestations. The new socialist experiments in liberated Africa, Tito's Yugoslavia, Mao's China and Castro's Cuba captured the attention and affection of the developing new left in Europe. The United

States, which epitomised for many post-war liberals the ideals of freedom and enlightenment, started to lose its aura for them as the war in Vietnam grew increasingly bloody.

Many on the Guardian editorial staff were among the disillusioned, but not Hetherington. For him, there was a right side and a wrong side in the cold war, and supporting America, or its representatives in regional conflicts, was the obvious choice. The problem was producing a truly liberal newspaper in a complex international and political arena. This debate inflamed the relationship between the editor and his staff time and again, and had a crucial influence on the paper's contents during Hetherington's tenure.

In earlier days, dissent could have gone unnoticed. Editors were powerful and newspapers were small, so they could keep an eye on everything that went into the paper. When CP Scott was editor, he was said even to dislike the term sub-editor, as a likely infringement on his prerogatives. But from the 1960s advertising was booming and newspapers began to put on pages; there were more features pages, more sport, more financial news and more international news. No editor could any longer supervise all the content, and the different Guardian editorial departments were increasingly run by relatively autonomous desk editors. Until now reporters were rarely credited with their names at the head of their stories. Instead, there was an arcane code of credits to "our own reporter", "our own correspondent", "our reporter", or "our correspondent", subtle distinctions understood only by desk editors at best. But with the increasing use of actual bylines reporters became household names, felt they had messages to convey, and grew freer with their opinions. Bias control, or keeping the right kind of bias, became a big part of the editor's work, and it was not an easy one.

In the Middle East, tension was permanent, and the outbreak of war between Israel and its neighbours was merely a matter of time. The founding of the Palestine Liberation Organisation in 1964 made the Palestinian refugee problem more visible and harder to ignore. The Arab states (mainly the host states of the refugees, Egypt, in the Gaza Strip, and Jordan, in the West Bank) saw the refugee problem as a major part of their grievance against Israel. At the Arab summit in Cairo that year

President Nasser made it clear that his army was not ready to challenge Israel again. The summit was united, though, in its determination to stop Israel's plan for pumping water from the river Jordan into its national pipeline.

The Guardian viewed the summit optimistically. The delay in action, a leader said, gave Israel time to start pumping, but also "the opportunity of making their own gesture of reconciliation. The means lie ready at hand; they concern not the waters, but the Palestinians who have lost their homes".[1] Hetherington was later to change his mind about Israel taking Palestinian refugees back into its territory, but for the time being he stuck to it, as he expanded his view:

> But here we approach the point of the Arabs' case too. It lies in a complaint in large measure justified, although they have not the knack of putting it in a way that wins in the West the sympathy it deserves. "Return" for the Jews in the diaspora is a figurative term; they have not actually lived in Palestine before. But several hundred thousand Arabs also, like the Jews, refuse to forget what they consider to be their homeland. And for them it literally is their homeland; they were born and grew up there. "Return", for them, is no metaphor. Whatever caused them to leave in the first place [...] the state of Israel was founded at their expense; if its population is to be enlarged they have the first claim to be admitted [...] Would not the inauguration of the Jordan waters scheme give the Israel government the opportunity for a new approach: an expression of its willingness to do its best to comply with the resolution? [UN 194, on the right of the Palestinian refugees to return] This announcement could probably not be very specific at first [...] But it would be an acknowledgement by Israel of its responsibility for the existence of the refugees and its duty to right their wrongs. Since those responsibilities are absolute — not conditioned by any responsibilities that the Arab states may bear in addition — the offer would have to be unconditional too.[2]

This article marked a revolutionary line not only for the Guardian, but in the international press in general. For a rare moment in history it touched the balance of Israel's right to exist and the right of Palestinians to their land. It attributed the responsibility for the creation of the refugee problem to Israel, and demanded from Israel an unconditional expression of willingness to solve it. Nothing, of course, was further from Israeli perceptions. In fact, Israel's refusal to admit any responsibility to the refugees has remained a principle obstacle to peace ever since. Zionist readers were enraged, and Hetherington, who was by then already irritated by letters from angry readers, took care in this leader to anticipate their antagonism:

> By acknowledging its responsibility towards the exiled
> Palestinian Arabs Israel cannot compel them to be friends. But
> by refusing such acknowledgment — by maintaining the self-
> righteous attitude all too evident in the sort of letters that flow
> into this office after every such comment as this — Israelis will
> ensure that they will continue to be enemies. And in the long
> run Israel can afford this hostility less than the Arabs.

But Hetherington's diplomatic editor had very different ideas. Terence Prittie joined the Guardian as a cricket writer early in 1946 after being a prisoner of war in Germany during the second world war. Geoffrey Taylor, who was foreign editor from 1960 until 1969, described him as "a natural conservative who would occasionally wonder at the meaning of the strange signs of liberalism all around".[3] Though a gentile, Prittie was a Zionist who deeply believed that the Arab claims were not worth considering, and for a long time had expressed his views freely in the Guardian. In his back page prime slot Diplomatic Commentary column he referred, though indirectly, to his editor's suggestions as "nonsense":

> The Arabs, in fact, oppose the Jordan waters plan because it
> could make it more difficult for them to destroy Israel — when
> they are militarily strong enough and politically united enough
> to do so.

This bald fact — which has been proclaimed often enough by
the Arabs themselves — makes total nonsense of suggestions that
Israel can buy peace with the Arab world by, for instance, settling
Palestinian Arab refugees in the Negev, to which the waters of
the upper Jordan will begin to be pumped and piped in June [...]
Israel, with a population of 2.4 million, already has an Arab
minority of around 250,000, which is subjected to a flow of Arab
propaganda as constant as that of the Nile, and which presents a
permanently nagging problem. No one in his senses would try to
solve a minority problem by increasing its scope.[4]

Prittie's solution was to distribute refugees among the Arab states.[5]
Hetherington himself later backed off from his demand for the
settlement of Palestinian refugees in Israel, and actually adopted Prittie's
ideas of settling them in Sinai and Jordan, with Israeli and international
help. Although the Guardian never again advocated the right of return,
Prittie's obvious pro-Zionist bias was becoming a problem for
Hetherington. Prittie kept bombing Hetherington with letters of
complaint about the writings of other Guardian correspondents,
especially when they had attributed to the Arabs any intention but the
total extermination of Israel. In May 1964, for example, he protested
because John Maddox suggested that there was a chance that Egypt
might return to a "more rational military policy". He also complained
because John Grigg's column suggested that the unity of the Arab world
would be an advantage to Israel. Prittie claimed that Egypt obviously
planned to attack Israel, and that Arab unity could produce nothing but
a unified attack on Israel.[6]

Hetherington replied by warning Prittie against his intention of
travelling to Israel as a guest of the Israeli government: "The real point,
however," he wrote, "is my concern to avoid the impression that we are
using the news columns to publicise select evidence that fitted in with a
preconceived editorial policy. While any such suspicion would be wholly
unjustified, it's easy to see how it could gain currency [...] I think it would
be foolish of you to go as the Israeli government's guest just now, and I
think we should call off the trip [...] [your objectivity] was not, and is still

not, in question in my mind, but inevitably it has been questioned by others, inside and outside the office [...] Hence my insistence on the need to avoid giving the appearance that we are in anyone's (Israel or other) pocket."[7]

In fact, Prittie did not find it necessary to go in person to Israel to be involved in its official information campaigns. An Israel embassy official from 1964 to 1966 remembers him as a vivid participant in the weekly internal meetings with the Israeli ambassador, Aharon Remez, and his staff — notably the press attaché Emanuel Sharon — planning the *hasbara* (Hebrew for "explaining" — in England, propaganda).

Hetherington's faith in Prittie's objectivity died a slow death during the coming years. In 1965 he rejected Prittie's proposal to write features from Israel while spending a sabbatical there fearing "too strong an Israeli aspect to what is written for the Guardian". [8] In 1967 he asked John Cole, then news editor, not to allow Prittie to go to Israel in Guardian time. "It is a delicate matter," he added, "but I fear that anything he wrote which appears favourable to Israel might not be taken by a number of our readers as objective."[9] A year later Hetherington wrote in a memo marked Confidential: "We ought, I think, to be wary of anything Terence Prittie writes about Israel."[10] Eventually, Prittie left the paper to become leader of a pressure group called Britain and Israel and promote Israeli propaganda in a more straightforward way. In his new position he continued to propose articles which the Guardian cordially rejected; and he continued to criticise the paper's position on the Middle East.[11]

1967 was another watershed in the prolonged tension between Israel and its neighbours. On May 12 the chief-of-staff of the Israel Defence Force, Yitzhak Rabin, threatened in a newspaper interview to march his troops into Damascus and overthrow the Syrian regime. In Egypt Nasser, well aware of his army's weakness but pressured by Jordan and Syria to show leadership, had sent a large body of troops into the Sinai desert, demanded the removal of UN forces, and on May 22 closed the Tiran Straits for Israeli shipping. A nerve-wracking three weeks, known in Israel as the waiting period, followed.

Levi Eshkol's Labour government was under enormous pressure from David Ben-Gurion, Moshe Dayan (now formally a politician), Shimon

Peres and their new opposition party Rafi, to launch a war. The three had abandoned the Labour party to form their own hawkish pressure group in the Knesset, and they kept up an attack on the government for what they called its appeasement policies. The government knew as well as Nasser that the IDF was stronger than all the surrounding Arab armies put together, but among Israeli citizens panic and fear of imminent Armageddon prevailed. On June 1 Eshkol, a man of moderate tendencies, bowed in the political heat and formed a national unity government, including Menachem Begin's rightwing party Gahal, and Rafi with Dayan as minister of defence. The tension in the Israeli leadership was as intense as that between Israel and Egypt. Eshkol felt that Dayan had been imposed on him, and on top of putting up with a man so alien to his nature, he now also had to endure the grievances of his foreign minister, Abba Eban.[12]

Four days later, war broke out and brought Israel's most brilliant military victory. It became known to history as the six day war, but as Hetherington noted, it was effectively won within six hours. In the early hours of June 5 bombing attacks wiped out the air forces of Egypt, Jordan, and Syria and destroyed a major Iraqi military air base near the Jordanian border. The Israelis, surprised by the swift collapse of their rivals, advanced at speed, and by June 10 had captured the Gaza Strip and Sinai desert from the Egyptians, the Golan Heights from the Syrians, and the West Bank and east Jerusalem from the Jordanians. A million and a quarter Palestinians, most of them refugees who fled or were driven into the West Bank during the 1948 war, were now again under the sway of Israel. "How do we control a million Arabs?" Yitzhak Rabin asked on the last day of the war.[13] Thirty six years later, with the number of Palestinian inhabitants of the occupied territories numbered at 3 million, Israel still seeks an answer, and still refuses to let go the bitter fruits of victory.

Israel fell in love with the territories it had occupied. On June 6 Dayan still thought it was a bad idea to conquer east Jerusalem, believing it wrong to waste soldiers' lives on a territory Israel would surely be forced by international political pressure to evacuate. But on June 7 he had marched into the occupied old city, and declared: "The IDF liberated

Jerusalem this morning. We reunited divided Jerusalem, the bisected capital of Israel. We have returned to our holiest places, we have returned in order not to part from them ever again."[14] On June 18 the Israeli government had already decided to annex east Jerusalem to Israel. Ideas for long-term keeping and settling in the West Bank and Gaza were soon to follow. The Israelis, many of them convinced that the shadow of a new Holocaust was replaced by the light of a new Jerusalem, were drawn into six years of euphoria, feeling invincible, celebrating Arab humiliation. Posters of generals were sold in memorabilia shops as if they were pop stars.

Back in the Guardian offices in London, the "waiting period" exposed growing gaps between Hetherington and his highly esteemed leader writer, Frank Edmead. Hetherington believed that Nasser had trapped himself into war with Israel, and thought that Israel would be justified in an attack on Egypt in response for the closing of the Tiran Straits. He was also concerned for Israel, which at the time "did not appear the invincible military genius that she later seemed".[15] Edmead, for his part, was certain that it was Israel, with its retaliatory raids on Jordan and Syria, which had trapped Nasser into aggression. The only tenuous agreement between the two journalists was that an attempt should be made to solve the crisis by diplomatic means, through the UN. The tension between the editor's views and his leader writer's was played out in the leader columns.

On May 18, one day before the surprise of Nasser's demand for the UN to evacuate its forces from Sinai, the Guardian's leader criticised Israel's reprisal attacks on Syria and Jordan, and called upon it to agree to UN forces on its borders:

> [...] Israelis say that reprisal attacks are necessary to deter the Syrian government from sending raiders across its frontiers. If this is their purpose, they are most ineffective [...] should they not try a new line that might give better results? A UN force, for instance, like the one in Egypt? [...] They [the infiltrators] used to abound on the Israel-Egyptian frontier until UNEF came there.[16]

The next day, the leader addressed Nasser's demand for the withdrawal of UN Emergency Force as "an act of sovereignty [...] but we can still regret it, most profoundly". It reiterated its opinion on the counter-productiveness of the Israeli raids, and denounced the threats from Israel towards Syria.[17]

On May 29 the Guardian placed most of the blame for the crisis on Egypt's blockade of the canal.[18] But in his signed personal column the same day, Edmead had made plain his feelings of frustration over Israel's actions:

> At the receiving end Zionism looks just like any colonial movement: settlers flowed in, to acquire eventually much of the land and all the political power. Throughout most of the colonised world, including Algeria and other Arab lands, the indigenous peoples have either checked or reversed that process. In South Africa, Rhodesia, Palestine and few other places they have not [...] In any case, acquiescence in what they take to be the injustice of a permanently Zionist Palestine seems as much out of the question for many Arabs as acquiescence in Mr Ian Smith's Rhodesia to many Africans.[19]

Edmead added, "Even those who most critically accept the justice of Arab claims must realise that their fulfilment would generate infinitely more misery than it would remedy — among Arabs as well as Israelis". But still, as Taylor remarked, it was "not the done thing in those days".[20] Smith's Rhodesia was criticised often and harshly by the Guardian, while Israel was still seen by majority British public opinion as the good, if bold, player in the game. Depicting Zionism as part of the colonial movement and indicating its racist nature was new in the pages of the Guardian, and was an implicit indictment of the paper helping to form those attitudes in past years. It fell on attentive ears in the new left.

However, it was clear why Edmead was feeling increasingly uncomfortable with Hetherington's editorial line. Even when criticising Israel, the editor was clinging to an optimistic interpretation of the power struggle in Israel between hawks and doves. His line was conspicuous in the next day's leader:

> We must hope that Mr Eshkol's statement to the Knesset
> yesterday at least served the function of enabling him to stay in
> power to continue his policy of relative restraint. The world has
> reason to be thankful that he and Mr Eban [Abba Eban,
> foreign minister] have been in charge in Israel, and not — as
> many Israelis are demanding — the team that launched the
> 1956 Sinai campaign, Messrs Ben-Gurion, Dayan, and Peres
> [...] The resources of diplomacy are far from exhausted.[21]

It was in vain. The next day was when Dayan, Meir, and Rabin became part of the coalition, with Dayan in defence (above, page 99). The road to war was paved. On the morning of June 5, when war was already launched, the Guardian leader, written, of course, the previous night, was still calling for private diplomacy to prevent fighting. On the second day, it expressed hope that the antagonists would settle for a draw:

> The Arabs' immediate aim is an Israel as weak as they can
> make it; the Israelis may be seeking to round out their frontiers
> (either for ever or until the bargaining) by seizing the west bank
> of the Jordan. Neither will feel inclined to stop if it feels it is
> getting its way at not intolerable expense. Thus a military
> balance would offer the greatest opportunities for
> peacemaking.[22]

The Guardian reporting team for the war included Michael Wall in Cairo — who, like Michael Adams in the previous war, was prevented by the Egyptian censorship from filing any stories until the fighting was over — David Hirst in Beirut, and Richard Scott in Washington. Harold Jackson was in Israel, overworked and bouncing from front to front to file his vivid eyewitness accounts of Egypt's hasty flight from Sinai, the muddy and bloody fierce fighting in the Golan Heights, and the Israeli celebrations over the capture of east Jerusalem. Hetherington was very happy with Jackson's versatility, which, in his opinion, enabled the Guardian to compete with the better-off daily papers, who each had three or four reporters in Israel.[23]

The reporting gained in depth from the work of the military analyst Hugh Hanning, who, using his access to military intelligence which monitored radio traffic in the battle areas, followed the strategic development of the campaign; Victor Zorza, an expert on Russia who supplied the Soviet aspect, and Bill Papas, the illustrator and cartoonist who flew to Israel at his own expense, and sent over illustrations of Israelis rejoicing in Jerusalem, Egyptian soldiers wandering in the desert, and views from the Golan Heights. Terence Prittie used his Israeli sources to outline the way Israel would deal with victory; Michael Adams portrayed the Arab response to defeat.[24]

The Guardian's attempts at balance were not appreciated by many Zionist readers. A Mr Cole thought that the "anti-semitic" paper should be destroyed[25] and John Cohen wrote: "Sir, that does it! As a Yorkshireman and a Jew, the Guardian is obviously not the paper for me."[26] Paul Rose MP had contributed what seemed a paraphrase of Harold Lever's speech in the Commons over Suez: "There is undoubtedly a danger that Israel, attacked on all fronts and devoid of diplomatic backing, may retreat into an arrogant and defiant posture. But the blame for this will rest upon those who [...] would have wept bitterly at Israel's funeral while refusing the guarantees which could have prevented bloodshed and who now self-righteously take Israel to task for having dared to refuse suicide."[27]

But there were other responses. Many readers, Jews as well as non-Jews, were horrified by Israel's display of force. "I write as a member of the Jewish community in Great Britain and as such I wish it to be known that I strongly condemn the aggressive and acquisitive measures taken by the rulers of Israel," wrote Margaret Lewis.[28] Others felt the need to defend their paper of choice: "I, too, have much sympathy with the Israeli point of view. Unlike some of your correspondents, however, I am aware that there are two sides to this, as to every other question. Not every newspaper has the courage and honesty to print them both. I am accordingly taking out an extra subscription to the Guardian," announced Dr Basil Dean. And David Rubinstein, a historian at Hull University, wrote: "May I briefly add my name to the list of those who have praised the informative and impartial nature of your news coverage and leading articles on the crisis in the Middle East."[29]

Hetherington, though many of Israel's most zealous supporters must have missed it, had shifted. He, too, was attracted to the idea that Israel would be justified not only in using the conquered new lands as a bargaining chip, but also in annexing some of it. Immediately after the ceasefire he wrote the leader himself, conveying some careful sympathy for Israeli expansionism:

> Their minimum demands must be free passage through the Tiran Straits [at the mouth of the Gulf of Akaba] and the Suez Canal, a more logical frontier east of Tel Aviv, ready access to the old city of Jerusalem, dissolution of the Palestinian Liberation Army, and agreement on the future of refugees. These were the kind of terms that the Israeli government appeared to have in mind a few days ago. The champagne of victory, however, has gone to some heads. Voices have been raised in Israel to insist that the old city must be held, that most of Jordan's west bank must become Israeli territory, and that an Israeli garrison must be stationed at the Tiran Strait. It will be neither surprising nor wholly wrong if these demands become government policy. But the chances of successful negotiation have to be weighed.[30]

It was no coincidence that this leader was written by the editor rather than by the specialist Middle East leader writer. Edmead was becoming increasingly upset by Hetherington's supportive line on Israel. In his signed column the same day Edmead wrote that one condition for Israel's acceptance by the Arabs was that it should be believed when it denied being expansionist.[31] He sensed a looming catastrophe brought about by Israel's insistence on retaining the occupied territories. Hetherington offered Edmead a break from leader writing in the reporters' room, but instead he resigned. The break was amicable, and Edmead said that the editor had treated their differences very fairly.[32] In an article he wrote for the Guardian after his departure he expressed the fear that Israel would still be occupying the West Bank "in 1970 and 1980 (although probably not in 2000) [...] however conciliatory the Arabs are now, the Israel government can still find reasons for not withdrawing. Yet if it does not, it will have fallen into the deepest trap of all."[33] In retrospect, even this grim prediction sounds over-optimistic.

Frank Edmead's departure, and the strong feelings it aroused within the paper, should be seen in a wider context than simply Middle East coverage. He was only one in a line of veteran and esteemed staff members who had resigned from the paper because of political friction with Hetherington. The three most inflammatory issues were the Middle East, Vietnam and Ireland, but there was also the general political and cultural stance of the paper. The features editor, John Rosselli, who left the paper in 1964 to become an academic at Sussex University, had a vision of the Guardian as "Le Monde in an English setting".[34] He wanted it to be essential reading for what he was not afraid to call the intelligentsia, whether they liked its politics or not. "It would be radical, vigorous, philosophical, inquiring." He felt that Hetherington was pulling the paper in too commercial a direction. The science correspondent John Maddox and leader writer David Marquand, who shared Rosselli's view, left at around the same time. It was not part of a concerted defection, but since all three men were much respected, it left its mark.

Hetherington's change of heart and editorial line in the midst of the Vietnam war added to the feeling of discomfort among staff. Until May 1967 the Guardian spoke up against the American involvement in Vietnam, carrying a series of articles by Martha Gellhorn in 1966, a powerful account of North Vietnamese suffering. In May 1967, Hetherington himself went to Vietnam. "The American officers managed to impress him, being a military man himself," concluded Martin Woollacott, a veteran Vietnam correspondent. This was the sentiment among most members of the Guardian's foreign desk at the time. They had to read in the Times, of all papers, a report about their editor's new convictions, as he expressed them in an editors' conference in Kyoto, before he returned home:

> Mr Hetherington admitted that his South Vietnam visit had left
> him no longer quite sure that the Americans ought to leave Asia
> to the Asians, and cease propping up helpless regimes. He had

been impressed by the civil effort, and the extension of the areas of security. He reckoned that for more than half of the South Vietnamese people the likeliest way to a peaceful life lay in "the Americans completing their military preparations".[36]

The report, conflicting with everything the Guardian had stood for on the subject, hit the newsroom hard. Upon his return Hetherington wrote a few signed articles and numerous leaders in the same spirit. Harold Jackson, who covered Vietnam for a period after Hetherington's visit, said that the editor never interfered with his own reporting, even though it was based on a very different assessment of events.[37] Edmead opposed Hetherington on Vietnam no less than over the Middle East, and it seems that the disagreement over Israel was simply the last straw. Hetherington, while admitting the disputes, summed up the Edmead affair in his memoir by saying, "university teaching claimed him as, from personal preference, it had claimed John Rosselli three years earlier".[38]

Other staff members took it less lightly. "You can't hire people like that; you have to grow them," wrote Rosselli's successor as features editor, Christopher Driver, in an angry letter to Hetherington, which seemed to sum up the criticism of many fellow journalists:

> Since I've started speaking out of turn, can I also suggest that your own interests and sympathies are now too narrowly focused for the paper's good (mine, perhaps, too widely). We are shaking off irreplaceable individualists at an alarming rate and the latest and most lamentable, Frank's, looks to the rest of us directly attributable to the fact that generals and politicians have your ear more than historians or students of Asian behaviour. (I doubt whether your argument on Vietnam will outlast a year, let alone a decade)...[39]

Edmead's resignation was not the last split within the paper over disputes about its Middle East policy. But for the first post-war months Hetherington was carrying the paper in the same direction: further understanding for Israel's dilemmas, combined with attempts to convince it to seek peace for its own good. This was radically accentuated in a series of features by Martha Gellhorn from Israel and the occupied territories, published in July 1967. Gellhorn fans, who cherished her courageous and humane account of the agony in North Vietnam, might have been surprised by her refusal to recognise any Palestinian suffering. Sitting calmly in a cafe in Bethlehem, while 250,000 refugees were making their way from the West Bank to Jordan across the Allenby Bridge, Gellhorn denounced "Arab propaganda" and allowed more than a few racist slips to filter into her writing:

> For the best part of a month I have been listening to Palestinian Arabs in West Jordan and the Gaza Strip. It always started well. Arabs have charming manners, though somewhat less charming to their own women, and are often fine to look at [...] then suddenly all was lost. "Bethlehem was bombed all day!" one cries. But there is Bethlehem, intact and rosy in the afternoon light [...] Fortunately, Israelis are not addicted to propaganda. Propaganda is the begetter of hate and hate is the begetter of killers. Perhaps, as time goes on, the Arabs in Israeli-held territory will decide that peace is more rewarding than propaganda. There are hopeful signs: Bethlehem is a joyous boom town, full of Israeli tourists; and the Israelis cannot squeeze into their municipal swimming pool in Jerusalem because it is full of Arabs.[40]

These visions of paradise didn't abandon Gellhorn even when she visited the refugee camps around Jericho, from which Palestinians were fleeing as she arrived. An Israeli official propagandist couldn't have done a better job. Gellhorn blamed the Arabs for the plight of the refugees:

> [...] blind fear of the Israelis, not the danger of war, was their driving emotion. Radio Cairo had promised destruction of the Jews [...] now the Jews had won, so the Jews would kill them instead.[41]

Even the sight of Israeli military vehicles driving refugees to Allenby Bridge to speed their departure moved Gellhorn to portray it as an act of kindness on the part of the occupiers:

> The commander had provided a car for their work, and truck transport for refugee women, children and old people to the Allenby Bridge. I surprise her [an Arab woman Gellhorn had met] by remarking that this truck transport, a gesture of decency in the white heat of summer, had been transmuted through propaganda into forced expulsion. If the Israeli army had tried at any moment to prevent the exodus, that would have been treated as forced detention.[42]

Abu, the brilliant Indian cartoonist and illustrator working in London for the Guardian and the leftwing weekly Tribune, illustrated Gellhorn's articles with a rather more sceptical view of the incident. One drawing showed two Israeli soldiers watching a Palestinian family flee. "That's the trouble with the Arabs," one soldier says to the other, "they won't integrate!" (see page 97).

Gellhorn advised the world "not to harass Israel for an overnight solution of the 19-year-old refugee problem":

> With time, work and money, the Israelis will manage simply by treating their acquired Palestinian refugee population as people, not as political pawns. During these 19 years Israelis gained much useful experience through resettling half a million Jewish refugees who fled to Israel from the Middle Eastern Arab countries.[43]

A month after the war was over, Gellhorn already took as given Israel's intention to hold on to the West Bank. The idea that Israel might welcome the Palestinians as it had welcomed the Jewish immigrants from Arab countries could hardly be entertained. It would be unfair to Gellhorn to attribute her advocacy of Zionism merely to her Jewish origin. As we have seen, in 1967 idealisation of Israel was a widespread trend among liberals, including a majority in the British Labour party.

But Gellhorn was not to have the last word on the matter. Gellhorn's articles were greeted by an angry letter from Michael Adams. From 1956-62 Adams was a staff correspondent of the Guardian, and, among other missions, had covered the Suez crisis from Cairo. Upon his return from the Middle East in 1964 he discovered that the post of diplomatic editor, for which he applied, had been filled by Terence Prittie, and chose to leave. His relationship with the newspaper remained cordial, and he contributed articles occasionally. On June 15, 1967, three days after Hetherington's leader that indicated the change of editorial line, Adams published in the Guardian an article in a very different spirit, headed The foundations of peace. Read today, post 9/11, it is chillingly prophetic:

> When the fighting started, Mr Eshkol's government disclaimed
> the intention to [take over] even one foot of Arab territory.
> A week later, General Dayan was talking casually of absorbing
> the Gaza Strip, the old city of Jerusalem, the whole West Bank
> of the Jordan, and the heights beyond the Syrian frontier. I have
> no wish to argue about these claims, only to state as forcefully
> as I can that they will destroy any chance of creating in the
> Middle East an environment in which Israel will be able to live
> at peace [...] If Israel now seizes the first opportunity since
> 1949 to expand [...] it will only confirm this deep-rooted Arab
> suspicion, and persuade the Arabs that not merely their best
> hope but their only one lies in rebuilding their shattered strength
> and waiting for the next round — when perhaps it will be they
> who will adopt the Pearl Harbour technique, with what may be
> deadlier weapons and in a suicidal mood of disregard for the
> consequences to themselves or to the rest of the world [...] We
> in the West, and Israel too, and possibly the whole world, will
> live in the shadow of these consequences — and it is at least
> conceivable that out of them will emerge a people as tempered
> by adversity, as hard and determined as the present generation
> of Israelis [...] But there is an alternative. It too demands vision,
> but of a different kind. It too is beset by difficulties, but they are
> no greater [...] Its starting point would be a disposition on the

part of the Israelis to conciliate rather than any further to
antagonise and humiliate the Arabs. Its essential condition
would be the willingness to acknowledge with no lessened
emphasis on Israel's rights that the Arabs have rights too.
Its intention would be to right wrongs and remove grievances,
rather than create more of both. Its conclusion would be a
settlement, rather than a "solution", a bargain, if you like, since
nothing else can reconcile claims so conflicting and where each
side is so much in the right.[44]

In 1968 Adams, who was travelling the Middle East preparing a series of
documentary films for the BBC, was commissioned at his suggestion to
write a series of four features for the Guardian about the occupied
territories and the Palestinians under Israeli occupation. By then, he was
already active in the Council for the Advancement of Arab-British
Understanding. His first feature described defiance of the 1949 Geneva
Convention by the Israeli army in Gaza, manifested in punitive curfews,
house demolition, and shooting in civilian territory. The last lines of the
article, given in a personal note, caused an outcry, which prompted
Hetherington to tell Adams that he regretted publishing it:

I had my ups and downs during four years as prisoner of war in
Germany, but the Germans never treated me as harshly as the
Israelis are treating the Arabs of Gaza Strip, the majority of
whom are women and children.[45]

Adams's second feature described further violations of human rights in
the West Bank, including a story of a woman who was thrown on to the
street with her five children while her husband was arrested and her
house blown up. These realities, combined with the continuing flow of
refugees towards Jordan, brought Adams to the conclusion:

The result — and it is difficult to believe that it is not the result
intended — is to terrorise the local population, especially those
who have small children or elderly dependents, and to

encourage them to leave the area and make the sad pilgrimage to safety beyond the Jordan.[46]

Adams's next story dealt with house demolitions in the old city of Jerusalem, and the house building for Jews on Arab land beneath Mount Scopus. Whether because he had a hard time believing what he himself saw, or because he was aware of Hetherington's apparent scepticism towards him, Adams sent the report with a private letter to the foreign editor, Geoffrey Taylor. "I cannot overemphasise," wrote Adams to Taylor, "the seriousness of the situation of the Arab inhabitants under Israeli occupation." He listed the names of neutral witnesses (diplomats, UN employees, medical workers), who could supply "verification of a state of affairs which I only came to accept after much scepticism". Adams added: "I realise very well how difficult it is to believe many of the allegations of ill-treatment, but I know that many of those listed above here have first-hand and incontrovertible evidence."[47] In a letter to Hetherington a few days later, Adams mentioned his letter to Taylor, and thanked him for "the confidence that you and Geoffrey showed in me by publishing my article from Gaza. I certainly realised that you would be criticised for doing so".[48]

Being so grateful might have been a tactical mistake by Adams. Hetherington was doing him no favours, and he was reporting the truth. Maybe the fact that his findings matched his own beliefs, and his sense of personal duty to alert the world to an unfolding tragedy had contributed to his appreciation of the paper's willingness to publish him. But he knew that his editors were under enormous pressure to stop his reporting, and some of this pressure was soon to come his way.

Hetherington's reply carried early seeds of distrust. "Have you, I wonder, seen the piece in this week's Jewish Observer?", the editor gently inquired, "[...] is it true that alternative accommodation of at least comparable or better standards was made available to those turned out of their homes? This has been alleged in one or two other letters I've read and was also put to me by Lord Sieff when I happened to see him a day or two ago. It's certainly true that the bulk of Jewish readers here believe that the Israelis have behaved with astonishing restraint. That's perhaps why they find it difficult to accept at face value your reporting of intimidation."[49]

In a long and elaborate reply Adams explained that even Jerusalem's mayor, Teddy Kollek, had complained to him that the government failed to compensate the victims of evacuation, and that only a minority were given alternative housing. He also wondered where Jewish readers in England derived such confidence in their information about events in Jerusalem, while Adams himself was the man on the spot. Adams remarked that he had difficulty understanding Hetherington's assertion in the same day's leader, that "there is much justification to Israel's reprisals".[50]

It can hardly have been accidental that in this exchange Hetherington mentioned Lord Sieff, the young Manchester businessman in Weizmann's and CP Scott's circle, and by 1968 the powerful president of Marks & Spencer and as much a Zionist as in his ardent youth. It is hard to assess the extent of economic pressure that was put on the Guardian at the time over its coverage of Israel, and even harder to estimate how much, if at all, it influenced Hetherington. Both Adams and Harold Jackson say they saw in the Guardian office a letter from Lord Marks to Hetherington threatening an organised boycott of the Guardian by Jewish businesses. No such letter is filed in the Guardian's archives; not surprisingly, perhaps, since when Jackson saw it the editor was nonchalantly, in the circumstances, using it as a bookmark in a volume of Keesing's Archive, the reference work on world affairs. Neither does the Marks & Spencer archive hold correspondence between Marks, or Sieff, and Hetherington.

What is incontrovertible is that in 1967 the Guardian had planned a special feature in connection with the 50th anniversary of the Balfour Declaration, which was to be supported by advertisement revenue. Marks & Spencer and other mainly Jewish-owned businesses made provisional bookings for advertisements in the supplement before the June war, and refused to confirm their bookings after the war. "I went to see Lord Sieff," Hetherington wrote in his memoir, "the only time in my years as editor when I undertook such a mission. He was reluctant to discuss the matter, but eventually said that he and others had disliked the way the Guardian reported the June war; and he made clear that, had I not pressed him, he would never have stated the reason behind M&S's action."[51] The special feature had to be cancelled, though some of the articles designated for it were published in the Guardian itself. Adams, though wounded by these events to this day, does not believe that it was merely, or even mainly, economic pressure that led Hetherington to doubt his reporting. "He was in London, surrounded be important people like Sieff, Marks, members of parliament, and angry leaders who told him I was in the wrong, and he believed that indeed I was."[52]

It was Adams's fourth story that led to final split between him and the paper. In May 1968 Adams discovered that three villages in the Latrun area west of Jerusalem, Imwas, Yalo and Beit Nuba, had been demolished and their population expelled weeks after the war. The story had been exposed already by the Israeli author Amos Keinan, who belonged to the military unit that demolished the villages, but refused to take part. Adams had access to the area and could record the evidence of demolition. The facts of the story were hardly controversial, but Adams wrote with biblical resonance and selected quotations from the book of Jonah. Taylor, the foreign editor who acted as a buffer between editor and reporter, was away in eastern Europe, and Hetherington, who dealt with the story himself, snapped. He had a noisy row over the telephone with Adams, and eventually told him that he no long felt complete trust in what he wrote. Hetherington said he did not doubt that the facts of the story were true, but accused Adams of concealing from the readers important facts, including that the destroyed villages were used as bases for attacks on Israel. It is not known (though not very hard to guess), where Hetherington derived these "facts" from, and Adams's riposte that it was undisputed by Israeli officials that the villages were quiet throughout the war failed to convince the angry editor. He refused to print the story or to receive any more features or articles from Adams. A subsequent series of meetings and letters failed to bridge the gap.

Adams later sold the story of the three villages to the Sunday Times, but the Guardian ended up publishing it first anyway. Harold Jackson, who, shortly after Hetherington's break with Adams, revisited Israel on the first anniversary of the six day war, which he had covered; while he was there he independently tracked the villages story, wrote it straightforwardly, and it was published in the Guardian on Friday June 5, 1968, a week before Adams's feature appeared in the Sunday Times.[53] Adams noted bitterly that Jackson's story included no mention of "attacks from across the border or other contributory factors".[54] "Alastair was not the man to apologise," says Adams today, "but he rang me before Jackson's story was published, and said, 'We are carrying a story by Harry that you might find interesting.' When I asked what it was about he said, 'It's about these villages of yours'. It was as apologetic as he could get."[55]

Adams returned to Britain and became editor of the pro-Palestinian publication Middle East International. In the 1980s, especially during the Lebanon war, he wrote for the Guardian again, though the desk editors were instructed to use him as writer of opinion pieces rather than as a reporter.[56] His relationship with the paper remained sour. He reads the Times and the Independent.

In 1972 Adams gave evidence for the defendants in a libel suit by the Guardian against the BBC and Richard Ingrams, then editor of Private Eye. In October 1971 Ingrams appeared in the BBC programme, A Chance to Meet, and claimed that the Guardian intended to print reports or articles about Israel but then decided to drop them because a number of advertisers threatened to withdraw their advertisements if the articles were published. Ingrams referred to the cancelled special feature of 1967, and apparently to Adams's Latrun feature. Adams said in his testimony, "It is impossible for anyone except the editor to say with certainty what impelled him to stop me writing for the paper. What is certain is that there was pressure and that he did stop me."[57] He also told the court that Hetherington said to him that the Guardian was in a specially difficult position "because of our large Jewish readership in the north-west of England".[58]

The Guardian emphasised in court that the articles were printed in the newspaper even though the special feature was cancelled, and that among them was an article by Michael Adams. The defendants withdrew, apologised to the Guardian publicly, and paid its legal costs. Ingrams undertook to the court that he would not repeat rumours of the kind. In its report of the trial the Guardian issued a statement explaining its decision to sue: "In the circumstances the plaintiffs had felt obliged to take the firmest action to scotch once and for all rumours of that kind, all of which were wholly without foundation, as the defendants now acknowledged."[60] This explanation strongly suggests that remarks by Ingrams were only the most public of the allegations on the subject to be directed at the Guardian.

The Hetherington-Adams affair raises intriguing issues. The Israeli-Arab conflict engages journalists very deeply, and usually commits them to one or other of the struggling parties. The conflict has become almost central to life for some of them. Terence Prittie became a propagandist for Israel, Adams for the Palestinian issue. Michael Wall left the Guardian, joined the Middle East International staff and, like Adams, became its editor; David Hirst, who was a Guardian staff correspondent and covered the Arab world for years, still lives in Lebanon. His book *The Gun and the Olive Branch*, which accuses Israel of stirring up violence in the Middle East but remains highly critical of the Arab regimes and the Palestinian leadership, was reprinted in 2003.[61] Eric Silver, staff correspondent of the Guardian in Israel from 1972 to 1982, remained in Israel as a freelance writer and a citizen. Except for Silver, who is a Jew and a Zionist, none of the above mentioned is either Jewish or Arab.

At the core of the heated dispute between Hetherington and Adams, was the very definition of an objective view of the Israeli-Arab conflict. Hetherington voiced the opinion that one who personally believed that Israel should not have been created as a separate Jewish state could not claim the position of an objective journalist.[62] "If you believe, rightly, that the Arabs have no right to drive the Israelis into the sea [...] you must agree that the Israelis have no right to drive the Arabs into the desert. Yet this is what they have done to many hundreds of thousands, and they are still doing it at the rate of about 5,000 a month," answered Adams.[63]

The argument continues along the same lines, which are whether acceptance of the basic Zionist claim to a Jewish state — which carries inherent justification of ethnic cleansing during the 1948 war and to a smaller extent following the 1967 war — could be regarded as more objective than the rejection of these claims. After the 1967 war it seemed to become consensual that almost any questioning of Israel's existence as a Jewish state was illegitimate. Israel's insistence that any discussion of the right of return for the Palestinian refugees was a threat to the state's existence had prevented such a discussion in the international media for many years to come. Hetherington believed that accepting Israel did not preclude finding a solution to the refugee problem somehow, sometime, somewhere. The debate over whether it is legitimate to express non-Zionist and even anti-Zionist views continues years after Adams's retirement and Hetherington's death. As this chapter was being written, Benny Morris, a revisionist Israeli historian who has dedicated his life's work to proving that an ethnic cleansing of Palestinians took place in 1948 and post-1967, said in an interview to Ha'aretz: "That has to be clear. It is impossible to evade it. Without the uprooting of the Palestinians, a Jewish state would not have arisen here."[64]

A third question is, assuming that all journalists have their preferences and biases, what is it that makes their work credible to their editors and readers. In other words, what was it that made Harold Jackson's account of the demolished villages, though nearly identical in its details to Adams's, being published in the Guardian? Taylor, the foreign editor at the time, Woollacott, a colleague and later foreign editor, and Adams himself, all agree that style has a lot to answer for. Hetherington, as well as his Zionist critics, couldn't stomach Adams's biblical indignation; Jackson's straightforward account of the facts seemed less inflammatory. One could argue that readers do not like to be preached to, which is the sentiment of many editors. On the other hand, articles which reflect their writers' horror of what they witness, especially in war or disaster, are often more memorable and influential. The two attitudes live side by side, and stir internal debate within the media and between the media and the public. However, in the Guardian of post-1967, the Jackson style of accurate and carefully pitched reporting seemed to have won. But Hetherington was yet to discover that this was not enough to make his paper immune to stern scrutiny.

CHAPTER SEVEN

Shock and awe

Towards the Day of Atonement 1973

When I'm Big I'm Going to be a Hijacker, What Else?, Papas, 18 September 1970

L EVI ESHKOL died on February 26, 1969 and Golda Meir succeeded him as prime minister of Israel. Her period of power marked the end of fluctuation between Eshkol's relative moderation and the Ben-Gurionist "activism". The hawkish line, as it was to be called from now on, prevailed and dominated in government. Negotiating the future of the West Bank and the Gaza Strip were now out of the question.

Plans for full or partial annexation with settlements of Israeli citizens in the occupied territories gathered momentum. Yigal Allon, deputy prime minister and minister of immigration absorption, presented a plan for partial annexation of the West Bank and the return of the densely populated areas to Jordan. Moshe Dayan, the defence minister, had more ambitious designs for a Greater Israel, from the river Jordan to the Tiran Straits, including the Syrian Golan Heights. Yet Dayan always opposed formal annexation and spoke of a functional plan, aiming to give Israel control without granting any but local political rights to the Palestinians. Meir herself was a hawk. She had no faith in any chance of peace with the Arabs, and believed that Israel was destined to rely solely on its military might.

The six day war of 1967 was followed by a limited war of attrition with Egypt between 1969 and 1970. It took the form of mutual bombardments between both banks of the Suez Canal. It caused heavy Israeli military losses, and led to the Soviet Union supplying Egypt with surface-to-air missile batteries, radar systems, and MiG fighter planes, eroding the superiority of Israeli air power.[1] Meir had rejected all negotiating initiatives. She prevented a meeting between Nahum Goldman, chairman of the Jewish Agency, and Gamal Abdel Nasser, initiated by the Egyptian president, and after Nasser died in 1970, she rejected the offer by his successor, Anwar Sadat, to open peace negotiations in return for Israel's withdrawal to the pre-six day war lines. Meir also rejected Egypt's suggestion for an interim settlement, involving a partial withdrawal in Sinai and the reopening of the Suez Canal.[2] Meir frequently expressed her willingness to negotiate, but her constant rejection of overtures combined with Israel's policy of building settlements in the occupied territories, made her declarations sound hollow. "For Mrs Meir there was something called 'the Arabs' — the adversary, the foe, the architect of our destruction," said her foreign minister Abba Eban.[3] She was incapable of viewing any Arab government or organisation as a suitable partner for negotiations, and her fears made her increasingly close to the hawkish military establishment and the defence minister, Moshe Dayan.

The Arab humiliation in the 1967 war turned out to be more dangerous to Israel than to the Arabs themselves. The air of euphoria infiltrated into the army, the government and the public, and created a consensus according to which the Arabs would never dare launch a serious attack on Israel again. The "conception", as this misconception was called in Israel, collapsed with the sudden and unheralded attack on Israel by Syria and Egypt in October 1973. The "conception" could be narrowed down to this dubious logic: if our neighbours are too weak to attack us, what could be the point in giving up territory in order to reach peace with them?

The Israeli occupation regime in the West Bank and Gaza was beginning to take shape. Settlements authorised by the government started to appear, at this stage still mostly ideological, populated by national-religious rightwingers. The project of mass settling non-ideological Israelis in the occupied territories was to start only under the first Likud government in the late 1970s, but the seeds were sown by Meir's government.

In January 1970 the novelist, playwright, and sometime academic David Caute wrote a three-feature series for the Guardian about Jews and Arabs in the occupied territories. He discovered that among all but a tiny minority of Israelis the words "new left" had recently come to acquire the force of an obscenity, and that critics of Israel's policy were depicted as anti-semites. The similarity to the situation today is glaring. Caute discovered the pioneering protest culture in Israel. He wrote about the public outcry over Hanoch Levin's political satire show, *The Queen of the Bathroom*, and the establishment's attempt to prevent it from being staged.[4]

After visiting the occupied territories, Caute treated with great suspicion Palestinian allegations about the torture of prisoners, even though Amnesty International found the evidence of torture sufficient to warrant an independent commission of inquiry. The Guardian allowed Caute some colonial condescension, and he felt comfortable enough to conclude, "No doubt the Arabs are partly governed by their own imaginations [...]" He did note, though, a policy of deportation, arrests without trial of workers for the United Nations Relief and Works Agency (UNRWA), and fines and confiscations as punishment for political protest strikes. "The Arabs — Israelis will tell you — respect strength and exploit weakness," Caute explained, without attempting to substantiate this observation. He also noted the danger of a flourishing economy in the occupied territories in creating Arab dependency on the Israeli occupiers.[5]

Caute commented dryly that the new Nahal settlements in the Jordan valley were "an engaging spectacle, except to the Arabs who have lost their lands". When he asked the Israeli minister Shimon Peres whether the settlements would not affect the political future, Peres said that they would introduce a "dynamic" element into the situation. Caute concluded:

The assumption that Arabs, but for their own obstinacy and bellicosity, could and should have lived as peaceful citizens of the Jewish state is quite simply an arrogant one [...] But if the permanent exclusion of refugees from Israel is yet another necessary injustice, the government's refusal to readmit to the West Bank those who crossed the Jordan in June 1967, is intolerable [...] Of all the creative options open to Israel the most dangerous is creeping annexation of the West Bank [...] Palestinian nationalism, of course, is precisely a Zionist creation. A people pushed, bought out, expropriated and forced to move on, finally evolved a national ideology and identity powerful enough to withstand that of the invader. If Zionism was a response to persecution, so is Palestinianism. But this is something that Mrs Meir has still got to grasp.[6]

Caute's conclusions demonstrate the line which the Guardian was to take on the Israeli occupation of the West Bank and Gaza for the next few years: gradual disengagement from Israel's original sin of creating the 1948 refugee problem as a necessary wrong; weighing in the balance rejection of Israeli refusal to give back the occupied territories and understanding of the reasoning behind the refusal; and anxiety over creeping annexation.

Alastair Hetherington himself moved from his 1964 position — calling on Israel to absorb the refugees — to the idea that most of the 1948 refugees should be resettled in Arab states, mainly in the Sinai desert after its return to Egypt. He was impressed by Israeli irrigation methods, and had a vision of Israeli-Arab cooperation on it for the benefit of the refugees, of "seeing the desert bloom, whether through Arab or Israeli skill, and realising what that can mean in a better life for peasants and refugees".[7] At the same time he thought it inevitable that Israel should accept at least a partial return of refugees to its territories.

Hetherington wrote in a leader:

Many refugees would refuse to be resettled, as would the guerrillas. But if there is tact and imagination, some would cooperate — and Israel will have usefully extended its policy of "creating facts" in occupied lands.

At the same time the broader problems of the refugees beyond the West Bank can be studied now. The Arab governments are bound to insist on the right of those who once lived in Israel to go "home". The Israelis must equally object that after two decades of Jewish immigration and development most of the refugees no longer have a "home" to which to return; that to retain its character Israel must remain predominantly Jewish; and that a large influx of Arabs will create a potential fifth column. The remedy can only lie in acceptance by Israel of the principle of a choice to return home, even if annual quotas at an agreed figure and prior security clearance are required. At the same time, resettlement outside Israel's own territory must be made more attractive [...] None of these, however, is likely to be adequate unless international assistance is forthcoming.[8]

The political stalemate between Israel and Egypt preoccupied Hetherington more than the plight of the Palestinians. It prompted him to launch an ambitious venture in the Middle East, motivated only partially by his role as journalist and increasingly by political involvement and diplomatic pretension. In January and March 1970 the editor embarked on successive visits to Egypt and Israel, conducting official and unofficial talks and interviews with political figures, and in the course of the visits, attempting to bridge the gaps between the Israelis and the Egyptians. Most of his discussions were not for publication. In his memoirs Hetherington describes his efforts humbly:

These journeys began as normal journalism; but because, as editor of the Guardian, I had access to people at high levels on each side I found myself being questioned on my impressions of the prospects for peace and war almost as frequently as I put questions.[9]

In Cairo he found himself at the same hotel as the maverick former foreign secretary, George Brown, who was by then on a one-man mediation mission funded by a private foundation. Cairo didn't seem big enough for both men, and Hetherington complained that Brown's presence complicated his inquiries. He found Brown "maddening to deal with, because he expected me to tell him everything that ministers and others said to me, but was not prepared to tell me all that Nasser had said to him".[10] However, Hetherington's cordial relationship with Mohammed Heikal, editor of El-Ahram and the closest man to Nasser, was instrumental in gaining him classified information.[11]

In Israel Hetherington held meetings with the foreign secretary, Abba Eban, deputy prime minister Yigal Allon, minister without portfolio from Menachem Begin's Herut-Gahal party, Chaim Landau, and the minister of police, Shlomo Hillel. His notes of these meetings display a mixture of diplomatic ambition, a genuine attempt to understand the complexities of Israeli politics, and a certain amount of naivety.

Shlomo Hillel, an Iraqi Jew, served as minister of police as part of a long tradition in Labour governments to have a token Mizrachi Jew in this post. Hetherington realised that Hillel was in the cabinet "primarily as a representative of the non-Western Jews". In this capacity, "he is said to be more closely in touch with Arab opinion than most other members of the cabinet". Hillel told him that the Druze in the Golan Heights were persecuted in Syria and preferred being under Israeli rule. They stayed, he said, while the Muslims all went. Hetherington also met Knesset members like Landau, who voiced support for the annexation of all occupied territories, and Israel Barzilai of Mapam, the party to the left of Labour that supported the Allon plan for future dispositions along the river Jordan.[12]

Hetherington identified Allon and Eban as moderates and saw his meetings with them as the most important he had set up in Israel. He had formulated a peace plan and hoped they might use their influence to persuade Meir and adopt it. Before his visit to the region, Hetherington wrote a leader in the form of an open letter to Allon and Eban, who were on separate visits to Britain. He welcomed them as "highly intelligent and reasonable men". He urged them to adopt a plan with two main components: the first was that Israel should confirm its acceptance of UN resolution 242, which defined the principle of "land for peace"; the second was that Israel should drop its insistence on face-to-face meetings with Arab leaders as a condition for peace negotiations.

Hetherington understood both the Israeli and the Arab positions on face-to-face meetings: the Israelis saw them as a test of the peaceful intentions of the Arabs; but the Arabs felt that to agree to meetings before Israel had withdrawn from the occupied territories would put them in the position of supplicants. Hetherington believed that if the moderates in the Israeli government were persuaded to abandon the demand for face-to-face negotiations, they would be able to convince the rest of the government to follow suit.

> The need now is for agreement that the talks can begin by being indirect, and that, if progress is achieved, then its results will be confirmed and concluded in face-to-face meetings and a signed agreement. The Egyptian government seems ready to accept this approach. If Egypt leads, other Arab states will follow. To avert war, will Israel not agree too?[13]

As Allon was leaving Britain and Eban was arriving, they met at Heathrow and read the article together. Allon told Hetherington later that Eban had teased him, saying that being described by the Guardian as a "moderate" would weaken his position in Israel.[14] Eban himself was comfortable with being perceived as a peace maker. For years he had been accustomed to being the velvet glove of iron-fisted Israel. Born in South Africa and educated in Cambridge, he knew the byways of British diplomacy, had a clever way with words and a sharp ironic sense of humour. He knew how to sweeten the most bitter of pills. He epitomised the diplomacy of Israeli Labour governments, which gave moderates the role of addressing the world, while persisting with hawkish policies.

Eban privately criticised the pig-headedness of his colleagues and masters, but in public never failed to defend their policies. On January 1956, after the unprovoked Israeli attack on Syria known as Operation Kinneret (see chapter 5), Eban defended the action before the UN security council, then dispatched an enraged letter to Ben-Gurion, condemning the operation. Ben-Gurion's reply was a classic: "I must confess that I, too, began to have my doubts about the wisdom of it. But when I read the full text of your brilliant defence of our action in the security council, all my doubts were set at rest. You have convinced me that we were right, after all."[15]

Eban viewed the defence minister, Moshe Dayan, and the growing political and public influence of the military establishment after 1967, as obstacles to Israel's diplomatic efforts. "There was one minister who said to me that a cabinet majority that does not include Dayan is not a majority at all," he complained in an interview in 1976. "My objection is not that Dayan spoke to people, but that he did not say the right thing."[16] Indeed, Dayan's straightforward belligerence contradicted Eban's conviction that engaging in diplomacy could gain Israel international support, regardless of the actual outcomes of such endeavours. "We should have been looking at the non-Arab world, and not the Arab world itself," he said. "Even diplomatic activity that is not leading anywhere is better than no diplomatic activity at all."[17]

When he met Hetherington in March 1970, the urbane Eban cast his spell. He charmed the Guardian editor with jokes and gossip, inside stories, mainly concerning the "common enemy", poor George Brown, then Harold Wilson's Jewish foreign minister. He told him how Brown got drunk at a dinner party in Eban's home and insistently tried to kiss Eban's wife Suzy.[18] In his memoirs Hetherington described a similar experience he had when he and his wife Miranda were with Brown in Egypt when Brown "arranged one talk with me in a nightclub around midnight, but the band made coherent conversation hard; I suspected that he really wanted to dance with Miranda, who was with me". But when it came to hardcore Middle East politics, Eban was unable to deliver. He rejected Hetherington's plan for indirect negotiations as a first step to reconciliation "on the grounds that nothing would be achieved until the Arabs and Israelis met face to face".[20]

Much as Hetherington enjoyed Eban's conversation, the man who made an unforgettable impression on him was Yigal Allon. Allon was one of the first Palestine born, or sabra, Israeli leaders. He was born in Kefar

Tavor in the Lower Galilee in 1918. Hetherington's conception of him as a moderate was hopelessly off-target. In the 1930s, Allon (then Pykowitch) joined the Special Night Squads, highly mobile offensive groups set up in 1936 by Orde Wingate (a Zionist British officer and later a charismatic leader in the Burmese jungle against the Japanese) to pre-empt Arab attacks during the outbreak of violence towards both Jews and British troops; Allon became known for his cruelty towards Arab civilians.[21] In 1941 Allon was one of the founders of Palmach, an elite strike force across the borders of Syria and Lebanon (Dayan and Rabin were fellow commanders with Allon). During the 1948 war he was in charge of ethnic cleansing, driving away the Palestinian population from the upper Galilee, Ramle, Lydda, and Be'er Sheva.[22] After the six day war in June 1967 Allon's plan, which was informally adopted by the government, led to the construction of militant Jewish nationalist settlements on the West Bank, including Kiriat Arba next to Hebron, and the notorious settlers' block at the heart of the city of Hebron. But unlike Dayan, Allon was willing to return a portion of the occupied territories, and that was enough to qualify him as a dove.

> "He was a man whose courage and sanity brought an instinctive response, or so I felt," wrote Hetherington. In 1970, when Allon was deputy prime minister to Golda Meir, he invited Hetherington to his home in a kibbutz at Ginosar in upper Galilee where he told Hetherington of his undying yearning for peace. "He said that a solution must be reached that would last not just for this generation and the next but for 200 years and beyond. He did not want his children and grandchildren to have to fight. When he himself was fighting in 1948, his son had been an infant. That son had been a corporal in the six day war and was an officer now. Allon did not want his grandson to be in the same situation."[23] He also said: "We can compromise on territory; we cannot compromise on security."[24]

So touched was Hetherington by this that it is doubtful whether he fully appreciated the implications of the political vision Allon had presented to him. Allon said that most Israelis would never support withdrawal from all the occupied territories, and that therefore only the question of how much territory Israel might yield could be discussed. He said that Israel might agree to give back two-thirds of the West Bank, providing that it could keep "security belts" of settlements in the Jordan valley. Allon said that "for religious reasons a Jewish community must be re-established in Hebron, south of Jerusalem, for one had existed there throughout the ages until the massacre in 1929".[25] He did not mention restoration of the Palestinian towns and villages destroyed in 1948.

As far as Hetherington's peace initiative went, Allon said he did not see why Israel should restate its commitment to UN resolution 242. "We adhered to it in the past, why should we say it again?" he wondered.[26] As for Nasser, Allon insisted that he should accept face-to-face meetings.[27] Hetherington was not taken aback by this chilly response to his plan, accepting that Allon had reaffirmed Israel's attachment to resolution 242 and that indirect negotiations could begin as long as Nasser committed himself in advance to negotiations across the table.[28] "Few meetings in my life have left me with as strong an impression as that morning at Ginosar," Hetherington concluded about his encounter with the architect of Israel's settlements policy. "Only Willy Brandt and Jack Kennedy had as powerful an effect."[29]

Hetherington aligned the Guardian with the policies of the doves in Meir's government, following, as always in the Guardian, the moderate tendency within the Israel Labour party in particular, and "soft Zionism" in general. Even when Israeli politics lurched to the right, taking the so-called moderates with it, the editor continued to see them as political allies. But Hetherington was not blind to the dominance of the hardliners Meir and Dayan, as much as he was impressed by his meeting with Allon, he saw that the desired peace process was unlikely to be pushed forward by politicians like him or Eban and could not help wondering how much chance there was of persuading Nasser or Hussein to accept it?[30]

During his journey to the Middle East Hetherington met no Palestinians and avoided the occupied territories. For him, as for most of the world at the time, the Palestinians did not exist as a political entity. But this attitude could not survive the combination of airplane hijacking and international terrorism that turned the Palestinian problem into a household issue in Europe during the early 1970s. Terrorist attacks inside Israel and the growing political and diplomatic dimension of the Palestinian Liberation Organisation drew growing attention to the Palestinian plight.

Despite Hetherington's enthusiasm over his Middle East journeys, he became disenchanted with the prospects for peace. Israel's refusal to engage in peace talks, its determination to build more and more settlements, and the measures it took to strengthen its grasp in the occupied territories, were all a bitter disillusionment. The Guardian seemed for a time weary of the whole subject, and reporting gradually declined. Nasser's death in September 1970 was an additional blow to the Guardian's interest in the conflict. Nasser was an exciting and engaging character, and his successor, Anwar Sadat, seemed to lack charisma and daring. As it turned out, Sadat proved to be bold and courageous in war as in peace, but his advent was seen at first as an omen of further stagnation.

As the Guardian's view of the conflict evolved, Hetherington felt unjustly attacked by advocates of both sides. He felt that the Jewish groups which disapproved of the Guardian were blind to the benevolence of his criticism of Israel, and that the new left and pro-Palestinian groups, who regarded the Guardian as biased in favour of Israel, were ignoring his attempts at even-handedness.

A feature by David Hirst, the Guardian's celebrated Middle East correspondent, triggered one of the major outbursts. Hirst visited Jerusalem in 1972 and reported on the Israeli disregard of Muslim heritage and the demolition of historic buildings during the excavations around the Western Wall. But in his anger over this brutality he misguidedly wrote a disrespectful description of Jewish worshippers at the Wailing Wall, a description sharpened by his obvious regard for the Muslim worshippers:

> The two great mosques, Al-Aqsa and the Dome of the Rock, still summon the faithful to prayer, but from below, the confused murmur of the Jewish worshippers, swaying and chanting at the

vastly enlarged Wailing Wall in their ungainly black garments, disturbs the exclusive sanctity of the Muslim shrines, while thousands of Jewish visitors, forbidden down the centuries, daily invade the sacred precincts themselves.[31]

This unfortunate paragraph, which was immediately branded anti-semitic, blurred Hirst's basically just complaint over Israel's treatment of the holy quarters of Jerusalem's old city. It was highly untypical of Hirst, who had an impeccable reputation even among opponents for his fairness and for cleaving to facts. His attacks on Arab regimes caused his deportation from all Arab states in the region at various times. He did not spare any leader in the region, including Yasser Arafat, and his resentment of Zionism never blurred his hatred for anti-semitism and racism. Nevertheless, this was a bad slip, and Israel's advocates were fast to respond. Among the angry letters to the Guardian was one from Terrence Prittie, the former diplomatic editor in his new role as a pro-Israeli propagandist.

Prittie was a frequent fault finder, and his letters of grievance often landed on Hetherington's desk. In May 1971, for example, he complained about a column by Peter Jenkins, who claimed that Golda Meir intended to keep all the territories which Israel occupied in 1967. Prittie behaved as if this accusation was unthinkable. "Peter's piece looked to me like a somewhat uninformed piece of writing, intended to fill up his column," wrote Prittie, ignoring the reality that Jenkins' depiction of Meir's policies was strikingly accurate.[32] But in the case of Hirst and the Wailing Wall, Prittie certainly had a case, and Hetherington was quick to redress the wrong using a favourite Guardian method — assigning another reporter to write the same story from a different angle. A "balancing" feature by Walter Schwarz, which appeared 10 days after Hirst's controversial piece, stilled the anger for a while, and Prittie thanked Hetherington.

On October 6, 1973, in the midst of Yom Kippur, the Jewish Day of Atonement, Egypt and Syria attacked Israel without warning. It was a rude awakening for a country still absorbed in its post-1967 euphoria and contempt for the Arabs and their military abilities. The so-called Yom

Kippur war did not end later that month in any Arab territorial gain but Israel had been taken by surprise, had suffered the loss of 2,569 soldiers and had faced an impressive military performance by Egypt and Syria. All this restored Arab pride, honour and self-confidence and caused a political, cultural and social earthquake in Israel.

The Guardian almost welcomed the war as a potential icebreaker. The leader on October 8 seemed nearly optimistic:

> If it [the Egyptian offensive] succeeds even to the extent of securing one or two firm bridgeheads on the canal's east bank, the effect on Egyptian morale will be enormous. That could, paradoxically, make negotiation between the Arabs and Israel easier [...] If Egypt were to decide to come to terms with Israel, all the others would follow, however protestingly [...] Syria's objectives are probably limited to support of Egypt and embarrassment of Israel. The Golan Heights have been well fortified by Israel since 1967, and that barren plateau is anyway of little more than symbolic significance to President Assad and his colleagues [...] It is significant that Arab broadcasts, unlike those of 1948 and 1956 and 1967, no longer proclaim any intention to try to drive the Zionists into the sea. That may only show a more discreet prudence than in the past, but it may also indicate that after 25 years of living alongside Israel most Arab leaders now recognise that they will have to come to terms. The Palestinians differ from them in this, but the Palestinians are a declining force. Resolution 242 — the well-devised UN basis for a settlement — may yet come into its own.[34]

The leader was right about the effects of the rise in Egyptian morale on the chances of peace. Previously they had been beaten out of sight in any conflict of arms with Israel; now, they could speak on equal terms. The leader tactfully did not mention the useful effect of Israeli humiliation on the chances of peace, though that too was a factor since the supposed impregnability of Israel had been shown to be a mirage. It was wrong both in the assessment that Syria would follow Egypt's road to peace as it had in war, and even more so in disregarding President Hafez Al-Assad's deeply serious intention of regaining the Golan Heights. The fierce fighting of the Syrians and the huge losses Israel suffered in the battle over the Golan Heights in 1973 traumatised a generation of Israelis, and it was now clear that peace with Syria would not be possible without returning the heights. But the Guardian's most conspicuous error was the assessment that the Palestinians were a "declining force". Their stubborn struggle for freedom soaked in Palestinian as well as Israeli blood remains at the centre of the Middle East imbroglio 30 years later.

Eleven days into the war, the Guardian speculated about what would be the best result to keep resolution 242 alive:

> If the battle eventually goes Israel's way, and if the Egyptians
> are thrown back across the Suez Canal, then there will be no
> hope whatever of negotiation [...] But, no less dangerous, if
> diplomacy is left until the Egyptians have driven the Israelis out
> of Sinai, it will again be too late. The Arabs will then demand
> punitive terms for making peace, which the Israelis are bound
> to refuse. Resolution 242 will have been mainly destroyed.[35]

In other words, Israel should lose a little, to prevent it from returning to its arrogant rejection of peace, but it should also keep occupied territories, to be used as bargaining chips for peace. Hetherington was obviously worried about Israel's fate, and wanted it to be in an advantageous post-war situation; but as always, what he saw as objectivity was perceived differently by many readers. The Guardian's line on the 1973 war provoked more long-running animosity from Zionist circles. In January 1974 the Jewish Gazette, a north of England publication, ran the headline Boycott Guardian call by Degroot — Mr Degroot was the chairman of the Zionist General Council political committee, and the story beneath the headline reported that, because the Guardian had allegedly deteriorated since the days of CP Scott, Jewish readers should switch to the Daily Telegraph.[36]

A few days later the Guardian rejected an advertisement by the Committee for Justice in the Middle East, a body which Hetherington described in his book as a Jewish group of anti-Zionists. Hetherington had previously laid down a policy that political advertisements should not be censored unless they clearly carried misleading or incorrect information, and he steadfastly maintained that whatever the political agenda of proposed advertisements. In the case of the advertisement proffered by the Committee for Justice in the Middle East, the Guardian executive editor, John Ryan, whose job included liaising between editorial departments and the advertising department, rejected the advertisement and then discovered to his surprise that the Times would be running it. He sent a note to Hetherington, who replied: "The Arab ad: quite right to keep it out, though in itself it contains no evident inaccuracies. We ought to keep a log of these that we are refusing."[37]

On another occasion, the Guardian felt obliged to apologise for an advertisement placed by an organisation called Free Palestine. The advertisement accused Israel of dropping booby-trapped dolls and teddy bears on a refugee camp in Lebanon on May 17, 1974, causing the deaths of two children. The Guardian decided to run the advertisement since the pictures it contained were issued internationally by Associated Press (AP), and accompanied reports in a number of newspapers quoting Palestinian allegations of the use of booby-trapped toys. A protest by the Israeli embassy and the Board of Deputies of British Jews, and a campaign by the Jewish Gazette for a boycott of the Guardian, led Hetherington to retract and publish a statement saying that while verification could not be obtained, the Guardian thought it highly improbable that the government of Israel had employed booby-trapped toys. He expressed regret for printing the original advertisement. "That, of course, brought on Arab complaints that we had yielded to Israeli pressure," wrote Hetherington.[38]

During 1974 the Guardian gave less space to the precarious ceasefire between Israel and the Arab states, and engaged a little more with the Palestinian struggle. In April a leader congratulated the Jewish Chronicle for publishing an interview with Said Hammami from the PLO, and the Israeli daily Yediot Aharonot for carrying an interview with Nayef Hawatma, leader of the Democratic Front for the Liberation of Palestine. The Guardian saw it favourably that two Palestinian leaders, "a minimalist and a maximalist", had addressed Jews and Israelis directly, and added:

> [...] the interviews indicate a recognition of an Israeli entity. In return, the Palestinians deserve to be recognised as being more than refugees with terrorist fringes. If these interviews lead to dialogue, it will be a start on the heart of the Middle East problem.[39]

In November, the Arab summit in Rabat established the PLO as the sole representative of the Palestinian people. The PLO moved towards a demand for a Palestinian state in the West Bank and Gaza.[40] The Guardian called upon Israel to recognise the PLO and engage in negotiation with its leader, Yasser Arafat:

> For Israel the next step towards settlement must be to recognise Arafat and the PLO. No government enters gladly into talks with terrorists. But talking to terrorists is a hurdle which any government in Israel's position has to face, as the British have discovered many times. The PLO can also legitimately say, as other terrorists cannot, that there is no government to speak for them. The Israelis must of course keep their country. They must be allowed to live in it in peace. But the Palestinians, too, must have a home and a peaceful one. What everyone has to realise, even if they do not admit it, is that there is no warlike way of achieving these ends. The solution has to be political. It must lead to a position in which the peoples of the Middle East live and prosper together — as they can.[41]

With this leader, the Guardian's attitude to the Palestinian question was crystallised for years to come: recognition of the PLO as the representative of the Palestinian people, demand from Israel to engage in negotiation with it, and encouragement of any act which might lead to dialogue or further understanding. But the idea that the Palestinian right to "a peaceful home" equalled that of the Israelis seemed to Israeli and

British Zionists outrageous. Even the notion that Israel should negotiate with the PLO was perceived by some as anti-semitic. The Guardian, in spite all its efforts, was gaining a reputation as anti-Israeli on one hand, and over-sympathetic to Israel on the other.

The experience distanced the Guardian and its editor from the paper's traditional cooperation with the Jewish community. In January 1973 Benjamin Gill, the general secretary of Zionist Central Council of Manchester, wrote to Hetherington, suggesting that the Guardian should publish a special supplement for Israel's 25th anniversary. He offered to supply a list of businesses in the Manchester area, likely to place advertisements in it. He also offered his help with facts, figures and statistics.[42] But Hetherington had not forgotten the fiasco of the cancelled 1967 supplement.[43] "I am grateful for your readiness to assist," he replied. "However, remembering what happened last time we undertook such a special feature, I think it unlikely that we shall repeat the attempt this year."[44]

In August 1974 Gill asked Hetherington to be the patron of the centenary events for Chaim Weizmann's birth, which the Zionist Central Council of Manchester was organising.[45] Hetherington offered to do "all we could do to help with the preparations", but declined to become the patron of the event. "I hope you will not misunderstand," he wrote, "when I say that in view of the crossfire of Jewish and Arab criticism in which we have been caught in the past 12 months, I really think that it would be inappropriate. People on both sides have accused the Guardian and me personally of hostility, misrepresentation and malice, although we have done our best to be fair and thorough both in reporting and in comment. I have been particularly saddened by some of the criticisms from Manchester."[46]

The years which followed the Yom Kippur war signified major and significant changes inside Israel. The war led to social unrest, and the rise of the Israeli peace movement on the one hand, and on the other the national religious settlement movement Gush Emunim, which held that the occupied territories had been divinely ordained. The second generation of Mizrachi Jews in Israel started to rebel against discrimination and social injustice, and formed the Israeli Black

Panthers. The accumulating resentment against the Labour regime was enhanced farther by the publication of the Agranat commission of inquiry report, which placed the blame for the Yom Kippur setback on the army rather than on the government. In 1977 the first Likud government of the right, led by Menachem Begin, was formed.

The 1973 war, as Hetherington foresaw, had paved the way to a peace agreement with Egypt, but these events were to be covered by a new editor. Hetherington left the Guardian in 1975 to start a fresh career with the BBC in Scotland. One of the last leaders he wrote for the Guardian denounced the UN assembly for the resolution that defined Zionism as "a form of racism and racial discrimination", calling it a wild swipe at Israel.[47]

CHAPTER EIGHT

Sour Grapes

Likud Years

We did not know what was going on, Gibbard, 20 September 1982

"I SRAEL's voters pull away the peace rug. Menachem Begin elected prime minister," ran the heading and subhead of the Guardian leader on May 19, 1977.[1] The headline marked a new era in the Guardian-Israel relationship: post-Hetherington for the Guardian; post Labour governments for Israel.

Begin, leader of the rightwing Likud party, was not a new name to the British public. As leader of the Irgun rightwing underground militia during the years of British mandate in Palestine, he was responsible for the bombing of the British headquarters at the King David hotel, and the hanging of two British sergeants kidnapped by his organisation. The 31 years that had elapsed between the King David bombing and Begin's premiership did not wipe the blood from his hands in the eyes of many British people. The Irgun's slogan, "there are two banks to the river Jordan, one is ours, and so is the other", echoed again. Begin's adherence to the ideology of "the whole Eretz Israel" (Greater Israel), which included, at the very least, the West Bank and Gaza, made peace seem more remote than ever. It was inconceivable at the time that Begin would be the first Israeli prime minister to sign a peace agreement with an Arab state, and to give away some of the territories conquered in 1967.

The Guardian, which had habitually supported Labour party "moderates" against Labour party "activists", had to get used to a new Israeli political reality for which it had little sympathy.

But the paper's changing line on Israel had a lot to do with the personality and convictions of Peter Preston, who replaced Alastair Hetherington as editor in 1975. Preston was neither a Zionist nor an anti-Zionist. Like Hetherington, he believed that Israel had the right to exist within the pre-1967 boundaries acknowledged by the UN, and that the West Bank and Gaza should be a matter for negotiation with the Palestinians through their representative, the Palestine Liberation Organisation. Unlike his predecessor, Preston did not believe that Israel should be treated with kid gloves. During his tenure the Guardian shifted from benevolent criticism that aspired to save Israel from itself, or from its leaders, to a harsher form of scrutiny, pointing out the danger that Israel's policies might hold for the Middle East, or even for world peace.

In part, the swift change in the Guardian's attitude towards Israel resulted more from the departure of the old editor than the advent of the new one. Hetherington's authoritarian style of editing had cast a heavy shadow on his experienced foreign desk. "He didn't have a vision of a newspaper as a community of people who think and act together; he was arbitrary," says Martin Woollacott, who was foreign correspondent in Vietnam under Hetherington, and was later appointed foreign editor by Preston. "I don't think the change was necessarily created by Peter Preston, He was less authoritarian and demanded less blind submission, but insisted on making major policy decisions himself. However, he liked to portray himself as a hapless cruiser, sitting in a boat floating downstream rather than holding the steering wheel."[2]

And unlike Hetherington, Preston did not engage in active diplomacy as a part of the duties or privileges of a newspaper editor. "I was and am still of the opinion that newspapers report and analyse the news; they are not supposed to engineer or manufacture it. Alastair in the Middle East and in Vietnam was sometimes in the position of making the news.

Editors are not diplomats. They shouldn't travel around the world in order to fix it. They could go and write about things they know but for me that's enough. I don't think I ever embarked on a peace mission. For me such missions are not under the definition of what's important," he says.[3]

Preston's main interests were India, Cyprus and Africa, where he had worked as foreign correspondent before becoming editor. "I never pretended to be an expert on everything, and I was a bit concerned that an editor needn't march in and start doing too much on a subject he's not familiar with. I was also a bit scarred after the big dispute with Alastair, who went to Vietnam, changed the paper's line, and got it wrong. I didn't have any crystallised opinion about Israel at the time, and I was aware that there were people on the team who were committed to the Palestinian issue. I also appreciated the difficulties of appointing an objective correspondent in Jerusalem".[4]

Preston left the problem of the Jerusalem correspondent's objectivity pending for a while, and let his staff steer the ship. The first sign that a new wind was blowing was a change in the advertising policy. While Hetherington, wounded by his experiences, shied away from political advertisements and supplements, in May 1976 Preston's paper published a multi-page advertisement bought by Free Palestine and entitled The Palestine Report. It included a feature about Palestinian poetry with poems by Mahmud Darwish, a report on "educating a nation in exile", memoirs from Palestine, traditional food recipes, and an article on "the Palestinian potential" to run an independent state. It also referred the readers to organisations who promoted the Palestinian cause by humanitarian aid or political activity.[5]

The Guardian devoted a leader column to the Free Palestine advertisement:

> The publication [...] is one more piece of evidence of the
> Palestinians' growing self-confidence. This advertisement,
> treating as it does such varied aspects of Palestinian life as
> history and education and embroidery and cooking, asserts that
> the Palestinians are a people, an ethnic group which should be
> treated as a nation [...] The Palestinians have also made violent

and grisly assertions of their presence – the Ma'alots and the Munichs.[6] Nevertheless, even their foes have begun to acknowledge them as more than hard-done-by refugees [...] If the PLO, difficult and as divisive as it would be, were to recognise Israel, then the tangible recognition of the political and human rights they claim would also become possible.[7]

In November 1977, not long after the Likud government was formed in Israel, the Egyptian president, Anwar Sadat, announced his willingness to come to Jerusalem and speak to the Knesset. The Guardian cheered "a brave man and a brave gamble":

> But even if President Sadat meets criticism and resistance from other Arab leaders, he has accomplished a great deal already. He has not just broken the ice, he has conceded a principle – the principle that Israel has a right to exist, a Parliament which represents a Middle Eastern nation, and a government which speaks for this nation.[8]

The leader reflected the Guardian's view that any peace negotiation in the Middle East would necessarily involve the PLO. The equation seemed clear: in response to Egypt's recognition of Israel, Israel should recognise Palestinian rights, and the PLO as their representative:

> The Arabs have so far refused to agree that the Israelis have a right to be where they are. The Israelis have refused to admit that the Palestinians, as represented by the PLO, have a comparable right to a state of their own. This particular obstacle has now been undermined. President Sadat's gesture calls for an Israeli answer. Which ought (however wrapped) to be the recognition by Israel of the PLO.
>
> This is not something that can come easily from Mr Begin above all Israeli politicians. The PLO has sworn, and still swears, to destroy Israel altogether. But there cannot be a peace conference in Geneva or anywhere else as long as Israel refuses

to talk to a Palestinian spokesman [...] If Mr Begin wants to get off the hook on which his past has impaled him, he could not wish for a better time. [9]

It remains virtually certain that the violence in the Middle East will never end without a viable solution to the plight of the Palestinians, but in the case of the Israeli-Egyptian peace agreement the Guardian got it wrong, at least over the intentions of those involved. Sadat was more than willing to settle his differences with Israel and even to conclude a peace agreement with it, in return for the Egyptian lands in Sinai occupied by Israel in 1967. The fringe benefit of a warm, sustainable and profitable friendship with the US was far more appealing than any urge to solve the Palestinian problem, or any fear of hostile reaction from other Arab states. The American administration of President Jimmy Carter felt that dragging a reluctant Begin to Camp David and getting him to sign the peace agreement with Egypt was sufficient for the time being. The agreement was signed by Begin, Sadat and Carter on March 26, 1979, paying lip service to the Palestinians by promising future discussions between Israel and Egypt about Palestinian autonomy in Gaza and the West Bank. The Guardian's disappointment was apparent in every step along the way to the agreement:

> The two questions of an Israeli-Egyptian peace and a settlement
> on the West Bank were treated separately in the Camp David
> peace framework. Moreover the working out of the two
> agreements was stretched across quite different timescales [...]
> Arabs opposed to the settlement will thus suspect that once in
> possession of its treaty Egypt will have no further interest in the
> Palestinian cause [...] It is for President Sadat to convince the
> other Arab heads that this is not the case, but to do that he will
> require the full cooperation of Israel. Will that be forthcoming?
> [...] A reversion to the oratory of Judea, Samaria and Eretz Israel
> could seriously harm Mr Sadat's standing and make it impossible
> for him to win wider Arab sympathy for what he is doing. [10]

Other articles criticised Carter for not insisting on Palestinian involvement in the peace talks, and Israel for not creating a suitable atmosphere for peace, particularly by persisting in building settlements in the West Bank.[11] The criticism of Egypt in this particular leader over abandoning the Palestinian cause in its own interests, was in general neither as fierce nor as consistent. The urge to encourage peace seemed stronger than a willingness to promote Arab solidarity.

The paper did, however, praise Israel for any little step in the right direction in the occupied territories. In a leader on Israel's decision to court martial an officer and two of his men for throwing tear gas grenades into a Palestinian school in the West Bank the pedagogic spirit of the article is telling:

> Israel is so frequently berated, both for its occupation of the West
> Bank and for the way the occupation is administered, that to
> dismiss the senior officer responsible might have been resisted as
> a sign of weakness. On the contrary, it is a sign of strength and a
> vindication of Israel's wish to live by the democratic rules. [12]

There was nothing "democratic" about military rule over the West Bank. But the Guardian seemed to feel the need to demonstrate that it could recognise and praise Israel for signs of good behaviour, however marginal, as well as pour scorn and contumely upon it when it tightened its grip on the occupied territories.

The change in the Guardian did not halt at editorial comment. A series of features from Israel by Martin Woollacott, published in May 1979, re-examined the role of Zionism in the light of developments in Israeli society and the Jewish diaspora. The paper dispatched Woollacott to Israel in April 1979, just after the peace treaty with Egypt was signed. "I'm not quite sure to this very day why the paper wanted me to do it," he says. Apparently, the old Guardian pattern — if you're not sure your correspondents are getting it right, send in another reporter — was at work again. "The Middle East reporting was much polarised between David Hirst, the Middle East correspondent in Lebanon, and Eric Silver, who covered Israel from Jerusalem," Woollacott adds. "The paper might have felt that a fresh view was needed, since they had a very pro-Palestinian reporter like David, and then Eric who was the most sympathetic to Israel of all correspondents, and a representative of the old Guardian approach of identifying with Israel's Labour party line." [13]

After the foundation of the state of Israel in 1948, the Guardian would intermittently commission from a single correspondent a series of features attempting a grand overview of the young country. Arthur Koestler in 1949, Martha Gellhorn in 1967, and David Caute in 1970 were all impressed by the developing agriculture and the very undiasporic chutzpah of the sabras and were barely critical even in the face of an army almost free of formal discipline. Woollacott's features were very different. The long, hard look he took at Israeli society yielded disappointed and sour conclusions.

His first article dealt with Russian Jews who were allowed to emigrate from the Soviet Union but preferred the US to Israel as their destination.[14] The second described the decline of the moral ethos of the kibbutzim: "Israeli farms are based firmly not only on advanced technology but, in flat contradiction to their founding principles, on hired, often Arab labour."[15] The third feature examined the Israel Defence Force as "the institute which defines the character of the state". Woollacott observed:

> From Israeli writing and thinking about armies and war, there is
> an almost complete absence of approaches common in other
> countries: there is no Schweik or Gunner Asch, there is no
> rejection of war, except in the shallower senses, there is no
> praise of the more stolid military virtues. The men who set the
> pace in the Israeli military establishment are what the
> Americans call 'Gung Ho' to a man.[16]

The fourth article concentrated on "the colonial situation developed in the occupied territories". It touched on the settlements, the realities of life under occupation, and the growth of racism and disregard towards Arabs in Israeli society as an outcome of the unequal encounters between soldiers and occupied Palestinians. [17]

Woollacott, demonstrating again that times had changed in the Guardian, did not buy into the notion that the Labour government would have dealt with the situation differently. And unlike Hetherington, he was far from enchanted by Yigal Allon's expansionist plan: "The Labour party, in opposition, can enjoy the luxury of vaguely suggesting that it would handle the negotiations on the basis of territorial concessions rather than a fake autonomy. But the various versions of the Allon plan which float around in discussion are almost equally unacceptable."[18]

Woollacott concluded:

Israel was the result of a brief coincidence of interests and ideals between an east European nationalism and the declining British empire. Its existence must thus be recognised both as an accident, and as an injustice to those who were displaced by its creation.

That does not mean it has no "right to existence". The thing is done: 3 million people live, marry and raise children within a state for which they have paid much in blood and effort. Or, as a young Arab lecturer said: "It would be a terrible tragedy for humanity if the Jews were pushed into the sea." […] What must change, the lecturer seems to suggest, is an Israel structured for war and basing its national mission on obsolete Zionism.[19]

The Israeli ambassador in Britain, Avraham Kidron, responded in a long, angry, yet eloquent letter to the editor. Kidron was a remnant representative of Labour-style diplomacy; he made no knee-jerk accusations of anti-semitism, but he exposed a fear which is at the core of the predicament of Israel's critics, and of the state itself: the notion that acknowledging wrongdoing or error questions the state's basic right to exist, or its chances of survival.

A good deal of what Mr Woollacott wrote is acceptable as journalistic impressions. But the basis of his argument is false because he has not presented Israel's current problems in the context of the past, her fight for survival as a state, and before that, the fight for survival of the Jewish people. He has sought to show that the social and political malaise which he says is now afflicting Israel is a sign of disintegration of the country and all it stands for. He does not allow that the current mood in Israel might be an expression of self-questioning – which is a sign of moral awareness in any decent society; not even a state of temporary confusion in the face of cataclysmic events.[20]

If there was any doubt that Woollacott's series, and his critique of Zionism, reflected a new spirit abroad in the Guardian, the leader which concluded the debate supplied final proof. First, it explained the justifications for the paper's attempt to "come to grips with the feelings about itself of an entire society":

A lesser one is that much statecraft and idealism have been invested by western countries, notably this one and the United States, in the creation and maintenance of the Jewish national home. A greater one is that the decisions taken by the leaders of Israel could influence and even determine the direction of international affairs for the foreseeable future.[21]

The article went on to defend the paper from the charge of anti-semitism brought by one of the readers, "as usual on these occasions". The leader writer explained that "to bring a charge of anti-semitism (which would in any case be hard in view of this paper's past) it is necessary to impute motives based on outworn stereotypes of Judaism". That settled, the leader went back to the constituting moment of British-Israel and Guardian-Israel relationships, the Balfour Declaration. In breach of the declaration, it determined, "the rights of non-Jewish communities have been prejudiced".[22]

What, therefore, are the remaining ambitions of Zionism? A state stretching from the Euphrates to Suez for which Zionist oratory (doubtless carried away) could be cited? The incorporation of the West Bank into Israel "without prejudice to the rights" of the Arab people there? The withdrawal of Israel into the pre-1967 boundaries and the negotiation of Jewish (as opposed to Israeli) settlements outside? The Israel government does not answer these questions directly, though incorporation of the West Bank is as near as they come.[23]

But the most important part of the article is its conclusion, in which the Guardian formulates for the first time the deal that the liberal West was, and still is, offering Israel:

> When Israel has defined its frontiers to the satisfaction of its neighbours, how it pursues its Zionist ambitions within its own frontiers will be of less pressing concern to anybody else. Until that happens it is crucial to know which direction Zionism is taking and if necessary to say that certain directions cannot be allowed for the sake of the peace of the world.[24]

The hidden agenda here is simple: should Israel give up its expansionism, negotiate with the Palestinians and withdraw from the territories occupied in 1967, its legitimacy in its post-1948 borders would be accepted. No hard questions would be asked about the moral validity of the idea of Jewish statehood, the constitutional discrimination against Palestinian citizens of Israel, or the ethnic cleansing of 1948. But should Israel insist on its belligerent and expansionist practices, than its past with its implications on its "right to exist", would become fair game. Whether the enlightened West, or the Guardian as its representative, was entitled to offer such absolution at the expense of the Palestinian people or on their behalf is of course a moot point. But with every new cycle of violence and expansionism involving Israel, the probe into its legitimacy and its past goes deeper, nourishing Israeli defensiveness that often verges on paranoia.

As Israel settled Jewish citizens in the heart of Hebron in 1980, the Guardian's leader column observed gravely:

The new and assertive policy at Hebron is one more act to slow down the peace process, which has never reconciled the two meanings of the word Israel. It cannot be both the territory of the sovereign state before 1967 and the land bestowed "on Abraham and his seed for ever". The Arabs of Hebron are equally his seed.[25]

The small, radical and religious settlement in the heart of Hebron was only the tip of the iceberg of Israel's settlement policy in the West Bank. Under Likud, settlements were no longer small enterprises of the marginal rightwing movement Gush Emunim, constructed with the government's silent consent. They became a massive state enterprise, promoted and marketed by the government. Tens of thousands of Israeli Jews were persuaded to move to the newly built settlements, which were advertised as suburbs of Jerusalem or Kefar Saba, a town in the centre of Israel.

The vast majority of the new settlers had no ideological inclination to populate "Judaea and Samaria" in the service of Israeli expansionism. They were tempted by the low-interest loans, grants and mortgages, compliments of the government. The idea of moving from a three-room flat in Jerusalem to a "quiet" detached house in the occupied territories was irresistible for many families. Settlements built around Jerusalem, marketed as "new neighbourhoods", were the most attractive. The ideological Gush Emunim settlements thrived alongside the more established enterprises, receiving similar encouragement from the establishment. Palestinian resistance concentrated outside Palestine, and the "new Jerusalem" settlers, ideological or otherwise, had no reason to feel threatened by the indigenous inhabitants of the West Bank and Gaza. The humiliated Palestinians, robbed of land and subjected to the new neighbours, turned their fury into action only more than 10 years after the first settlement was built.

In July 1980 Israel formally annexed occupied East Jerusalem, by way of a law passed in the Knesset, without giving full citizens' status to the Arab inhabitants. The Guardian, dubious from the start about the chances of Camp David yielding a viable solution to the Palestinian problem, now despaired of it altogether. "[...] Israel has created another fact," said the Guardian's leader, [...] "Camp David having achieved all it is ever likely to achieve, there would be value in a European reading of the situation to put to the next American administration. It is likely to lean further towards the Arab standpoint, and Israel's current actions will help it along the way".[26]

The Guardian, in spite of its criticism of Israel's Labour party, wrongly saw Begin's government as a temporary radical anomaly, rather than a permanent shift in Israeli politics. A leader in December 1980, prompting Labour leader Shimon Peres to prepare himself for the role of prime minister, demonstrated this type of wishful thinking:

> The latest date for an election is November 1981 [...] Mr Peres could, however, put the time to good use by mobilising Israeli opinion against the way in which the occupation is being managed. It is no longer, if it ever was, a benevolent administration seeking to govern Arabs for their own good. It is growing in severity, in some instances brutality, [...] and some cries of real alarm from Mr Peres about the dangerously provocative policies there would not be premature.[27]

The self delusion in this approach was double. The assumption that Begin was about to fall proved wrong; peace with Egypt, and Begin's decision to attack Iraq's nuclear reactor on June 7, 1981, three weeks before election day, won him a second term. The idea that Peres, who was indeed leading in the polls for a few months, might consider a serious anti-occupation agenda was utterly wide of the mark. Human rights violations in the West Bank, severe as they were, were a non-issue in the Israeli political debate of the early 1980s. Most of the public knew nothing of them, the media ignored them, and Palestinian protest in the West Bank was non-violent and therefore invisible. Security threats, including those involving Palestinians, were perceived as lurking outside Israel's borders, and manifesting themselves in terror attacks committed by Palestinian groups penetrating Israel from Lebanon, Jordan or Egypt. Peres kept nurturing his vague "Jordanian option", a plan for a confederation between densely populated parts of the West Bank and

Jordan, which the Guardian acknowledged as a non-option due to Jordanian lack of interest.[28]

Peres, who launched the first Gush Emunim settlement in Sebastia in 1976, was hardly one to object to more settlements.

The election of July 1981 increased the power of Likud from 43 Knesset members to 48 (of 120). The Labour party also grew in power from 32 representatives to 47 – a classic close finish that remained a nearly constant pattern in Israeli politics until the mid-1990s. And while Begin's first government had signed a peace agreement, his second took advantage of the now peaceful southern border to launch a war in the north.

On June 3, 1982, the Israeli ambassador in London, Shlomo Argov, was shot by a Palestinian assassin and severely injured. This was the pretext for Israel's pre-planned invasion of Lebanon on June 6, 1982. The invasion was presented to the government by the minister of defence, Ariel Sharon, as a limited operation, in which the army would penetrate 40 kilometres into Lebanon, and "clear terrorist nests", namely, chase out PLO fighters based in south Lebanon. Ariel Sharon, a hardline veteran of several Israeli wars and a founder of the Likud party, reassured the cabinet that the operation was to take no longer than 48 hours, that Beirut was out of its range, and that there was no intention to engage in fighting Syrian forces in east Lebanon. The attack came after 11 months of ceasefire between Israel and the PLO along the Lebanese border. Palestinians in Lebanon, who had committed themselves to refrain from shelling Israeli villages in northern Israel, did not violate the agreement. Regardless of this, the operation was given the name Peace for the Galilee, and gained the support of the opposition Labour party. The title didn't stick. It is remembered in Israel as the Lebanon war.

Sharon's real war plan, concealed from the cabinet, was far more ambitious. It included an attempt to help Bashir Gemayel, the leader of the Christian Phalange, a political party opposed to pan-Arabism, to take over the country. Sharon aspired to control Gemayel as a puppet president, and to encourage him to deport the Palestinians from Lebanon into Jordan, which in Sharon's vision was to become the Palestinian state. IDF forces did engage in fighting with the Syrians, and did get as far as Beirut, which was put under a cruel and long siege during the heat of

August 1982. American mediation ended in Yasser Arafat's agreement to leave Lebanon with his men and relocate PLO headquarters in Tunis. Gemayel was elected president under Israeli guns, but was murdered two weeks later on September 14, 1982, apparently by a Syrian agent. The IDF allowed the enraged Phalangists to enter Sabra and Shatila refugee camps in west Beirut, to "hunt PLO terrorists" who were allegedly still hiding there. IDF forces tightly encircled the camps while the Phalangists raided them, embarking on a carnage that lasted from Thursday night to Sunday evening, massacring children, women, the elderly and whoever else they could find. The number of dead in the camps was estimated by Israel at 700 to 800, and by the Palestinian Red Crescent at around 2,000.

This time international outrage was joined by protest within Israel. Both the atrocities in the camps and the great number of Israeli losses in the war induced a public outcry. An unprecedented number of Israelis protested against the government's policy in Lebanon in a Peace Now demonstration in Tel Aviv. It was followed by parliamentary pressure and some dissident voices were heard even inside the ruling Likud party. The government responded by appointing an official commission of inquiry to examine Israeli responsibility for the Sabra and Shatila massacre, headed by a supreme court judge, Ytzhak Kahan.

The commission's report was made public in February 1983, and stressed that Israel bore indirect responsibility for the massacre, since the army, with the knowledge of cabinet ministers, had prompted the Phalange to enter the refugee camps. It recommended that Sharon should be removed from his post as defence minister, and some senior army officers dismissed.

The invasion of Lebanon was the first Israeli war that provoked controversy while it was still going on, and which was not presented or perceived as a "no-choice war". It gave an immense boost to the Israeli peace movement. During the war the Yesh Gvul organisation, supporting conscientious objectors and refuseniks, was established. Many of its members were inspired by the refusal of the Givaati division commanding officer, Colonel Eli Geva, to enter Beirut. Another new phenomenon was the involvement of soldiers' parents — mainly, but not only, mothers — in political protest. Until the invasion of Lebanon the

Israeli ethos required bereaved parents to carry their grief with restraint and to conduct themselves with "dignity" rather than blame politicians for their loss. This imperative was gone for good.

Until the invasion of Lebanon, the use of images and symbols of the Holocaust was commonly used by the establishment to serve political ends. All prime ministers described Israel as the only way to prevent another Holocaust, and the alleged danger of another Holocaust was the pretext for many controversial military actions. But no one ever took it as far as Menachem Begin. In a telegram to President Ronald Reagan during the siege of Beirut, Begin wrote:

> I feel as a prime minister empowered to instruct a valiant army facing "Berlin" where among innocent civilians, Hitler and his henchmen hide in a bunker deep beneath the surface. My generation, dear Ron, swore on the altar of God that whoever proclaims his intent to destroy the Jewish state or the Jewish people, or both, seals his fate, so that which happened once on instructions from Berlin – with or without inverted commas – will never happen again.[29]

As the historian Avi Shlaim remarks, this message enraged many Israelis, who felt that it was a sign that their prime minister had lost touch with reality.[30] But after the horrors of Sabra and Shatila were exposed to the Israeli public, the officially sanctified invocation of the Holocaust turned sour for the first time. The wave of protest, in political poetry, journalism, and protest posters, against Begin and Sharon incorporated a jargon that was formerly used only to describe the Nazi and pre-Nazi pogroms. Many turned to earlier sources of writing about the Holocaust, and rephrased the texts to encompass the current issue.

One of the main sources was Nathan Alterman, the unofficial poet laureate. The columnist Amnon Dankner published an update of Alterman's poem about the silence of the world in the face of the Holocaust, Of All People; Dankner's version described the silent collaboration of Israeli soldiers with the Phalange butchers. Another Alterman poem (taking its title from what a little girl had asked after her release from a Nazi concentration camp), Mother, is it permitted to cry already?, was rephrased by the popular satirist Yehonatan Gefen into Mother, is it allowed to speak already?, mocking the silence of Israeli intellectuals during the war. *On Slaughter*, a poem by Haim Nahman Bialik, describing the atrocities of the Kishinev pogrom in Russia at Easter 1903, was printed in Hebrew and Arabic on anti-war posters.

These were models for a style of writing and speaking which became dominant on the Israeli left during the invasion of Lebanon, and reinforced itself during the first intifada. It was both a reflection of the writers' horrified helplessness and sense of guilt in face of atrocities committed in their name, and an attempt to move their readers to dissent. It was picked up in international media coverage of Israel, to the dismay of many Israelis and Jews who thought such invocation was legitimate only in Hebrew and only for internal consumption.

On the eve of the Lebanon war, the Guardian denounced the shooting of the ambassador in London and paid tribute to his diplomatic skills. It went on to argue that his death might cause Europe and America to try to persuade Israel that there was a way to arrive at a better alternative than a resurgence of terrorism:

> That cannot yet be peace by negotiation but it can be an agreement by Israel and the Palestinians to start recognising one another's rights: secure and peaceful existence, free from terrorism on the one side and freedom from foreign occupation on the other. Such conclusions may seem far distant from the murderous exploits outside the Dorchester or the gathering, bloody momentum of yesterday's reprisals over Beirut. But there is no end to the nightmare down the barrel of a gun.[31]

On the second day of the war, the Guardian foresaw an Israel that would become "four times an occupying power; in the West Bank, Gaza, the Golan Heights and Lebanon. Peace with Palestinians is nowhere to be found on that route, but the sad fact is that peace with the Palestinians seems to Israel too impossible an item to put on the agenda".[32] The

Guardian saw the invasion of Lebanon as another distraction from the path of righteousness leading to mutual recognition between Israel and the Palestinians, and a two state solution.

The war had brought the work of the Jerusalem correspondent, Eric Silver, under close scrutiny. Silver, appointed in 1972 by Hetherington, was a Zionist Jew who never thought that this interfered with his work as a journalist. "When I work I'm not there as Eric Silver from Manchester, son of immigrants from Lithuania, a member of Hashomer Hatsair. I was there as Eric Silver of the Guardian, whose role is to tell the editor, and then the readers, what they want to know about events. I would never censor myself on account of a story being 'damaging to the Jews'; if you do that you are finished."[33] Silver became an Israeli citizen and an integral member of the society he covered. He was far more interested in internal Israeli affairs than in the situation in the occupied territories. "It was very hard to get him to go to the West Bank often enough," says Peter Preston. Silver foresaw the criticism against him before he even went to Jerusalem. "I told Alastair Hetherington that people will say that my being a Zionist is a problem, and he said that I don't write propaganda." And people, indeed, did speak ill of Silver. The veteran correspondent is still bitter about the fact that he was mentioned in a book written by Michael Adams and Christopher Mayhew as a Zionist reporter, and about a Private Eye story saying that he was off to Israel to work at "Israeli public relations". "I felt that people were always looking for Zionist bias in my writing, but it doesn't happen to gentile reporters who cover the Arab world. People are far less judgmental of their prejudices. Michael Adams and David Hirst are not Arabs, but they did have crystallised opinions when they started covering the region."

Political hostility between Silver and Hirst was common knowledge. On one of Hirst's visits to Jerusalem, the two had a tough confrontation in the lobby of the American Colony hotel in east Jerusalem. "One of the foreign reporters who watched it said that it would be easier to reconcile the Israeli-Palestinian conflict than the war between the two Guardian correspondents," says Silver. The editor, Peter Preston, saw some advantages in the situation. "When the Board of Deputies [of British Jews] would summon me to tell me off, always over something David

Hirst wrote, I could tell them, 'but you have Eric, your guy, in Jerusalem'." Silver resented this attitude: "I didn't want to be a 'house Jew'. This is not why I wanted to become a journalist and work for the Guardian. When Peter said that to the Israeli ambassador, Gideon Refael, Refael replied: 'It's you who have Eric Silver in Jerusalem'."[34]

Martin Woollacott, foreign editor at the time, says: "Eric always saw himself as fighting against British criticism of Israel on one hand, and against the Israeli right wing on the other. He was always a peace-supporting Labour party person, and he was impressed by many good things he encountered in Israeli society."[35] This attitude, combined with the reputation the Guardian was gaining as highly critical of Israel, caused Silver trouble from the Israeli side too. "When I went to Hebron Mrs Levinger [wife of rabbi Shlomo Levinger, a radical prominent figure in Gush Emunim] said, 'So, you are the nice Jewish boy who works for this anti-semitic newspaper'," he recalls.[36]

The Lebanon war sharpened the discrepancies between Silver's reporting and the Guardian's change of approach to Israel. "I don't think you could say I supported the war, but I didn't write very critical things right from the start. I just reported what happened. I became more critical after Sabra and Shatila. I don't think I was a 'gung-ho march on Jewish soldiers' kind of reporter," he says.[37]

On June 8, two days into the war, Silver reported the battle over the ancient crusader fortress, Beaufort Castle, "a symbol of safety for Galilee". He mentioned that the battle turned "harder than the Israeli army had bargained for", but not the death of six soldiers, nor the embarrassment caused to the government when Begin visited the occupied castle and announced that there were "no losses to our forces". Parents of the soldiers killed in that battle became prominent figures in the anti-war movement in Israel. The report included mainly quotes from Israeli officers and ministers congratulating themselves on being "ahead of schedule". Rather than wonder whether the operation wasn't actually heading far beyond its 48-hour schedule, Silver described the joy of Galilee civilians in the face of war: "I drove through Kyriat Shmona in the middle of a convoy of armoured personnel carriers," he reported. "The children rushed waving out of the shelters and plied the young infantrymen with orange juice".[38] Silver's report, headed Israeli invaders get a Christian welcome, of June 23, 1982, is typical of his writing about the early phases of the war:

> In Jounieh a girl aged about 18 came up and tried to talk to us in Hebrew. While we were eating somebody scrawled "Victory for Israel" in bad French in the dust covering our rear window.
>
> On the way back we stopped to ask the way of half a dozen Israeli paratroopers. Three or four young Lebanese of the same age as the paratroopers came to shake hands and exchange newspapers [...] Some Israelis are beginning to worry about the very exuberance of the Christian welcome.
>
> "It's going to our heads," suggested a reserve officer. "It's encouraging the hawks to go all the way."[39]

This report is similar in spirit to the way doveish Israeli papers such as Ha'aretz covered the war at this stage, but Silver, as he sometimes seemed to forget, was not an Israeli journalist. Even though the report suggested that the Christian welcome might encourage Israeli hawks, another Guardian journalist remembers "Eric Silver describing the Lebanese cheering for the Israeli liberators". He was, indeed, under scrutiny, at least by his colleagues.

At the same time, David Hirst described from Lebanon how the Arab world "is ready to abandon the Lebanese – and the Palestinians – to the fate which Israel has so obviously had in store for them". Hirst made an accurate forecast of Israel's intentions – pushing the Palestinians out of Lebanon and helping Gamayel to become president. "Since, it is argued, there is so little danger of concerted Arab retaliation against the western backers of Israel, the US can permit its unruly protege to get away with more than ever before."[40] Subsequent articles described civilian suffering under the siege of Beirut, Israeli attempts to pretend that the cutting off of water and electricity from the besieged city was the deed of the Christian Phalange, and the tough, desperate defiance of Arafat's people in the city.[41]

Ian Black, sent over to Jerusalem to back up Silver, and possibly to balance his perspective, reported growing resistance to the war, which started during the siege of Beirut. He provided his readers with a key to understanding the nature of the protest:

> The peace camp is no longer just against the war. It wants peace – and peace with the Palestinians. The soldiers and civilians who demonstrated in Tel Aviv on Saturday carried a message that will echo far beyond the immediate aftermath of this war: "Enough! We can no longer ignore the other people who claim this sad land for their own. There is no military solution."
>
> It is a novel approach. The Zionists have always sought to make peace with the surrounding Arab countries and thus bypass the intractability of the Palestinians.[42]

The massacre of Sabra and Shatila was reported in the Guardian on Monday September 20, a day after the Sunday papers and the BBC had already exposed the horrors. Lebanon accuses US and Israel, ran the headline, and other news stories covered the atrocity in detail. The leader examined Israel's responsibility:

> Lebanon has just seen one of the most barbarous events of our time, and the Israeli authorities, to their perpetual shame, presided over it. There are not many adequate words for what the Christian(!) militias did to the defenceless refugee families in the Sabra and Shatila camps. The massacres of the second world war – Lidice, Warsaw, Oradour – provided a recent parallel, and one which Israelis may find poignant [...] It was, of course, the Lebanese who did the slaughter [...] But Lebanon is far gone in civil war and the nature of the state now defies definition. Israel, on the other hand, which allowed the massacre to happen, claims to be a democracy. Democracies do not allow their leaders to behave like this. Unless the Begin government is voted out of office for what it has permitted at Sabra and Shatila there will be serious doubt whether Israelis have not surrendered their democracy into the hands of a fanatical elite.[43]

Martin Woollacott remembers this leader mainly for "being very fair on Israel, and mentioning that it was the Phalange forces which carried out the actual killing". He says that the evidence disclosed later by the Kahan comission of inquiry further enhanced the hostility to the Israel government. The leader demonstrated that the shadow of the Holocaust over Israeli history was fast to enter the media debate following the massacre and that the world clearly expected higher moral standards from Israel.

Melanie Phillips, who was a leader writer for the Guardian at the time (though most leaders on Lebanon were written by Woollacott), says that both phenomena encouraged anti-semitism. "There's racism in the assumption that Arabs who kill other Arabs are not as appalling as Jews killing Arabs," says Phillips. "The invasion of Lebanon was a huge watershed. It gave the left a villain – Sharon — and a symbol. Israel to them was no longer just an occupier but a war criminal, something diabolical, and it was seized upon by some people in Britain, because if the Jews are as bad as the Nazis, it allowed the complicity of Britain and Europe during the Holocaust, and their treachery towards the Jews in Palestine to be negated."[44]

It could, however, be argued that higher expectations of Israel indicate a sense of partnership, even if a paternalistic one, by committed supporters of the foundation of the Jewish state on moral grounds. In the case of the leader on the massacres, it is also very clear that the comparison of Sabra and Shatila to Nazi massacres was made to touch the conscience of Israelis and Jews, who might find it "poignant".

Phillips claims that during the Lebanon war she was subjected to "anti-semitic remarks" from fellow workers at the Guardian. A colleague, she says, referred to the Lebanon war as "your war", on account of her being Jewish, hence "denying me my Britishness". There were also "remarks on the fact that I eat kosher". She refuses to name names. In 1985 Phillips wrote a play that ran for a short period in a fringe London theatre. It was about a newspaper, evidently the Guardian, during the Lebanon war, and included allegations of anti-semitic conduct by colleagues. Phillips says that "many people, who had made remarks themselves, came to me after the play and said they could not believe that anybody said such terrible things to me". The anonymous and general nature of her allegations make it impossible to seek a response to them from her colleagues. Phillips remained on the Guardian staff until the early 1990s as news editor and later a columnist, and then left for Daily Mail via the Observer.

Two other allusions to the Holocaust were to be found in the post-Sabra and Shatila massacre issue of the Guardian. One was a cartoon by Les Gibbard, in which Ariel Sharon sits in a tank and Menachem Begin, in despair, gazes at a heap of bodies. The caption was: "We did not know what was going on"[45] (see page 139). Michele Kohler of Surrey responded in a letter to the editor: "Like many right-thinking people, I abhor what has happened in the Lebanon during the last few months, and I have not refrained from saying so. However, the offensiveness of the cartoon and the ignorance of other people's religious practices that informs it, leave me at a loss for words."[46]

A coincidence – if coincidence it was – was the publication on the same day of an article by Michael Adams, headlined Why Israel's moral blackmail has backfired. The article was obviously pre-ordered, and it did not mention the massacre. It consisted mainly of a translation of an article by the Israeli columnist Boaz Evron, which appeared in an Israeli literary magazine, and dealt with "the use made of the Holocaust as a means of propaganda". Evron warned that time was running out, and that the stock of guilty feelings in the West "is like a limited bank account that one keeps drawing on".[47]

Then the Kahan commission report was published in February 1983, and the Guardian approved of it as a manifestation of democracy:

> Much credit flows to the state of Israel for the vigour of the
> Kahan commission of inquiry and the rigour of its conclusions.
> There is not another country in the Middle East (and not
> too many beyond) where the rulers could be subjected to
> questioning of such a kind, and in Lebanon, at whose citizens'
> hands the massacre was committed, the parallel inquiry has
> turned into a charade.

This leader called for the committee's recommendations to be implemented, and turned to what had been the consistent line of the paper ever since 1974 which was accentuated in every leader about the Lebanon war: the necessity of a solution for the plight of the Palestinians in the West Bank and Gaza.

> Yet all this is a feint in comparison with the real thrust, which is to retain the West Bank and Gaza at all costs. In one respectable school of thought the entire Operation Peace in Galilee was a distraction from the race against time to make the West Bank unevacuable […] Israel is indeed Judaising the West Bank to the point where Palestinians can no longer be at home there. The project began in 1967 but has quickened immeasurably under Begin. Has this been the inevitable expansion of the Zionist universe for which the Balfour Declaration provided the big bang?[48]

As during the Suez war, the Guardian was not alone in its criticism of the invasion of Lebanon. 1982 is seen by many in Israel and beyond as the watershed both in the coverage of Israel by the international media, and in the way Israel was perceived by liberals and by the left. The Times, for example, was extremely critical of the invasion from the beginning. Even before the massacre of Sabra and Shatila Robert Fisk, reporting from Lebanon, compared the heavy bombardments of Beirut to El Greco paintings, scenes from Federico Fellini films and "a lunatic cameo of old photographs of the London blitz".[49] His reporting drew fire from Jewish Zionist organisations, and so did the Times's position in general.[50] In a strong leader column in August, "The pathology of persecution", the Times stated that Israel's policies made it "impossible just now to be her friend".[51] In May 1983, the Times addressed its Israeli and Zionist critics in a leader article, saying: "To suggest that it was Israel which was a greater victim than the thousands of innocent people who died is to reveal, on the part of spokesmen in Jerusalem and their apologists in the West a reluctance to take criticism and an inability to be fully aware of the consequences of one's own actions – let alone accept responsibilities for them – which is truly alarming."[52]

The BBC, too, found itself under bitter attack from Israel over its reporting. It was the first Israeli war to be covered by modern television, and the pictures from Lebanon were not pretty. Even the Daily Telegraph felt obliged to shift towards a more critical line on Israel after the September massacre. The media shift was only one manifestation of a larger political earthquake. Traditional supporters of Israel within the Labour party responded with disgust and disillusionment to the images from Lebanon. Strong condemnation of Israel in Parliament followed angry demonstrations in European capitals. For the first time in its existence Israel was portrayed as an aggressor by most of the world media, including the usually supportive Americans, the Germans, previously silenced by guilt, and the remote and normally disengaged South Americans. In this new reality the Guardian's criticism was less conspicuous than before, even though its coverage remained the most extensive.

Ian Black replaced Eric Silver as the Guardian's Jerusalem correspondent in the middle of 1983. Martin Woollacott says that it was "just time for Eric to move on".[53] Preston, who started his career as a reporter in the Guardian alongside Silver, says that the main reason was the latter's tendency to avoid the occupied territories. Silver was offered a senior position in London, but opted to stay in Israel. He lives in Jerusalem and works as a freelance for various British newspapers. The manner of his departure was impeccable. "They did have a feeling that I was becoming too close to the story, and it is their right. I have no grievances against the Guardian," says Silver.[54] Preston still struggles to find the right professional and political terms to explain Silver's removal from his position in Israel. "When Eric was nominated for the job they didn't foresee the difficulties. He's a very good reporter but when he moved to Israel he became too identified with the Israeli cause. I am not knocking him in any way, but I felt at the time that you could anticipate which kind of story you are likely to get from each reporter. I don't think that this problem existed with the reporters who came later. For the last 25 years the Guardian has not had a correspondent in Israel whom it could not be proud of."[55]

After the 1984 election a national unity government was formed in Israel, a guaranteed recipe for political stagnation. Shimon Peres led the government for two years, to be replaced according to a rotation agreement by Yitzhak Shamir. In 1985 Israeli forces retreated into a "security belt" in Lebanon, along the southern border, where they remained until 2000. But as the Guardian leader articles never stopped pointing out, the ordeal of the Palestinians in the occupied territories was far from over.

CHAPTER NINE

Raining Stones

The First Intifada And the Oslo Accord

Steve Bell, 1 September 1993

THE summer of 1987 was long and boring. Ian Black, by then a veteran Jerusalem correspondent, felt burdened by a sense of stagnation. His predecessor, Eric Silver, met him in Jerusalem and remembers him saying, "the story here is done".[1] "Nothing was changing, and it didn't seem as if anything was about to change," Black reflects today.[2]

The Israel national unity government seemed locked into immobility. On the Palestinian side, Yasser Arafat's Palestine Liberation Organisation was yet to recover from the consequences of the 1982 exile from Lebanon to Tunis. Ronald Reagan's American administration refrained from a new diplomatic initiative in the Middle East. In the military courts Israel had imposed in the occupied territories, Palestinians were prosecuted for security and political offences and Black would go there to cover some of the trials. Unlike most other foreign correspondents, he had social and political relationships with Israeli journalists, Danny Rubinstein and Yehuda Litanny of the Israeli liberal daily Ha'aretz. The two were pioneers in coverage of the West Bank, a wilderness neglected by both Israeli and international media during the pre-intifada years. "At the time, it was brave Israeli reporters who defined new basic notions about the reality of occupation, and I have learned a lot from them," says Black.[3]

The Yellow Wind, a book by the Israeli novelist David Grossman documenting Palestinian lives under occupation, made an impact on Black as it did on a generation of Israelis. Everybody knew that a few kilometres from Tel Aviv a whole people robbed of civil rights lived, a silent army of obedient workers showing up in Israeli cities every morning to wash the dishes in the prosperous restaurants and clean the streets. Hardly anyone foresaw that after 20 years of relying on the external activities of the PLO and on the ever changing whims of the occupation authorities this mute mass was about to rebel.

When the first intifada erupted in 1987, Black made good use of his acquaintance with both the occupied territories and his Israeli friends. The fact that it took him by surprise, just as it had the Israeli government, the PLO, and other Palestinian leaders of the community, is hardly evident when reviewing his reporting from its early days. "I thought it was a temporary unrest which was to die out soon enough," admits Black, "but Martin Woollacott, the foreign editor, realised immediately that this was a historical change, and I was encouraged to cover it extensively."[4]

It began with a road accident in Jabalya refugee camp in the Gaza Strip on December 9. An Israeli truck driver ran over and killed four Palestinian residents of the camp. A false rumour that the killing was intentional brought hundreds of Palestinians on to the streets, where they launched what was to become the pattern of Palestinian resistance for the following years. They threw stones and Molotov cocktails at Israeli vehicles, set tyres on fire, and rallied in the streets waving the Palestinian flag, an act forbidden by the occupation authorities. It took hours for the spontaneous rebellion to spread all over the Gaza strip, and days to roll over to the West Bank. Tens of thousands of Palestinians took to the streets, many of them women and children. Strikes were organised and the Israeli economy, at this stage still heavily dependent on Palestinian labour, took an immediate hit. The Israeli army, under strict orders to quell the disturbance as soon as possible, used cudgels, batons, tear gas, water cannons, rubber bullets and live ammunition against the protesters. Many were killed. The image of a Palestinian boy challenging a fully armed soldier with merely a stone in his hand became the symbol of the uprising.

By December 11, after two days of reporting the casualties in Gaza, Black was in Nablus, at the north of the West Bank, from which he dispatched a thorough report and analysis of the new situation, clearly influenced by the new factor — publicity — that affected the approaches to their work of press and occupying authority alike:

> 'Don't hit him with your baton,' the Israeli officer screamed at
> the soldier as the photographer approached the Red Crescent
> ambulance where a dead girl's body lay on a stretcher, swathed
> in a rough checked blanket.[5]

Black noted that Yasser Arafat thought that a large number of Palestinian casualties would draw the world's attention to the Palestinian predicament. He observed that though the Israelis were under American pressure to keep the numbers of Palestinian deaths down, they translated this into an attempt to prevent cameramen from reaching the centres of violence. The unrest, Black reported, was not enough to make the cost of occupation unbearable for the occupiers, since "no one Israeli has been killed in Nablus or Gaza". The situation was not yet out of hand, but, Black added, "yet" was the key word:

> This week's unusually stern warning from Washington that
> the Israelis are overdoing their suppression of the trouble has
> already been noted and digested in Jerusalem. But its only
> practical effect, so far, has been a more than usually determined
> effort to keep the press and television cameras out of the hot
> spots – a South African-type solution to what looks increasingly
> like a South African-type situation.[6]

The inevitable comparison to South Africa, infuriating for many Israelis, was repeated in a leader two days later. Black says today that he was always able to defend his accounts by telling his critics that harsher words were being published in the Israeli press at the time. And indeed a Guardian leader at the time quoted the South African parallel from an Israeli daily:

> Five successive days of demonstrations, involving at least six deaths and many other casualties, have led Israelis to speculate whether the Palestinian resistance in the occupied territories is entering a new and more determined phase [...] Repeated incidents in Gaza and elsewhere have prompted the Israeli newspaper Hadashot to say that parts of the occupied territories 'have become more and more like Soweto, densely populated, poor, with shameful living conditions and full of hatred.' [...] The Labour party leader, Shimon Peres, has, it is true, made rather more running towards an international peace conference since he relinquished the premiership than when he held it, but he has been balked by his successor, Yitzhak Shamir.[7]

The last sentence signifies a weakening, rooted in the Lebanon war and the years of Likud governments, of the traditional link between the Guardian and the doveish wing of the Israeli Labour movement and Labour party. The reason for that was simple; during the 1980s the Israeli Labour party did not have a leftwing. Its integration in the national unity government was complete, and differences between Likud and Labour members of cabinet were mostly invisible. The defence minister, Yitzhak Rabin, was identified more than any Israeli with the iron-fist policies of attempting to break the intifada by force. The Labour leader, Peres, was a veteran Ben-Gurionite "activist", and his repeated talk about the "Jordanian option" and an "international peace conference" failed, at this stage, to convince anybody. Yossi Sarid, the most conspicuous Labour dove, left the party in 1984 and joined Ratz, a liberal-Zionist party to the left of Labour.[8]

The Guardian expressed hope for a Labour victory in the 1988 election, but when the power of Likud increased in the aftermath, the paper urged Labour to stay in opposition, and expressed disappointment with Shimon Peres's hesitant leadership, and his attempts to avoid formulating a decisive policy on negotiations with the PLO.[9] One leader article entertained the idea that the Likud leader, Yitzhak Shamir, was "better placed than Mr Peres would ever have been to deliver on any promise he can be persuaded to make."[10] Shamir's great care never to promise a thing kept this assertion from being tested.

But the Guardian was compensated for the loss of its old ally by the emergence of an Israeli peace movement, embodied not merely by the prominent Zionist Peace Now organisation, but also by the mushrooming of numerous movements and organisations like Women in Black, Solidarity groups with Palestinians, and Yesh Gvul, the refusnik movement formed during the Lebanon war. The intifada created alliances between Zionist and non-Zionist peace activists and the latter, while remaining a minority, had a significant influence on protest activities, mainly because of their political discipline and acquaintance with Palestinian activists in the occupied territories. The Guardian, which had ignored the Israeli left, suddenly took notice.

The growing interest in peace activities in Israel was not caused simply by the political disappointment with Labour party policies. During the years of the first intifada the focus, on both sides of the green line, shifted from the helpless political leaderships to the vibrant developing grassroots movements on the streets and in the public arena. While the PLO was trying to come to terms with a rebellion it had not fomented, a new local Palestinian leadership was forged in the occupied territories. And while Peres contemplated some new idle "formula", and Rabin prompted IDF officers to break the limbs of stone throwers, Israeli demonstrators, students, artists, musicians and journalists were responding to the Palestinian cry for human rights. For a long moment, the region did not seem to belong exclusively to formal leaderships.

The Guardian caught this development as it was happening. Black's knowledge of Israeli society, his fluency in Hebrew and Arabic, and the diligence which enabled him to move fast and be in three locations at the same time, were evident in his coverage. It was no less crucial that back in London, in the Guardian offices, there was a foreign editor who gave priority to the story. "There was great demand for these materials, and I was working hard and enjoyed it immensely," says Black.

Black wrote about politically controversial movies screened in the Jerusalem film festival, and that songs and television sketches were being censored by the broadcasting authority and the army radio because of their political content. The activities of protest organisations were covered extensively by the media, and Benny Morris, a young historian who wrote for the Guardian occasionally, published his prison diary after he was sentenced for refusing to serve as a reservist soldier in the occupied territories.[11] Other left activists, such as Yael Lotan and Amira Hass, emerged in the Guardian as writers and interviewees.[12]

Martin Woollacott notes that until the intifada, the Palestinian contacts of foreign journalists, Guardian correspondents included, were largely restricted, firstly to those who worked for the Israeli authorities and expressed very mild criticism if any at all, and secondly to the aristocratic Jerusalemite families, the Nusseibehs and Husseinis, who saw themselves as representing the national leadership, and indeed played a role in later stages of the intifada. But the uprising created a new reality. Local leaders, often teenagers or very young adults, controlled events. Reaching the true leadership of the intifada demanded contacts with stringers, informants and activists all over the West Bank and Gaza. Black ventured to spend a day with "an undersized Arab Rambo", a member of the Black Panthers, "the self-appointed guardians of the Palestinian uprising", in Nablus, and supplied many reports from the streets of the occupied cities.[13] Later into the intifada, Black described in a chilling feature the brutal killing of people suspected of collaboration with Israel, and the ruthless methods used by Israeli intelligence to recruit informers.[14] A local political leadership evolved in the territories, supplying a new type of Palestinian spokesperson, national, self-assured and eloquent, such as Hanan Ashrawi of Ramalla, Haidar abd El-Shafi of Gaza, and others. In 1988 Sari Nusseibeh published a few articles in the comment pages of the Guardian.

Even though it reported the new grassroots politics extensively, the Guardian pushed from the very early days of the intifada for the political leaderships to initiate diplomacy. "The occupied territories will not be liberated by throwing stones," said a leading article, which encouraged Arafat's initiative to form a government in exile, three weeks after the end of intifada.[15] The urge to push Arafat into diplomacy prompted the leader writer to argue from the foundations of Zionist history. International support for the Zionist enterprise might have been wrong from the start, he reasoned, but there could be no way back; therefore, a two state solution would be the only just and pragmatic option:

> If ever there were a situation where the legalities of past decisions were best left unexplored, this is it. Cogent arguments can be mounted, that virtually every international act towards the creation of the state of Israel, from the Balfour Declaration onwards, was invalid, even when proceeding from the UN general assembly and the security council. The one proposition on which a fair degree of unanimity can be reached is that there are now two separate entities in Palestine: Israel and the occupied territories. If the PLO, by promoting a government-in-exile, confines its ambitions to the latter it will, by more than mere implication, recognise the former.[16]

The paper's growing criticism of Israel's methods of oppression did not stop it from repeating an old theme – Israel's security fears should be acknowledged and answered to prevent further violence in the region:

> In short, the failure of statesmanship is not only Israeli. It is also the shortcoming of countries which, while professing Israel's right to exist, give such little thought to its security. It is a bad international bargain which makes Palestinians the perpetual losers in a contest no one can win.[17]

Another feature by Black described the predicament of soldiers trained to fight conventional wars, who found themselves policing a civil population. "A few years ago I did two spells of reserve duty in Lebanon," one of the soldiers told him. "Believe me, that wasn't easy and we ate shit there too. But if you ask all the guys in my unit they'd all choose to do two months in Lebanon instead of three weeks in Gaza. I break into cold sweat when I think I'll have to go back to this filthy place. I'm not the kind of guy who disobeys orders or refuses to serve in the [occupied] territories. But I doubt whether I'm emotionally capable of again seeing the terrible things I saw this time at close quarters. I'll be having nightmares for weeks to come."[18]

On the same day Black reported deaths, injuries and a violent Israeli Defence Force raid on a hospital in Gaza. "I don't mind them beating me, but if they stop me from treating people it is absolutely inhuman," a Palestinian doctor told him.[19] Another interviewee, a journalist from Jabalya refugee camp, encapsulated the sentiment of elation among Palestinians, typical of the first months of intifada: "An old woman told me she saw that the Israeli soldiers were afraid of demonstrators for the first time. There's a strange joy. Those who die – people will remember them forever."[20] A subsequent leader recommended Israeli withdrawal from Gaza, which would "relieve a lot of tension and be an earnest of good will towards the remaining Palestinians in occupied land."[21]

But the more violent the suppression of the intifada became, and as hardship intensified in the occupied territories, especially in the refugee camps, the Guardian penetrated more deeply into the heart of life under occupation, and its political implications. One anguished feature was by Swee Chai Ang, a British doctor who volunteered for duty in a hospital which served Sabra and Shatila refugee camps during the Lebanon war and the massacre of September 1982. Before she went to Lebanon, she "never knew there were people called Palestinians". Now, she was working for UN relief as a doctor in Ahli hospital in Gaza. After describing the hardship of Gaza, the density of the population, the diseases, the refugees, the dead and injured children, most of them shot or with with limbs broken by beating, she concluded:

> Getting rid of the occupation is not merely a matter of pride
> and dignity. In real life, it means running one's own country,
> building a modern sewage system, increasing the number of

hospital beds tenfold, repairing the roads. It means opening the
gates of the prisons so that those who have resisted the
occupation can be reunited with their loved ones, demolishing
the camps and building proper homes for the people. It means
labelling Palestinian goods with the words Made in Palestine,
an end to refugee identity cards, carrying a Palestinian passport.
It means no curfews, no arbitrary arrests, no beatings. It also
means the right of return for those Palestinians exiled in other
Arab countries. It means a home for the people of Sabra and
Shatila. It means flying the Palestinian flag freely.[22]

The intifada, and to a lesser extent the Lebanon war, gave a growing
number of European volunteers and charity workers a first-hand
experience of the Palestinian plight. Many felt cheated of the ideal of
Israel they had always carried in their minds. Dr Ang felt that "Israel, a
country which I have loved and respected for all my life, had suddenly
turned into a ruthless monster".[23] And although there weren't a huge
number of such volunteers, the impressions that they carried back to
their own communities, and their accessibility to newspapers and
television, had their influence on Israel's international image.

The violent events in the West Bank brought extensive coverage. The
space the Guardian devoted to the intifada was enormous even by the
standards of a paper that had covered Palestine extensively from the
early days of Zionist immigration. There were daily reports of clashes
between army and demonstrators, there would be a leader article at least
once a week, and feature stories, opinion pieces, and commentaries
appeared steadily.

By the end of the first year of the intifada, the PLO leader, Yasser
Arafat, seized the diplomatic initiative from the Israeli coalition
government. The Palestinian declaration of independence of November
1988, which included recognition of the state of Israel and willingness
for a peaceful resolution on a two state solution basis, was answered by a
grumpy Israeli refusal to "talk to terrorists", and an increase in settlement
building in the occupied territories. The measures against the intifada
were toughened. The IDF "elimination units", Duvdevan and

Shimshonwhich targeted intifada activists, were exposed by foreign media, and stirred an international outcry.

The Guardian welcomed the Palestinian declaration of independence, and the diplomatic initiative that accompanied it. The declaration text was published in the paper almost as prominently as the declaration of the formation of the state of Israel had been 40 years earlier.[24] At the same time, the editorial line expressed increasing frustration with the Israeli refusal to respond favourably.[25] "The Israelis, alas, have rather a lot of ground to make up before they convince world opinion of their sincerity in the cause of peace," said one leader.[26] Arafat's Geneva speech in December 1988 calling on Israel to make peace, and Israel's rejection of it as deception, added insult to injury.[27] It did not escape the Guardian that Israel's response to the US decision to talk to the PLO was wrapped up in an announcement on the construction of seven new settlements.[28]

For month after month the Guardian repeated the argument: Israel must come up with its own peace initiative and talk to the PLO, or violence in the region would increase yet further. This was combined with calls for international pressure on Israel:

> All experience of indigenous struggles against occupying forces
> suggests that – unless the Israel army declares total war on the
> West Bank and Gaza – negotiation is the only solution. A
> unified approach from everyone, including the EEC, the Soviet
> Union, the US and Sir Geoffrey Howe [the Conservative party
> foreign secretary] would help to concentrate Israel's mind.[29]

Another leader published before a visit by Shamir to Washington urged President George Bush Sr's secretary of state, James Baker, to take heed of Palestinian peace proposals. "So far they may only be dreams, but the alternative is another nightmare."[30] And another leader:

> There are many reasons why Israel should then respond
> creatively to the opportunity to deal with the PLO that
> American diplomacy has created. Not the least of them is that,

> if it does not, what is still a relatively limited conflict on the
> West Bank could become a far, far bloodier affair.[31]

The rising Palestinian death toll, and Israel's intransigence, led the Guardian to take a conspicuously dismissive approach to what may have been the first suicide attack on Israeli civilians. On July 6, 1989 a Palestinian man attacked a bus driver on the Jerusalem-Tel Aviv route 405, took hold of the wheel and diverted the bus off the road and into a ravine. Eleven passengers were killed on the spot; three others died later. The Guardian leader concentrated on Prime Minister Shamir's response to the event:

> A shocking disaster, the height of madness ... Prime Minister
> Shamir was not talking about the Likud party's scuttling of his
> peace plan, but about the tragic bus crash yesterday which
> killed 11 people near Tel Aviv [...] At least 533 Palestinians
> have died since the intifada began. But the image of the 11
> deaths in the red and white bus which crashed into a ravine
> near Abu Ghosh will divert Israeli attention from the profound
> crisis which they face.[32]

The next day, when details were clarified, the event was reported with little, if any, more sympathy. It was revealed that the Palestinian who diverted the bus was a member of a relatively new player in the Palestinian arena, the Islamic Jihad. Some details were given about the victims, and their accurate number, 14, was mentioned.[33]

An ironic, sometimes bitterly cynical tone, crept into some of the reporting about Israel. The Jewish state's reverence regarding its own dead seemed to stand in bitter contrast to its disregard of Palestinian lives and rights. A report about Israel's memorial day for IDF soldiers, by an Israeli freelance reporter, Guy Arbel, focused on the additional suffering caused to Palestinians by Israeli mourning traditions:

> Israel had sealed itself off from the occupied territories for 48
> hours to recall in tranquillity the creation of the Jewish state 41

years ago, and to honour the soldiers who fell defending it. Around 1 million Palestinians in the Gaza Strip and much of the West Bank were confined to their homes yesterday under a curfew that began on the eve of Memorial Day celebrations on Monday night and will last until tonight and the end of Independence Day.[34]

At the end of July 1989 the Israeli army kidnapped from Lebanon a local leader of Hizbullah, the Shia para-military organisation, Sheikh Abd El Karim Obeid, to be used as a bargaining chip.[35] This action was in total defiance of international law, and it also prompted Hizbullah to execute an American hostage, Lieutenant-Colonel William Higgins, a few days later. The Guardian responded with fury:

> There are times when it is desperately hard to hold fast to the principle that a terrorist crime is always the responsibility of the terrorists who committed it [...] But even though we must and do assume that the Israeli government does not want hostages, including its own three soldiers, to suffer needlessly, we do and must make a connection between the abduction of Sheik Obeid and the murder of Colonel Higgins. The connection is one of cause and effect. Those responsible for the former ought to feel very guilty about the latter and should at least have the decency to resign. This time "we blame the terrorists" simply won't wash.[36]

Many leading figures in Jewish communities in Britain and the US alike, horrified by the Palestinian death toll and the oppression of the civilian population, took a very critical view of Israel, as they had during the invasion of Lebanon. Jews were conspicuous in demonstrations against Israeli policies in the occupied territories. Many were disturbed by the sense that Israel's behaviour was creating hostility towards them.

The questionable link between anti-Zionism and anti-semitism was raised in the pages of the Guardian, and had come to stay. It was not focused on the media, but rather on trends on the left, and the ways in which sympathy for the Palestinians had influenced attitudes towards

Jews. Dr Henry Stellman, an academic at Tel Aviv University, argued in a feature that anti-Zionist discourse often slipped into anti-semitism. He quoted an article by Gore Vidal, who reminded American Jews that they live in a "host country", and accused them of giving their "first loyalty" to Israel. Stellman showed how sometimes the word Zionist is used as a cover for Jew. He added:

> This method of proving the relationship between anti-Zionism and anti-semitism is claimed by its proponents to be particularly useful with regard to those individuals whose anti-Zionism contains no noticeable anti-Jewish theme. For example, there are some leftwing groups who are genuinely opposed to all forms of nationalism and do not single out the Jews for criticism. Nevertheless, the unintentional consequence of their position is a threat to the Jews. Since most Jews identify closely with Israel, by accusing Zionism and Israel of Nazism, one is in fact accusing the Jews of the world of being Nazis.[37]

Grimly, the Guardian kept following regional politics as, after the first Gulf war in 1990-91, the US administration of George Bush Sr turned its attention to Israel and pushed for a settlement between Israel and the Palestinians. Shamir was dragged reluctantly to Madrid for peace talks with local Palestinian leaders after he refused to have any dealings with the PLO. It was clear to the whole world, including the Israelis, that Shamir was going through the motions of negotiation without any intention of reaching a settlement. It was time for a change.

The election of the new Labour leader, Yitzhak Rabin, as prime minister in 1992, raised hopes in Israel, and in the Guardian. Taking into account Rabin's hawkish convictions and his role in the harsh suppression of intifada, the leader which welcomed his election emphasised that his leadership brought some hope: "[...] Though opposed to a Palestinian state, he appears to envisage a degree of autonomy which may just lead in roughly that direction," it said.[38]

The first signs were not promising. After the intifada Hamas, a relatively little-known Islamic organisation, developed huge popular appeal in the occupied territories. Following the kidnap and murder of an Israeli border policeman, the Israeli government expelled 415 Hamas activists, to an outburst of international media outrage. The Guardian urged Rabin to restore his "peaceful credentials" by bringing the deportees back.[39] When the Israeli Supreme Court ruled that the deportation was legal, the Guardian responded:

> The Israeli Supreme Court has only compounded the damage
> already done to the prospects for peace in the Middle East. If
> Prime Minister Rabin had not dug his own trap by the original
> mass deportation, one might feel more sympathy as he sinks
> further into the sands. The court's decision to cancel the overall
> deportation order, but to allow the individual orders to stand, is
> a judicial conjuring trick which flouts both international law
> and considerations of equity.[40]

But within less than a year, Rabin precipitated a whole new phase of diplomacy in the troubled history of Israel and Palestine. While the Madrid process stagnated, Israeli and Palestinian negotiating teams conferred secretly in Norway. They presented a groundbreaking if problematic formula, which was sealed with the signing of the Oslo accords in Washington on the White House lawn, on September 13, 1993, with a historic handshake between Yitzhak Rabin and Yasser Arafat that was seen with renewed hope around the world.

The declaration of principles signed in Washington was an agenda for negotiations rather than a complete agreement. It stated that two months after the signing Israeli forces would withdraw from Gaza and Jericho and deliver them to the control of a Palestinian authority led by Arafat and secured by a Palestinian police force. In other areas of the West Bank control over civilian matters such as health and education was to be given to "authorised Palestinians". More areas of the West Bank were to be gradually transferred to Palestinian control, and a final settlement was to be reached within five years.

The novelty of the accords lay in their mutual recognition of the two national movements. The PLO accepted Israel as a Jewish state and Israel recognised the Palestinian right for self-determination, and the PLO as the representative of the Palestinian national movement. After 45 years of bitter struggle, this achievement could hardly be taken lightly, but there were gaping holes in the accords. The borders and nature of the Palestinian territory were not mentioned, and neither were other core issues: the future of Palestinian refugees, of Jerusalem, and of the Israeli settlements in the West Bank and Gaza, which by then were inhabited by over 100,000 Jews.

The historian Avi Shlaim remarks that had these issues been addressed, there would have been no accord. This may well be true, but the drawbacks are clear and should have been at the time. They enabled the Palestinians to continue to aspire to a sovereign state with east Jerusalem as its capital, to push for the evacuation of all settlements behind the 1967 boundaries, and for the right of return for refugees. They also enabled Israel to organise the scheme of bantustans heavily populated by Palestinians whose forces were handed the dirty work of keeping the peace. Israel retained the whole of Jerusalem as its capital. And the settlements remained.

During the early 1990s Israel recruited a labour force from the Far East, Africa and Eastern Europe, which meant it no longer depended on Palestinian workers. The two economies, of Israel and of the occupied territories, were no longer co-dependent. The Palestinians relied heavily on the need to find work in Israel, but the Israelis no longer needed them. This new reality enabled Israel to introduce a system of closures on the occupied territories, limiting under the pretext of security, and finally reducing to a trickle, the numbers of Palestinians allowed to enter Israel. A thin and fortunate layer of Palestinian bureaucrats, politicians and heads of policing forces were supposed to enjoy commercial franchises, import-export revenue, and VIP status that provided them with the privilege of entering Israel freely. It was this group which was charged with maintaining order among the impoverished and increasingly unemployed people in the Palestinian areas.

A further weakness of the accord was that its implementation depended heavily on Israel's goodwill. The collaterals given to the Palestinians by the international sponsors of the accords, it was to be discovered, were insufficient to ensure execution.

The opponents of the accord on the Palestinian side, mainly the Islamic forces, Hamas and Islamic Jihad, had sworn to stop the "treacherous surrender". Unemployment, life under, in a sense, lock and key, and the failure of Israel to withdraw from wider areas of the West Bank made Palestinians, who after the signing of the accord had marched the streets with olive branches in their hands, feel that they had after all gained nothing.

The Guardian, loyal to its tradition of embracing any "step in the right direction", welcomed the agreement, but asked many of the hard questions it raised. On the eve of signing, it argued:

> Neither secret diplomacy in Oslo nor fine statements before unfurled flags will be sufficient unless the rhetoric is translated into deeds without delay [...] Reports from the West Bank and Gaza yesterday suggested that many Palestinians were willing to give the news the benefit of the doubt. The Hamas activists did not attract a mass following. But if they continue to be shot down by the Israeli army while life remains miserably constrained, the suspension of disbelief cannot last for long.
>
> Israeli public opinion also has to be reassured. For the settlers in particular who have been encouraged to believe in a Greater Israel for the last 20 years, this deal seems an unholy and menacing alliance. The image of Palestinian enclaves which PLO terrorists can use as safe havens is powerfully disturbing. There are a host of practical difficulties about law enforcement by the PLO. Yet in the end the settlers' safety too depends upon the normalisation and "deoccupation" of the territories, without which Jew and Arab can never live in harmony [...] Foreign governments now have an opportunity to contribute something rather more useful. Monday's signing of the declaration of principles in Washington, already billed as a "historic ceremony", should not be an occasion for self-congratulation by those who over the decades have made their own contribution to the divisions of the Middle East and the misery of the Palestinians [...] History's verdict on the Middle

East policies of the great and glorious ex-presidents and prime
ministers now jostling to attend will be distinctly mixed. A more
humble approach to history would pare the list by half.[41]

Despite these misgivings, the Guardian covered the signing in
Washington with all due festivity, and reflected the hopeful and historic
atmosphere of the moment. But the comment pages during the post-
Oslo era contained many critical articles, mainly by David Hirst, still in
Lebanon, and the leading Palestinian intellectual and bitter opponent of
the Oslo formula, Edward Said.

On February 25, 1994, during the Jewish Purim festival, Dr Baruch
Goldstein, a settler, a medical doctor and a member of the racist party
Kach, entered the Tomb of the Patriarchs in Hebron, a sight holy to both
Muslims and Jews, and shot into a crowd of Muslim worshippers, using
his IDF-issued rifle and killing 29 Palestinians. Martin Woollacott wrote:

> The Hebron massacre has put a spotlight on the evasions and
> hypocrisies of both sides. The Oslo agreement is or was a
> device for allowing the Israeli government, and to a lesser
> extent the PLO, to talk about peace without talking about
> statehood, and to move toward statehood without saying they
> are doing so. That was earlier regarded as the genius of the
> arrangement. The two sides were to be enabled to avoid a
> dangerous confrontation with political opponents and attacks of
> panic and rage in both communities by blurring the real issues,
> using riddles and euphemisms, and putting off all the hard
> questions into the future. But Baruch Goldstein blew away
> more than just a political device with his assault rifle [...]
> Israelis are muddled and divided over the purpose of their
> country and its proper relationship with the world [...] A
> country where large numbers of new Jewish immigrants are not
> Jewish at all. A country where Arab votes may very soon be
> necessary if there is ever to be a centre-left government again.
> A country which lives in a world where the fourth largest Israeli
> — Israeli, not Jewish — city is Los Angeles. A country

desperately attached to hard, old things like territory and sovereignty and war-making capacity but also desperate to plug into the global economy, to master the new forms of power. Torn between a simpler past and a more ambiguous present and future, the tendency has been to locate the anxieties over these identity shifts in the peace process itself. Israel's muddle is especially apparent in the way in which political discussion, and action, is influenced by concepts from the past which operate sub-rational level. The concepts of dominance and division, for instance, are rarely absent.[42]

The Hebron massacre was followed by a chain of suicide bombings, carried out by Hamas and Islamic Jihad terrorists, mainly in civilian buses. This new, deadly and terrifying form of attack terrorised the Israeli populace and strengthened the vocal settler led opposition to Oslo. A suicide bombing at the Beit Lid junction in January 1995, which left 19 dead, most of them soldiers on their way back from weekend leaves, was the peak of a series of such attacks. There was a striking difference between the Guardian's compassionate editorial line on this incident and the remote attitude it adopted to the deliberate bus crash in 1989, suggesting that an Israel involved, however reluctantly, in a peace process, would be treated differently from the defiant country, led by Yitzhak Shamir, which crushed the Palestinians mercilessly while expecting the world to be shocked by its own pain. The Guardian wrote:

> Those who suffered in yesterday's appalling incident were, if possible, an even more sensitive target in Israeli public opinion [...] Israel is a small country where almost every Jewish family – or its nearest neighbours – has a son or daughter, a nephew or niece, going back to camp on Sunday in exactly the same way [...] The Islamic Jihad knew exactly where to hit where it hurts most Israelis most grievously – and therefore hurts the peace process most effectively.[43]

And yet, the Guardian fiercely rejected the "separation" plan Yitzhak Rabin proposed as a response to the bombing. The plan, which could be regarded as parent to Ariel Sharon's "Separation Wall", aspired to create a physical barrier between Israeli and Palestinian communities. It played a chord in the hearts of many in the Israeli "peace camp", whose wish somehow to move the Palestinians out of sight was always stronger than any vision of peaceful co-existence. The Guardian responded with a far sighted leader column headed Apartheid is not the answer:

> Separation could offer a tempting opportunity for the Palestinians to secure at least a slab of the land where sovereignty could no longer be refused. Palestinian critics of Mr Arafat have been arguing for some time that he should proceed at once to negotiate the final stage. Yet it is likely to remain an illusion, for them as well as for Mr Rabin. The real issues of Jerusalem and of the settlements would remain unsolved. Economic co-operation would be blighted. And separation would give a formal recognition to a geopolitical divide based on ethnic exclusivity. It may be an illusion to hope that Jews and Arabs can easily live together for a long time to come. But real peace will never be built upon the basis of permanent antagonism.[43]

And just as everything that could possibly have gone wrong with the Oslo accord did, while both Israeli and Palestinian leaderships struggled to maintain it against fierce and growingly violent opposition, three gunshots in Tel Aviv ushered in a sombre new era. On the night of November 4, 1995, Yitzhak Rabin was assassinated by Yigal Amir, a rightwing religious law student. A fresh era dawned for the Guardian too. After 20 years, it had a new editor once again.

CHAPTER TEN

Under Fire

The second intifada and the campaign against the Guardian

Steve Bell, 27 September 1996

IN 1995, his twentieth year in the position, Peter Preston retired from the editorship of the Guardian and the Scott Trust appointed Alan Rusbridger in his place. Like Preston, Rusbridger had seen service in the reporter's room; like Preston he had been the gadfly editor of the diary column, pricking the vanities and hypocrisies of public figures; like Preston, he had been a notably successful features editor; and like Preston, he came to the editorship with everything left to prove about whether he had the calibre to follow in the role of the great editors of the past, Scott to Hetherington, in the days when the wood and frosted glass panelled Corridor in Cross Street, Manchester, home of the editor and the leader writers, was the power centre of the Guardian. Not to put too fine a point upon it, Rusbridger was not considered a heavyweight in political journalism.

He had to prove himself fast. His first years saw the culmination of the libel actions brought against the Guardian by the Tory ministers, Neil Hamilton and Jonathan Aitken. The Guardian won both and Aitken went to jail for perjury, but had the paper lost, the financial burden would have been crippling, the cost in reputation incalculable. But from the beginning of the 21st century the stakes became even higher, for now the Guardian came under sustained attack, not for making a couple of misjudgments, but for abandoning its policies of the past and its reputation for backing incisive reporting with editorial wisdom. It stood accused of being anti-Israel and, worse, anti-semitic: this, in a paper which had been in at the birth of the Zionist dream.

The Rusbridger style is, for want of a better phrase, new Labourite, if not in substance, since the Guardian remains unattached to the agenda of a political party, and entertains growing criticism of Tony Blair's government. Either way, the hoary old lefties are cornered and on their way towards extinction. A new generation is becoming prominent in the Guardian, consisting of young liberals, whose claim for fame is more for brilliant writing, management skills and sharp eye for "concept" than for backbreaking service as news reporters in the world's darker corners.

Rusbridger likes to present his approach as non-hierarchical, a collegiate gathering of minds with the editor in the chair. This may well be what is meant in the trust's admonition to carry on the paper "as heretofore", but the way that has been interpreted over the years veers from the authoritarianism of Hetherington to the laid-back style of Rusbridger, with the editor in charge of strategy and not necessarily of day-to-day operations. This can, and to listen to some of the staff, does, create some bewilderment as to the paper's stance.

All the same, there is a core. Every one of the Guardian's current staff interviewed for this chapter mentioned the Balfour Declaration and the newspaper's involvement in the creation of Israel. Eighty-six years after it was drafted, Britain's approval of the creation of a Jewish national home in Palestine is still a part of the Guardian ethos.

The commitment to the heritage of the Balfour Declaration is used not only to underline the paper's support of Israel. The declaration also states, "nothing shall be done which may prejudice the civil and religious rights of existing non-Jewish communities in Palestine", and Guardian people proclaim commitment to that part of the document as well as to the others; now more than ever. As in the recent past, this obligation manifests itself in support for a two state solution for the Israeli-Palestinian conflict.

Simon Tisdall, an assistant editor and, until recently, leader writer, said: "This paper has a tradition of supporting Israel and supporting a Palestinian state. We always refer to the 1967 borders and we never made a big deal out of the Palestinian right of return, because it was obviously problematic for Israel, which fears losing its Jewish majority."[1]

Yet despite this history and these good intentions the Guardian is now subject to constant and violent attacks from a much broader base than its own Jewish readership. The intifada and, especially, the battle of Jenin, have had a powerful influence on this sea change. Jenin, particularly, solidified Jewish antagonism towards the Guardian, whose image as an anti-Israeli newspaper had gone so far that people would actually quote from it things which had never been printed. "They call suicide bombers 'freedom fighters', and they call suicide bombings 'alleged terrorist attacks'," one reader alleged, "and they are the only newspaper which referred to the battle in Jenin refugee camp as a massacre." Repeated and thorough scanning of hundreds of Guardian issues failed to detect any use of those terms. Moreover, the Guardian was probably the only British newspaper that never wrote of the battle of Jenin as a massacre. It used the word once, prominently, but in inverted commas (see appendix). Yet something about this newspaper led people to believe that it was highly biased against Israel.

Rusbridger was, by his own account, hardly an expert on Middle East affairs when he started his tenure, until events forced him to increase his involvement and recover lost ground impressively with the break of the second intifada. The Guardian mourned Rabin after his assassination and expressed hostility towards his enemies in Israel's hard-core rightwing. It watched with dismay the series of suicide bombings in the summer of 1996, which brought Likud and its new, ambitious leader, Binyamin Netanyahu, to power. "Mr Netanyahu's election will be bad news which at the very least must raise a large question mark about the chances for maintaining peace, let alone advancing further along the road," said the Guardian leader.[2] Ian Black, by then diplomatic editor, reported Netanyahu's election under the headline, Foreign leaders force smiles.[3]

The downfall of Netanyahu in 1999 and the rise of a Labour government, led by the no less ambitious Ehud Barak, was accepted by the Guardian as good news, more for the defeat of Netanyahu than for Barak's own merits. "His paper positions on the peace process and on negotiations with Syria do not differ much from Netanyahu's [...] A Barak government must show progress, if the world is not to conclude that no party and no leader in Israel can deliver a true peace to the region."[4]

The Guardian encouraged Barak's initiative at the Camp David talks with Yasser Arafat, sponsored by the American President Bill Clinton in July 2000, which was portrayed by Israel and the US "a generous offer" to be rejected outright by Arafat. While recognising that the offer shattered many Palestinian hopes, the Guardian urged them to make an effort:

> But for the Palestinians too, given willpower and a strong stomach, a deal is reachable and far preferable to what may otherwise follow. Up to 90 per cent control of the West Bank and Gaza; some form of limited power-sharing in east Jerusalem; the consolidation of the remaining Jewish settlements in the occupied territories into contiguous blocs; an international commission for the resettlement or rehabilitation of the estimated 3.5m Palestinian refugees: these are the rough outlines around which any second Camp David pact can be built. It is hardly heroic; not the stuff of celebration or even satisfaction. But it is the reality of the present. Like Mr Barak, Mr Arafat must find the strength to face it, manage it and then improve upon it.
>
> "Enough of blood and tears, I say enough," cried another former Israeli general-turned-PM, Yitzhak Rabin, when, rising to the challenge of statesmanship, he offered his hand to Mr Arafat in 1993. Mr Rabin paid an awful price. But his heartfelt message still stands.[5]

The argument over the amount of "generosity" in Barak's Camp David offer is still in dispute, but the failure of talks led directly to the second intifada. Just before it broke, a last attempt was made by the parties to prevent calamity in discussions in Taba, Egypt. The sides came nearer to bridging some of the caverns in understanding, but didn't make it to an agreement. The issues that were left out of the Oslo accords, Jerusalem, the refugees, the settlements in the West Bank and Gaza, now returned to haunt negotiators. Barak offered more on these subjects than any other Israeli prime minister before him, but, backed by Clinton, effectively presented his offer as "take it or leave it". As people tend to forget, the Palestinians also have a public opinion to satisfy and could not accept; and Barak, who did not have the parliamentary backing to support his offer even if it were accepted, was soon forced to call new elections.

The immediate trigger for the break of El-Aqsa intifada, or the second intifada, was a visit by Ariel Sharon, leader of the opposition, to Temple Mount in Jerusalem, which provoked a burst of violence around the site sacred to both Jews and Muslims that quickly spread throughout the West Bank, reviving memories of the first intifada and its harsh suppression. The Guardian leader said:

> The appalling explosion of Israeli-Palestinian violence over the
> past few days is the predictable consequence of the failure of
> men of peace to agree. The immediate spark was provided by
> last week's deliberately provocative incursion by Ariel Sharon,
> the hardline Likud leader, into the precincts of the Arab-
> administered Muslim holy site of Haram al-Sharif, also revered
> by Jews as Temple Mount.[6]

Barak rewarded Sharon for the provocation by inviting him and his party to join an emergency government until the new elections. The Guardian responded with anger:

> Ehud Barak, Israel's prime minister, would rather save his own
> skin than pursue the "peace of the brave" to which he
> committed himself after his election last year. That is the

distasteful conclusion that must be drawn from his decision to invite the hawkish Likud leader, Ariel Sharon, to join a national emergency government.[7]

To the Guardian's dismay, all too soon Sharon was elected prime minister, and violence erupted beyond any precedent. Stone throwing and tough oppression shortly intensified to shooting, raids on Palestinian cities by the Israel Defence Force, the renewal of suicide bombings, first by Hamas and later on by Arafat's own organisation, Fatah. Israel introduced "targeted assassinations": executions of Palestinian political figures and terror suspects, usually carried out by missile or, and causing, not just the death of the target, but family members and bystanders, often children. Another round of suicide bombings ended with reoccupation of most West Bank cities and Gaza, places from which the IDF withdrew during the Oslo negotiations and their aftermath. But this time, Israel occupied the land without forming a civil administration, without taking on the obligations of an occupier.

The Guardian columnist Jonathan Freedland said:

When the Israeli Labour party joined Sharon's government the paper found itself oddly out of date: we were still promoting the ideas that were crystallised in Taba and, to a lesser extent, Camp David. We still believed in those core ideas: land for peace and a two state solution. We were still holding on to Rabin's hopes of 1995. For sure, we gave some room to anti-Zionist voices on the comment pages, but as a paper our line was wholly in tune with that Rabin vision and was, therefore, pro-Israel.[8]

Just as Ian Black had been by the first intifada, the newly posted Jerusalem correspondent for the Guardian, Suzanne Goldenberg, was taken by surprise. She arrived on February 2001, after six years of covering India. "I thought the conflict was about to end, I thought I was covering the beginning of peace. Jerusalem foreign correspondents started wondering at that time whether we'd still have any work to do", she says. Soon enough, Goldenberg was not only snowed under by work, but also found herself at the eye of two storms: the rising violence in Israel and the occupied territories, and a hate campaign against the Guardian and against her personally. Swastikas were painted on her house in Yemin Moshe, an affluent neighbourhood in central Jerusalem, and she had to change flats. Her car was damaged, and she received death threats. Israeli officials threatened to take away her accreditation. Colleagues and interviewers heard from Goldenberg that much of this persecution was "due to my surname"; that is, she was Jewish. But there were other reasons.

When I first arrived in Jerusalem, there was no intifada, and I thought the conflict was about to end, and that I would be covering the beginnings of peace. That idea was so widespread in the summer of 2000 that foreign correspondents based in Jerusalem used to joke about whether we would still have work to do, or whether we would be made redundant.

Israeli officials often claimed they did not like the "tone" of my reporting, but my writing style was deliberately flat and descriptive. For the officials, 'tone' was a code word for their belief that I was writing too much about the Palestinians, and that I wrote about them as human beings.

It was not as if I described the Palestinians only as victims. I made a point of writing about Palestinians who were responsible for violence. Many of my stories were based on interviews with gunmen and other militants, because I thought it was important to talk to combattants, not just Palestinian civilians.

In retrospect, maybe I could have written more about Israeli politics and events. But news coverage often is driven by violence, and the impact of the violence on the Palestinian civilian population was far greater in the early months of the intifada than on Israeli society -- until the suicide bombings started and inflicted heavy casualties.[9]

Unlike the days of the first intifada, when Black could bounce from Jerusalem to Nablus and back to Tel Aviv, the second round of violence caused severe limitations on the free movement of journalists. In days of massive violence a journalist who managed to get into a remote West Bank town would often have to stay there for days. Despite new and advanced technologies, versatility seemed harder to achieve than it was 10 years earlier.

Goldenberg didn't realise, it seems, to what extent she was breaking the rules of the game as far as the Israelis were concerned. The terminology she used enraged many readers.

> Some Israeli government officials were angry because I used the term "illegal settlement" to describe Gilo, and the other Jewish settlements around Jerusalem. I used that terminology because Gilo is a settlement according to the United Nations, and international law, and there is no distinction in law between settlements around Jerusalem or deeper in the West Bank. Now, that is not how the Jewish settlements around Jerusalem are viewed by many Israelis, but it is not my role as a journalist to perpetuate that myth, which is a politically self-serving myth. The Israeli government put pressure on foreign journalists to adopt their terminology – neighbourhoods instead of settlements – precisely to obscure the fact that the settlements were illegal under international law.[10]

Gilo is a settlement by any international criterion. It is built on land occupied in 1967, and is a link in a chain of suburban settlements around Jerusalem. The Israeli consensus treats them as "neighbourhoods", and their inhabitants, middle class Israelis, do not see themselves as "settlers" at all. Some of them would describe themselves as leftwingers. Because Gilo is linked to other Jerusalem neighbourhoods and it takes less than 10 minutes to drive into the city centre, residents see themselves as legitimate Jerusalemites. All this had nothing to do with international law, but Goldenberg's adherence to UN definitions rather than to the Israeli consensus was seen as a wild provocation by her foes.

Ed Pilkington, foreign editor at the time, realised that some of the rage directed at Goldenberg had to do with the editorial treatment of materials:

We have listened to, and learned from, some of the criticisms levelled at our coverage. For instance, at the start of the intifada we would have a headline like 'Palestinians brace themselves for Israeli retaliation' after a suicide bombing. And yet, the story was about how many Israelis had been killed by a suicide bombing. We were too eager to look forward to the next news event rather than to mark the last, and as a result, unintentionally, we made it seem as though we were more concerned with Palestinian deaths than with Israeli ones. Now we make sure that we properly mark the suicide bombings in news stories and headlines, before moving on to any Israeli retaliation. We also make sure we give a human face to the Israeli victims of Palestinian violence, as we do for Palestinian victims of Israeli assaults. Many of the early complaints we received from readers have now stopped.[11]

Rusbridger said: "There have been days in which we have underplayed the Israeli casualties compared to the Palestinians. I'd be the last to claim that balance has always been perfect. Other days we have got it just right. The same, I guess, is true for all papers. I'm equally certain there have been days when we — and again, other newspapers — have not given enough prominence to Palestinian casualties."[12]

Seumas Milne, comment editor, remarked that it is more often Palestinians victims who are underplayed: "We report every suicide bombing in Israel, and often mention the victims' names, run colour stories about them, and interview families and eye witnesses. But when it comes to the day-to day death toll of two or three or six Palestinians a day, they are often not even mentioned."[13]

The Guardian staff gave full backing to Goldenberg's work. Rusbridger personally put out feelers in all directions, to his staff, to his readers, even to the more intemperate non-readers who attacked on the basis of what they have heard about the paper; from the beginning he has expressed his pithiest response to the criticism in two sentences: "This newspaper has always supported the right of Israel to exist. It does not mean that we must support Ariel Sharon's government."[14]

In 2001 Rusbridger made his first visit to Israel, to watch his correspondent in action, and was impressed. In an article for the Spectator he wrote:

> Some international correspondents, but only some, have made it their business to cultivate a decent range of contacts among the Palestinian community and to travel regularly to the occupied territories. The Guardian's correspondent, Suzanne Goldenberg, is one of them. It does not surprise me that her work is unsettling to people who are used to a rather more circumscribed view of the situation. She is regularly accused of being a self-hating Jew. She has been threatened with withdrawal of accreditation. Her email — much of it is organised by pressure groups from around the world — is so hate-filled and disturbing that she has been forced to change her address.[15]

Despite the backing for Goldenberg of all her Guardian colleagues, Linda Grant, a freelance writer, thought the final balance of reporting was problematic: "Suzanne is an excellent correspondent, but I think that she tried to do the same kind of work that Amira Hass does for Ha'aretz.[16] She did it very well, but in Ha'aretz there are many reporters who cover different angles of Israeli society, and the Guardian only has one correspondent. Maybe it would have been better if they had two."

While Goldenberg's critics were attacking her for writing a feature which gave a human face to the family of a female teenage suicide bomber, many of them ignored the two features in which she explored the "well oiled killing machine" behind the suicide bombers.[17] Goldenberg's reports went into the heart of darkness in which politics, religion, manipulation and hatred were all playing part.

In August 2002 Goldenberg was given the plum posting of Washington. Chris McGreal, who replaced her, has been subjected to less criticism. There seems to be various reasons for this. To start with, McGreal is not Jewish; but Rusbridger thinks that the principal differences have to do with the events covered.

Suzanne was there at a period of maximum violence. The fact that she was always present where things were happening enabled her to deliver a perspective you couldn't find in many other papers. It was very good reporting, but it was very different from what most others were doing, and it made her unique and a target for criticism. Chris, due to the decline in the level of violence, has more chance to get into Israeli internal politics, which might also be less controversial.[18]

And then there are certain differences in the reporting styles of the two correspondents. Pilkington said: "Chris inevitably has a fresh take on the Middle East process — inevitably because each reporter brings their own values and understanding to their work. He is keen to move beyond the day-to-day violence of the intifada and explore the politics that lie behind it, which I think is right. Two years into the uprising we can't devote as much space as we used to the violence and killings on both sides."[19]

McGreal, in covering the occupied territories, definitely quotes more representatives of the Israeli military. This doesn't necessarily put Israel in a more favourable light. "They are living in shit," Colonel Noam Tibon told McGreal after the killing of two Palestinian boys in Nablus by his soldiers. "We put pressure on the population [...] to show them that if they continue to cooperate with the terror they will suffer."[20]

McGreal said: "My experience in South Africa made me very aware that Israelis might behave in a certain way because they feel threatened. I realised that every story has various sides. I think that if you want to understand what the army is doing, then you should talk to them and let people decide for themselves what they think about this version. Of course, if you discover you've been lied to, you must write so."[21]

But the roots of the controversy lay not just in news coverage but also in feature articles, interviews, commentary and leader columns, which, being by nature more opinionated, were natural centres of dispute.

Ian Katz, the Guardian features editor, believes that the suspicious attitude of British Jews towards the Guardian was triggered by the publication in G2, the features section, of two chapters from the book *The Holocaust Industry* by the Jewish historian Norman Finkelstein.

Finkelstein criticises the commercialisation of the Holocaust memory by Israelis, Zionists and American Jews.[22] Jonathan Freedland responded with a furious article.[23] Only those who know how much Freedland hates being called "a self-hating Jew" could appreciate the rage that led him to use this insult against Finkelstein. The debate went on in the letter pages. "It was the first time I felt that serious liberal Jews felt that we had published anti-semitic material," says Katz, Jewish himself. "It is possible that some of the antagonism towards our coverage of the intifada derives from that episode."[24]

Five months later, the Guardian had hit danger zone again. In an article in the comment section, Jemima Khan examined why the press in the United States was heavily pro-Israeli and concluded: "The media are largely controlled by the Jews, as is Hollywood, and they account for more than half the top policy-making jobs in the Clinton administration."[25]

The Guardian readers' editor, Ian Mayes, responded in his column to the outcry: "There were remarks in this article which were quite understandably construed as anti-semitic. They caused offence not only to a large number of readers but to people inside the paper who also complained." Mayes explained: "The deputy editor, who saw the article before publication, gave an instruction for a passage which included these remarks to be taken out. Somehow it was left in." Khan, he added, wrote a letter in which she said that she had no intention of making an anti-semitic remark. The letter was not published because the letters editor "took the view that Ms Khan had already made her case".[26]

Two and a half years later Rusbridger was still ambivalent. "The problem with that sentence regarding the ownership of press is that is has such an unhappy history, which is directly related to anti-semitism," the editor says. "When I read the article I thought that this was not an absurd thing to say. The question of who owns newspapers is not irrelevant, it does affect what is written in the newspapers. On the other hand, maybe the history of this argument was reason enough not to print it."

Seumas Milne was not yet comment editor at the time Khan's article was published. He believes her arguments about the Palestinians, Israel and the US would have been both more acceptable and effective if expressed differently. "I would have asked her to write it differently and put her case more effectively without lapsing into these stereotypical phrases and caricatures," he says.[27]

Similar protest was aroused by Faisal Bodi's article, headed Israel simply has no right to exist. " [...] whatever God meant when he promised Abraham that 'unto thy seed have I given this land, from the river of Egypt unto the great river, the Euphrates,' it is doubtful that he intended it to be used as an excuse to take by force and chicanery a land lawfully inhabited and owned by others," wrote Bodi, a Muslim British journalist. He added: "However, take away the biblical right and suddenly mutual coexistence, even a one state solution, doesn't seem that far-fetched [...] Jews will continue to live in the Holy Land — as per the promise — as equals alongside its other rightful inhabitants.

"If that kind of self-reproach is forthcoming, Israel can expect the Palestinians to be forgiving and magnanimous in return. The alternative is perpetual war."[28]

An article two days later by Colin Shindler, author of *Israel, Likud and the Zionist Dream*, argued that "Mr Bodi's vision of the future is endless war until his version of history is accepted [...] As in Ireland, history eventually brings the participants back to the negotiating table. Better a flawed peace than a perfect war."[29]

"I have no regrets over publishing this one piece [Bodi's]," says Rusbridger. "I do not think that this is a point of view which should be excluded from the pages of the Guardian. But it is a marginal view, and naturally there is no reason to air it too often. There is such a view on the left — and of course, the Arab and Muslim world — that Israel shouldn't exist in its current form. It also had a perfectly respectable history within the British Jewish community."[30]

Upon his return from his first visit to Israel, in May 2001, Rusbridger wrote a long leader. While stressing Israel's existence as "a moral necessity", the leader continued: "A visitor to Israel today who takes the trouble to visit both the cosmopolitan and historic centres of Tel Aviv and Jerusalem as well as the captive degradation of the Gaza Strip cannot but think of the rottenest days of South Africa".[31] His leader concluded: "Jews the world over should think deeply about the terrible cost of securing their necessary sanctuary. Israel has accumulated massive power over the past two generations: it is not clear that it yet knows how to use it humanely."[32] The letters page the next morning had mostly supportive comments, most of them from British Jews.[33]

In August 2002, the Guardian published an interview by Jonathan Freedland with Britain's chief rabbi, Jonathan Sacks. The interview, pegged to the publication of Sacks's new book, *The Dignity of Difference*, concentrated mainly on Sacks's ideas for inter-religious dialogue. But one phrase by Sacks provoked a sensation: "[...] I regard the current situation as nothing less than tragic, because it is forcing Israel into postures that are incompatible in the long run with our deepest ideals."[34] A reference to that sentence was published on the same day in the Guardian's news pages with a prediction that it would "send shockwaves through Israel and the world Jewish community."[35] A few days later Freedland wrote in his column: "Jonathan Sacks made his choice this week, and came down on the right side of the line. Now the rest of the Jewish world has to decide where it stands" [over the occupation].[36]

Most of the postbag to the Guardian letters page was from supportive Jews, but Sacks himself received hundreds of hate letters and threats. To add insult to injury, he was also warned that he could be declared a heretic by orthodox rabbis in Britain and Israel, because of a paragraph in his book saying: "No one creed has a monopoly of spiritual truth. In heaven there is truth, on earth there are truths. God is greater than religion. He is only partially comprehended by any faith." The Guardian backed him in a leader column headed Courage to speak out.[37]

But towards the end of September the paper announced that Sacks had retracted the theologically controversial sentences of his book.[38] Then in January 2003, in an interview on BBC Radio 4's Today, Sacks denied ever having said the things quoted about Israel. The Guardian leader column reminded him that the interview was recorded: "The chief rabbi's Anglo-Jewish critics have often accused him of a lack of backbone; it would be deeply regrettable if a lack of truthfulness had now to be added to that charge sheet," it said.[39]

Of the many Israelis who contributed articles during the second intifada, most belong to the Israeli peace camp or to the left wing. The leftwing author David Grossman is one of the paper's favourites, and so is the author Amos Oz, a Zionist dove who is regarded in Israel as an oracle of the peace camp. The revisionist historians Ilan Pappe and Avi Shlaim, and Dr Menachem Klein, former adviser to Ehud Barak, then prime minister, are frequent contributors. Another important writer is Benny Morris, a revisionist historian who was known as a leftwinger until he converted to the radical right wing after the failure of the Camp David talks.

The prominence of this group does not stop at the opinion pages. Jonathan Freedland said in 2002 that the Guardian's interviews with Ariel Sharon, the leftwing activist Uri Avneri, Rabbi Sacks, the refusnik Rami Kaplan, the Palestinian politician Sa'eb Arikat, Yossi Beilin, an architect of the Oslo accords, and Shimon Peres as "some of the most important on this topic to have appeared anywhere in the British press during the past two years."[40] The only representative of the Israeli right on this list is the prime minister, Sharon.

But the current political debate in Israel is not being carried out between Zionist liberals like one of the architects of the Oslo accord, Yossi Beilin, and non-Zionist leftwingers like Pappe. In the midst of the second intifada the Israeli political arena was controlled by Sharon, advocating and practising an attempt to break Palestinian society and resistance by military force. On his right were the settlers and their representatives, pressing him to even harsher extremes or to attempt the mass deportation of Palestinians, also known euphemistically as transfer. On his left, the enfeebled Labour party was toying with ideas like dividing the Israelis from the Palestinians by building a separation wall. These kinds of ideas were not often aired in the Guardian, except the transfer, which was discussed in two articles by Benny Morris. In retrospect, maybe the Guardian was not so wrong to ignore the alleged differences between right and "left" in Israel. A few months later Sharon endorsed the separation idea, as well as the wall.[40]

Seumas Milne, the comment editor, says that rightwing Israeli writers "often seem reluctant to deal with the complexities of the arguments made against them or engage directly with what their opponents say". He sometimes turns to writers like the Israeli research fellow of St Anthony's, Oxford, Emanuele Ottolenghi, or the settlers' leader Israel Harel. "We have run a few articles by Jonathan Spire, who is prepared to engage with the more difficult questions for the Israeli right. We have the widest range of political opinion in the English language mainstream press, but the centre of gravity of our debate is left of centre."[42]

For Ian Katz, the shortage of rightwing writers and interviewees is "a problem I am aware of". Yet he states, "We are not trying to precisely reflect the whole spectrum of opinions. You also won't see a great number of British rightwingers writing in the Guardian; after all, it is a liberal newspaper." Katz says that he often uses diaspora Jews like the playwrite David Mamet to represent the point of view of the Israeli rightwing. Why not use Israeli rightwing writers? "It's a tough question. We are looking for writers with whom our readers could identify, and our readership is mostly liberal."[43]

This goes well with the editor's position, which is committed to balance in the news pages but not in the commentary section; however, the upshot of this policy may be that the paper does not reflect the true nature of the internal political debate in Israel, where the left and the doves are marginalised.

Rusbridger and Pilkington say that the debate as it takes place in Israel should be reflected in the news section, and in the news section, Pilkington says, "I feel that we have to be careful not to give the peace camp more prominence than they have in reality within Israeli society. That would be to give a false impression of the debate inside Israel itself."[44]

Rusbridger says: "It is possible that we were under-reflecting the views of Likud and the Israeli rightwing in comment terms. It leads us back to the matter of a wider concept of balance: to what extent should you do what the others are doing, and how much should you balance them."[45]

Freedland agrees that "people who read the Guardian might think that if all Israelis are so peaceful — if they are all like the Pereses and the Beilins we highlight on our pages — then how come Sharon came to power? Did he do it through some military coup? But it is essential to strengthen the Israeli peace camp. I suppose our presumption is that people are already quite familiar with the Israeli government point of view. It reaches people through other media like radio and television, where they are exposed to the likes of Binyamin Netanyahu or Raanan Gissin [a senior Sharon spokesman] all the time."[46]

Katz observes that the Guardian feels that it should supply a forum to Israeli peacemakers if they are being ignored in their own country.[47] This was the idea behind the alternative peace talks and a "joint shadow government for peace" suggested during a dialogue arranged, sponsored and covered by the Guardian in June 2002.[48] There were three days of discussion between Israeli doves and Palestinian mainstreamers, joined by representatives from Northern Ireland. Israeli representatives like Beilin, Amnon Lipkin-Shahak and Avraham Burg were indeed members of the Labour party, and though that was part of Sharon's coalition government, they hardly represented the mainstream. Jonathan Freedland, who chaired the meeting, explains how it represented the spirit of the contemporary Guardian: "Its importance was in the message that it is not enough to shed light on all the negative events. We should show that there is an alternative and promote it."[49]

However public spirited the motive, it did little to dispel the anger directed at the Guardian by Jews in Britain, Jews in the United States, and Jews in Israel. Each of the groups responded in its own way and with its unique style. In Britain a major part of the controversy was conducted in synagogues and other institutes of the Jewish community, and through the Jewish press. Israel acted through its officials. The Americans organised internet campaigns.

The common tool, used by all protest groups and individuals, was the email. "Email bombardment" is the first expression used by everybody in the Guardian when trying to describe the nature of the campaign against the newspaper. "A lot of flak is coming my way, hundreds of emails, many of them pure hate mail," says Freedland.

The flood was so strong that very word "email" developed a negative meaning in internal Guardian language. "In January 2001 I wrote that the Israelis were behaving badly in the West Bank, and received 800 emails," says the diplomatic editor, Ewen MacAskill. "Half of them were from the US, a quarter from Britain, and a quarter from Israel. A month or two later I wrote that it was not true that Israel had presented a generous offer in Taba, and I received hundreds of even worse emails."[50]

The violent email attack on Suzanne Goldenberg, a large proportion of it organised by the website organisation HonestReporting, was so intensive that it interrupted her ability to contact the newspaper in London. "There was a real hate campaign against her," says

Goldenberg's desk editor, Ed Pilkington. "It included murder threats, obscenities, and thousands of emails from HonestReporting. Quotes were taken out of their contexts. It became so bad we had to change her email address so that we could communicate with her."[51]

HonestReporting was established shortly after the second intifada broke out, and its declared purpose is to "scrutinise the media for examples of anti-Israel bias, and then mobilise subscribers to complain directly to the news agency concerned".[52] HonestReporting claims that its subscribers run into six figures: they receive press packages and are asked to email the news organisations that attract HonestReporting's disapproval. Samples of letters are attached to the packages, ready to be mailed. HonestReporting doesn't encourage its members to be abusive. "Stick to the facts," it recommends the website. "Preserve the integrity of the HonestReporting campaign by keeping your comments clean and respectful. Hostile or over-emotional language is counter-productive. Accusing the media of anti-semitism will always be met with great resistance (besides being frequently untrue). This is not the place to vent your frustration."[53]

Alas, while a large number of subscribers followed the instructions, many HonestReporting subscribers ignored the advice. "What is 'repellent' is the Guardian's shabby, irresponsible and blatantly anti-semitic reporting," wrote one of them in response to a leader of April 17, 2002 regarding Jenin. "You are a vicious lot. May you all be damned!" "Have you killed a Jew today?" inquired another.[54]

This might have something to do with HonestReporting's methods. In a list of "selected violations of media objectivity, courtesy of the Guardian", published in its website, the organisation claims: "When a Palestinian terrorist kills eight Israelis by ramming into a bus stop, the Guardian defended him as 'a sort of Palestinian everyman who finally snapped because of the combined pressure of the four-month uprising and Israel's economic blockade'."[55] The story was by Suzanne Goldenberg, and what she actually wrote was: "In the Gaza Strip, meanwhile, he is being seen as a sort of Palestinian everyman who finally snapped because of the combined pressure of the four-month uprising and Israel's economic blockade."[56] This sentence appeared after a quote from Israeli security sources saying that the man had confessed to having carefully planned the attack.

Curiously enough, HonestReporting does supply links to the Guardian's original texts alongside its own interpretation of selective quotes.

After the Guardian was deluged with emails regarding the bus driver story, the Guardian journalist David Leigh addressed the issue.[57] Leigh described HonestReporting's activity as "internet harassment", and exposed HonestReporting's contacts with Aish Hatora (Hebrew for the Fire of Torah), which he described as "an international group promoting Orthodox Judaism", and said that "they are widely regarded as rightwing extremists and they are certainly not people entitled to harass the media into what they would call 'objectivity'."[58]

Indeed, Aish Hatora is deeply involved in Israeli politics, and was under scrutiny in Israel's for allegedly financing illegally the election campaign of Israel's former prime minister Binyamin Netanyahu. They are also involved in enterprises for settling Jews in occupied east Jerusalem. But from the Guardian's point of view, it might have been helpful if Leigh had simply presented the original quote from Goldenberg story, hence exposing the manipulation.

When Goldenberg left Israel, HonestReporting hailed the "good news", and encouraged them to "send a friendly farewell message to Suzanne".[59] The real incitement was in the next sentence: "Goldenberg's incessant criticism of Israel's right to defend its citizens has undoubtedly emboldened Palestinian terrorists."[59]

The Guardian itself frequently addresses the problem of objectivity. Interviewees from the Guardian always mention the US press ethos as the one to avoid. The American-approach, embodied in slogans like "Only the facts, please", insists on a strict distinction between news and commentary, and demands an equal and non-judgmental representation of the claims of both sides. Some Guardian senior editors acknowledge the concept of objectivity, but try to supply a different formula for its practice. Others deny the possibility of objectivity, and strive to replace it with what they see as more relevant and morally justified values.

The editor himself says: "I don't believe that absolute objectivity exists, though I do believe that newspapers should strive to achieve something like it in their news reporting. Obviously, they are not committed to it in their commentary pages. But in situations when most of the media are biased towards one side, I sometimes feel a pressure for this paper to have some sort of obligation to produce a form of balance — to give more representation or voice to the events or views of 'the other', be it Muslims, Palestinians, the poor, or minorities inside the UK."[61]

Pilkington says: "Where I part company with some of the American media is the idea that events have to be given equal weight, irrespective of their significance. That can lead to a flow of stories that have no context and do not help readers understand what is going on. Suicide bombing, Israeli incursion, another suicide bombing, Israeli incursion, and so it goes on[62] […] When awesome events happen, it's the job of a newspaper not just to lay out those events in a cold factual way, but also to convey the awesomeness of what happened. And on occasion, to convey too a sense of moral outrage – not as commentary but as emotion. We do not ask our reporters to cease having human reactions and emotions when they witness and write about appalling things."[63]

The Middle East editor, Brian Whitaker, takes objectivity further. "I think objectivity is not about being neutral and standing in the middle. It is a matter of looking objectively into the facts, approaching them with an open mind, and drawing conclusions, which should be fair. It doesn't necessarily mean not taking sides, especially when atrocities occur, as long as you are fair and honest."[64]

MacAskill discounts the concept of objectivity: "Once editors make a choice what to cover and where to place it, it's already subjective. It is not honest to pretend to be objective. Being fair means presenting the positions of both sides in the most effective way."[65]

Simon Tisdall, assistant editor, columnist and former leader writer, stresses that the concept of objectivity should be replaced by more relevant values: "A paper should present its basic values and repeat them. For example, regarding the Israeli-Palestinian conflict, it means demanding from both sides to resolve it in a peaceful manner, and to judge them all the time according to how much they act in a way that gets them closer or farther to this principle."[66]

Chris McGreal, Goldenberg's successor in Israel, adds another component to the concept of balance. "It is wrong to strive for balance in every individual story. Coverage becomes balanced through a period of time."[67]

Martin Woollacott, columnist and a veteran foreign affairs correspondent, including the Middle East, and former foreign editor, thinks that keeping a "technical" separation between news and commentary doesn't give enough credit to the readers: "Readers got used to the idea that coverage will include a certain amount of comment. They are aware of signs in the text which indicate an attitude to the events expressed by the reporter, and they are able to accept or reject it. I think we have developed an established language for those things, which is more subtle and nuanced than putting the comment in one box and the news in another. It works well for intelligent readers and good reporters."[68]

But many writers and editors in the Guardian feel that they are often attacked by people who are not readers, particularly HonestReporting subscribers. "The people who complain don't necessarily read what you write," says McGreal. He had written about the army taking over buildings in Hebron, which, McGreal pointed out, "is a kind of ethnic cleansing." "I mentioned specifically that Sharon was using the fact that 14 soldiers and settlers were killed there in one attack as an excuse for this controversial act. I received about 50 emails saying 'how could you write about this without mentioning that 14 people were killed there?'" [69]

But are internet campaigns, annoying as they may be for journalists, illegitimate? "Campaigns like this one have their importance," Rusbridger admits. "The more I do this job the more I become uncomfortable with the huge power of the press, and the way it is used. And as much as I have tried to make the Guardian open and responsive, there is an obligation to check oneself. I think, though, that a great part of this lobbying campaign was counter-productive. It was plain that much of the lobbying activity came from people who didn't read the paper at all but felt free to criticise it."[70]

HonestReporting worries the journalists much less than the concern of British Jewry. After all, most of HonestReporting subscribers live in the US; British Jews are paying customers. "The assumption is that there is a very large Jewish left, and that the Jewish community is a relatively liberal broadsheet reading kind of group," says Katz. "It is worrying when those liberal Jews feel that we give Israel unfair treatment."[71]

Freedland has a personal take on this: "After my interview with Jonathan Sacks I went to shul on Rosh Hashannah," he says. "Someone confronted me and said 'I'm surprised you dare show your face here'. They feel that even as a journalist one is supposed to represent the community. I don't feel like that at all about my writing."[72]

Freedland acts unofficially, though vigorously, as a kind of ambassador for the newspaper within the Jewish community, and vice versa. He takes part in meetings with Jews, participates in panels, and promotes awareness of Jewish sensitivities inside the paper. Not everybody in the Guardian is happy with this undertaking, Freedland says. "After one of the suicide bombings we made a list of all the children, Jews and Palestinians, who were killed during the intifada. After it was published I realised that due to some mistake the youths who were killed in the suicide bombing at the Dolphinarium were missing from the list. I thought it was terrible, and that critics would focus on this one error. Somebody on the staff, a colleague, said 'You can't seriously think that this was in any way a deliberates act, as if there was some kind of conspiracy.' I said it's a matter of accuracy which is very important to those of us who are sometimes called on to defend the paper in public. And then I was asked, 'Who appointed you to defend the paper?' The answer is that I am in an unusual position, and I do often get attacked over the paper's views — and therefore am obliged to defend them."[73]

Rusbridger says he has lost count of the number of meetings with Jewish representatives he has attended over the past two years. Among them were the Board of Deputies, the Anglo-Israeli Society, rabbis, a policy group on the Middle East, and others. He has also engaged in long email discourses with concerned members of the Jewish community. When Rusbridger heard that Rabbi Tony Bayfield had spoken in his temple against the Guardian, he invited him to a meeting, and suggested that he should write an article for the Guardian. So far Bayfield has written three articles for the Guardian, and keeps in touch with Rusbridger by email.

One of the most highly charged issues in this debate is the extent to which criticism of Israel becomes anti-semitic. Many members of the

Jewish community, some liberals among them, adhere to ardent support of Israel, and view attacks on the Jewish state as attacks on Jews in general. In an article he wrote after returning from a visit to Israel, Katz tried to explain the syndrome.

> Israel exerts a strange power over Jews, however flimsy their
> identification, and mine is flimsier than most. It makes you feel
> proud, guilty, embarrassed, brings a lump to your throat at the
> most inconvenient moments [...] At some level, I suspect,
> feelings like these animate the attitude of most diaspora Jews,
> however disillusioned or assimilated, to Israel. You may despair
> over its idiotic invasion of Lebanon, its complicity in atrocities
> such as the massacres at Sabra and Shatila, its countless human
> rights abuses, its reckless and frequently disproportionate use of
> force, its paranoia, its sheer bloody-mindedness. But somewhere
> inside there is always a small, persistent voice saying: these
> people are putting their necks on the line, making sacrifices,
> doing ugly things so that there will be a sanctuary for you if
> ever you need one. Who are you to criticise?[74]

Rarely is the Guardian accused of anti-semitism over matters which are not connected to Israel. The readers' editor, Ian Mayes, cannot remember any specific complaint of that kind. He is sure that there have been some, "but not any more than complaints of offended Welshmen, or deaf people".[75] The major concern of the complaining Jews is obviously Israel. Whitaker says: "If we have an argument with the French regarding, say, importing meat from Britain, it doesn't make us anti-French. Some people just don't make this distinction."[76]

"The accusations of anti-semitism are pure nonsense," says McGreal. "It is an unfortunate reaction by a group among Israel's supporters who oppose any criticism of it. Israel should be judged according to its self-presentation as a western democracy. There are Jewish people in some key positions in the Guardian, and they are leading the paper in those directions. Surly they can't be blamed for being anti-semitic or anti Zionist."[77]

Actually, the belief that Jews must be pro-Zionist is exactly what triggers many Jews to see criticism of Israel as anti-semitism. Many Jews in the world see themselves as anti-Zionists or non-Zionists, in the sense that they do not support a state which accepts as first-class citizens only members of a certain religion. But in England, in the current atmosphere, anti-Zionism is perceived as objecting to the right of Israel to exist at all.

As HonestReporting anticipated, accusations of anti-semitism are highly infuriating, especially for liberals. Tisdall observes that the easy accusation of anti-semitism against critics of Israel simply prevents any further discussion. "Maybe this is the aim of the Israeli right wing," he adds.[78]

But Linda Grant believes that the matter is more complicated, and that some kinds of criticism towards Israel could indeed strengthen anti-semitism:

> Every Jew I know is talking about anti-semitism in Britain [...]
> The approach stating that all the world's problems derive in
> Israel found a warm home in the Guardian [...] It is not that
> the paper is promoting these points of view, but people who
> think like that read the Guardian, and are subjected to doses of
> articles about the Palestinian suffering. They feed their anti-
> semitism on this information. People start to believe that Israel
> is the most horrid, murderous and ethnic cleansing state in the
> whole world. It is wrong to dehumanise the Israelis, turn them
> into political causes, and it is wrong to think that it doesn't
> affect the attitude towards the Jews.[79]

Ian Black agrees that there are people in Britain who simply hate Jews. "And there's another thing. Because Palestinians are the main victims of this conflict, and they are, their victim status gets more attention. But there are also victims on the other side. I'm not talking only about the Israeli casualties, but also about a whole society, which suffers from a major leadership crisis. It shouldn't be ignored or delegitimised."[80]

Shortly after the Jenin crisis, the readers' editor devoted three consecutive columns to the Guardian's coverage of Israel. The first two columns concentrated on a survey Mayes conducted among the paper's staff, not only the journalists, asking for their opinion. Mayes was surprised to discover that only 30 workers bothered to answer his questions, given that 350 journalists work for the paper. One non-journalist thought that the coverage of Israel was "unfair to the Israeli side, anti-semitic and indulgent to the Palestinians". Most of the other workers thought that the coverage had been "good and generally fair".[81]

The second article invited readers to respond, and Mayes was flooded by 500 emails, which after the publication of the third column increased to 800. In his third column Mayes assessed that 400 out of the 500 letters came from HonestReporting members.[82] Mayes concluded: "Many of the 'readers' who responded have never seen the Guardian at all. Some read it online, but others saw only circulated articles." And yet he read them all because despite his reservations, the emails were individual and strongly felt, and the abusive ones were a minority. Mayes answered "even the most nasty ones. I wanted to check the theory, which Rabbi Sacks might have agreed with, that calm responses, even to the vilest attacks, might calm the whole discourse".[83]

A peek into Mayes's packed mail files puts paid to some myths. Not much more than half the letters were hostile, and not all the letters from the US or Israel attacked the newspaper. Many American readers thanked the Guardian for supplying them with a different view from their own press. A few Palestinians and many more Jews encouraged the paper to maintain its line. Most of the critical letters were not rude, though some were genuinely abusive. The most impressive and painful letters were from British Jews. Even those who declared that they had stopped reading the Guardian because of its attitude towards Israel, expressed a wish to "come back home", as one reader had put it.[84]

Israel's approach under Ariel Sharon towards foreign media is embodied in the character of Danny Seaman, the director of the government press office. Seaman is a typical though radical exemplar of Likud-type diplomacy, which views journalists as hostile in advance, and assumes a take it or leave it approach to them.

Seaman became notorious among news agencies after he confiscated press cards from all Palestinians who worked as reporters, technical staff or stringers for foreign or local media. The press cards enabled their holders to move from one curfewed village to another, and in their absence work became impossible. He also prevented some foreign photographers who left Israel for a few days from returning on the pretext that Israeli unions were pressuring him to do so, to provide local photographers with work.

In October 2002, Seaman launched a belligerent attack on the Guardian and its correspondent, Suzanne Goldenberg, as part of a general campaign he was conducting against the foreign media. In an interview he granted to the Jerusalem magazine Kol Ha`ir, Seaman accused the European press of reporting "every slander against Israel as if it was a fact. The negligence of their coverage contributed to the anti-semitism that is now making rounds on the continent". Seaman boasted that he was boycotting four journalists, Suzanne Goldenberg, Lee Hockstader from the Washington Post, Sandro Contenta from the Toronto Star and Gillian Findlay from ABC. "The editorial boards got the message and replaced their people," he declared.[85]

Rusbridger responded with a robust letter to Seaman. "This is completely untrue," he wrote. "We regard Suzanne Goldenberg as an outstanding correspondent and had every faith in her reporting on the Middle East. During her period in Israel, she won four prestigious awards from independent juries. The decision to promote her to a new role in Washington was mine alone, and was utterly unconnected with any view of her reporting which the government of Israel might or might not have had."[86] In an interview with the Toronto Star Rusbridger defined Seaman's accusations as "utter rubbish", and added that he received an infantile reply from Seaman to his letter.[87]

Seaman's letter said: "I would like to point out that besides the four awards you mentioned, Ms Goldenberg won the complete disdain and contempt of the Israeli authorities. As far as I am concerned, the reason for her relocation is irrelevant. I will happily withdraw any statement made about Ms Goldenberg when your newspaper withdraws the biased, sometimes malicious, and the often incorrect reports which were filed by her during her unpleasant stay in Israel."[88]

The Guardian defended Goldenberg in a leader headed Seaman lets it Slip, which skittishly described the press officer as "the Alastair Campbell of Israel":

Mr Seaman has at least been candid about his futile attempts
to bully and penalise foreign reporters and news organisations,
but he has done his organisation and his government no favours
at all.[89]

DJ Schneeweiss, spokesman for the Israeli embassy in London until the
summer of 2002, had, to say the least, a different style from Seaman's.
He initiated and conducted long and civil conversations with all the
Guardian staff who had anything to do with the coverage of Israel. His
opinions rarely convinced them, but he gained their respect, and made
some impact. "When DJ was here he made many comments, and I
found them very useful. We became friends and I respect his opinion. I
think he also developed respect towards our point of view," says Simon
Tisdall.[90]

Schneeweiss, though not enthusiastic about the Guardian's tone, never
indulged in a war with the media. "The Guardian finds it hard to share
its sympathy around," he said when asked by a Jewish news agency about
the paper's attitude towards Israel.[91] Schneeweiss left his post in the
summer of 2002, and was replaced by Shuli Davidovich. The contacts
between the embassy and the paper have dwindled.

The Israel foreign office, too, had a relatively civilised approach to the
press compared to Seaman's, but this distinction was soon to blur. In the
summer of 2003 the foreign office spokesman, Yonatan Peled, said: "We
don't have a different policy from Seaman, but we do not boycott
journalists or organisations".[90] But a few months later the foreign office
declared a boycott of the BBC after what they regarded as a hostile film
about Israel's nuclear power.

In November 2003 Seaman went too far. His initiative to get all
journalists, foreign and local, cleared by the general security services as a
condition for being granted press cards and accreditations, and his
demand that media organisations would pay for this "service", met fierce
resistance from both the Israeli press and the foreign media. He backed
off and was asked to retire although at the time this book went to press
he was still in his position awaiting his replacement. In April 2004 the
Israeli high court of justice ruled that his denial of press cards to all

Palestinian journalists was illegal, and that any such denial should be applied only to individuals and based on a specific security threat.

The campaign against the Guardian had a two-way influence as Alan Rusbridger and Martin Woollacott explain. The editor himself was driven to the view that he needed to see Israel at first hand, though his purpose was quite different from Hetherington's on his Middle Eastern visits in a quasi-diplomatic role (see chapter 7). Rusbridger says:

> About two years ago various lobby groups started to initiate contact through emails, letters and so on. I thought: I am nothing like an expert on the region and it is about to develop into a huge running story, and I should somehow get a first-hand impression. There's no other example, except maybe Northern Ireland, where I felt obliged to make two trips in order to see what's up. I'm happy I've done all this homework, otherwise you become very dependent on your correspondent. There has also been an ongoing dialogue here with the Anglo-Jewish community, we had open staff meetings here at the Guardian and Ian Mayes did his survey. There were also many hours of email debates with complainants. Including the trips, I would say that's disproportionate for such a small country.[93]

And Woollacott explains:

> It had an impact. The paper became more critical of Israel due to the criticisms and the attacks on Suzanne's integrity. The paper's leadership reacted by taking a careful look at our coverage. The editor took a close interest, convened meetings, and eventually went out there, coming back convinced that our coverage was indeed accurate and fair. In that sense the campaign against Suzanne was counter-productive. But we did also become more sensitive to the feelings of readers and to the unintended impact of headline and picture choices. We also were alive to the problem, which Linda Grant emphasised at a meeting she initiated with the editor and senior writers,

including myself. She felt we might be on the road that would take us from being critical of Israeli policy toward implying that Israel had forfeited its right to exist. The meeting took her point that criticism of the Israeli government should not slip or appear to slip in that direction. We had used some highly charged expressions, mainly in headlines and we determined to be more careful.[94]

Katz is very aware of the perils that derive from pressure:

There are two dangers here. The first is if a paper is attacked so relentlessly that its journalists are just driven to dismiss every comment, regard it all as part of an orchestrated attack and deny it. The other side of the spectrum is also problematic — all the analysis and arguments around every headline, word, photo, discussions of in which paragraph each of the story should or should not have been mentioned — it could also be unhealthy. Sometimes you do have to be bolder to make your point. There are periods when it seems that Alan spends half the time dealing with that thing, meeting people, and explaining our position. At some point you are in a danger of saying 'oh, the hell with it all'.[95]

Brian Whitaker, on the other hand, implies that scrutiny has made his writing more sophisticated: "I have been covering this conflict for a long enough time to know in advance what things will create an outrage. I can predict what the complaints will be about, and address it in the article."[96]

Rusbridger seems slightly frustrated over the way his attempts to be responsive to the public debate are sometimes treated, and fears that the repercussions might go beyond personal discomfort:

I do believe we are the most responsive newspaper in England. We have numerous mechanisms to explain, apologise, clarify and correct things when we are in the wrong. I never have a problem with apologising, only with the spirit in which the

apology is taken. We also recognise we are operating in a
political environment where some people see a newspaper as a
part of a war. So some people will never give you any credit:
they will simply see it as a weakness to be exploited. You try to
be honest and apologise or correct and some of these lobbying
groups simply say, 'Ah-ha! We squeezed an apology off the
Guardian, it just proves that they are always wrong'. These
people are not actually interested in fair reporting and balance:
they are open advocates for one side of the argument. The
same happens when you answer emails. You find yourself
sometimes conducting what you imagine to be a private
discussion with somebody via email, and then you discover that
selective parts of what you were writing in private, appear on
some website often wrenched out of context. So you end up
having a discussion which is not quite frank on either side.[97]

Politicians often have the same complaint about journalists. Isn't that a
taste of our own medicine? "It might be," Rusbridger says, "but it will
just have the effect of making newspapers less open and more tight-
lipped, fearing that any expression of honesty or self-criticism will be
used against them. I think that it did happen to politicians, and that it is
a loss to the press and the public."[98]

HonestReporting claims that it has succeeded in shaking up the media
and putting them on alert. "They think twice, knowing they may be
called to task for a particular article or headline,"[99] the organisation
boasts. If this was the genuine goal of their campaign, then it was a
success. But if, as many at the Guardian suspect, and the political line of
the website indicates, the true aim was to make the paper haul down its
flags and change its policies — than its success has been limited and
short-lived. But it did leave the paper and its journalists tired and wary.
Their beliefs may not have changed, but a number of them avoid the
subject when they can. The war on Iraq, in a way, broke at the right time
to set the Israeli Palestinian conflict to rest for a while.

CHAPTER ELEVEN

Aftermath

Exploring New Paths

Steve Bell, 5 December 2001

T
HE last chapter of this book does not enjoy the privileges of historical perspective. It is being written on the wing as the events that it attempts to capture are still happening. But one fact is conspicuous. During 2003 and the first months of 2004 there was a significant decline in the number of Guardian references to Israel.

Maybe one should start at the end. During the second week of April 2004, two Guardian leading articles, each of them accompanied by a powerful signed article, signified the conclusion of a long period of pondering. On April 15, 2004, the main front-page headline of the Guardian declaimed: Bush rips up the road map. The next day's leader criticised the US presidential endorsement of Ariel Sharon's disengagement plan:

It is hard to know which was more astonishing: The White House's endorsement of Ariel Sharon's ill-conceived peace plan, or Downing Street's decision to back it without hesitating for even the blink of an eye. Either way, the Israeli government's plan to retain settlements in the West Bank for itself and deny outright Palestinians' right of return should be rejected as a dangerous abrogation of the basis upon which negotiations for a peace deal in the region have aimed towards for so many years.[1]

On the same day, a column by Jonathan Freedland exposed the disengagement move as the opposite of a peace plan:

> [...] What's left of the West Bank will be sliced into a Swiss cheese that can never be the "viable" Palestinian state Bush still promises, thereby preventing the two state solution, which is surely the best hope for both peoples [...] This is a break not only from Bush's road map – which called for a negotiated rather than imposed settlement – but also from 37 years of US policy [...] It confirms the extent to which Bush's is the aberrant presidency, a period future historians will marvel at as a rupture from all that had gone before. The abandonment of even the attempt to appear to be an honest broker in the Middle East, along with the doctrines of pre-emptive war and unilateralism, are departures from the post-1945 US consensus with no precedent.[2]

The second set of two articles broadened the argument by contrasting the double standards involved in the approaches to the occupation of Iraq and the treatment of the Palestinians. The first, a leader, criticised the killing of 600 inhabitants of Falluja by the American forces in Iraq, describing the act as a "massacre in the making" and calling the UN to investigate "the deadly events in Falluja as it did in Jenin"[3]. The other article, by the novelist and screenwriter Ronan Bennett, questioned the silence on the Falluja massacre from Labour MPs from Peter Hain to

Chris Mullin and Harriet Harman; and then, he pointed out, there was Oona King, who "denounced the 'slaughter and oppression of the Palestinians in Jenin' ", and is now silent in face of Falluja's atrocities."[4]

These Guardian articles demonstrated the point that there wasn't a hair separating US foreign policies and Israel's treatment of the Palestinians. Despite Tony Blair's attempt on the eve of the war to present Britain's alliance with the US as an opportunity to push for progress in the famished Israeli-Palestinian peace process, it was now obvious that Israeli and American belligerence went hand in hand. It was not possible to be lenient towards George Bush's crusade, the "war on terrorism", while attacking Israel's similar policies and similar pretext. Israel's administrative detentions, house demolitions, air raids on residential compounds and "targeted assassinations", were the same in kind as the identical though much larger scale US actions.

Although the Guardian did not support the war on Iraq, many readers were not clear that this was the case, and many staff journalists, to the contrary, believed that the paper had raised outright objections. There are two reasons for the confusion. The first is that the Guardian, while rejecting the idea of going to war without a UN resolution, did not reject flatly the very idea of attacking Iraq, a secular though unattractive state, as a response to 9/11; nor did it raise the question of whether the supposed evidence of weapons of mass destruction in Iraq was irrelevant in a war supposedly against terrorism, when Stanley knives were the only weapons involved in the plane hijackings of 9/11. All in all, its pre-war stance was a cautiously liberal one.

Beyond the immediate reasons, the Guardian differs greatly in the 21st century from the Manchester Guardian in the time of the Balfour Declaration or even the Suez war, not in the general thrust of policy, but in presentation. The leader column, unsigned, deliberated over in conference each day, remains the editorial voice of the Guardian, but, from the single opinion page facing the leader page launched by Peter Preston, then features editor, in 1968, the subsequent proliferation of such pages and their star columnists has meant that the leader no longer appears to the reader as the sole measurement of the paper's position; while all opinion pieces other than the leaders are free agents in the market of opinions, their prominence can make them appear to be the authentic Guardian voice. At any rate, they carry the same weight, and though on balance some of the heavyweight columnists, like Martin Woollacott and David Aaronovitch, supported the war, others such as Jonathan Freedland were undecided for a long time. Unlike the Independent and the Daily Mirror, and in a very different spirit from that obtaining during the Suez crisis of 1956, the Guardian approached the war on Iraq as a mistake rather than a crime.

The Iraq war had a direct effect on the coverage of the Israeli-Palestinian conflict. The world's eyes focused on a new point of turmoil, involving the world's greatest power, aiming to create a new global order, and with Britain as its close ally. The Israel-Palestine story, which two years earlier was perceived as shocking in its violence, now became close to routine: another suicide bombing, another Israeli raid on Palestinian enclaves, more assassinations.

Civilians' lives are a much cheaper commodity in the post 9/11 era. A few politicians on the left wing of Labour might have thought that killing some 10,000 Iraqis was a reasonable price to pay to save the Israeli-Palestinian peace process, but even they came to their senses, as Clare Short demonstrated with her long-delayed resignation from government after the first phase of the war. But the death toll in Iraq made the deaths of Palestinians less central for the world media.

Behind the day-to-day violence in Israel and the Palestinian territories, prime minister Ariel Sharon shaped a new plan, typical of his approach of attempting to uproot regional axioms and replace them with new "facts on the ground". Conceding the widespread horror caused by suicide bombings, and adopting the "separation" slogan of the Israeli Zionist left, Sharon ordered the construction of a security fence, a massive wall built not on the so-called green line — the pre-1967 border that was internationally accepted as the prospective boundary of the Palestinian state to be — but along a perimeter cut deep into the West Bank, effectively annexing settlements, water sources and farmland. It created isolated bantustans in Palestinian territory, separating farmers from their fields, patients from hospitals, villages from cities. Movement of Palestinians from one West Bank town to another became virtually impossible. As the Israeli columnist B. Michael commented, about the only things it didn't separate were suicide bomber from victim.

Chris McGreal, who replaced Suzanne Goldenberg as the Guardian's Jerusalem correspondent in August 2002, was perhaps the first international journalist to notice that the construction of the wall had far-reaching implications beyond its defensive pretext. In a series of news reports and a feature he followed the dispossession of Palestinian farmers, the often lethal results of arbitrary limitations of travel inside the West Bank and into Israel, and the devastating life imposed on the West Bank's Arab population. His perceptiveness may well owe something to his 10 years' experience in covering South Africa, reporting the last years of apartheid. Bantustanisation, dispossession, and strict limitations on transport as means of oppression, often far more powerful than straightforward violence, were not new to him.

The deeper strategic implications of the security wall were exposed when Sharon presented his "disengagement" plan, involving the evacuation of Israeli settlements and a unilateral withdrawal of Israeli forces from the Gaza strip, which was already surrounded by a wall. The plan included dismantling four small settlements in the West Bank. In return, President Bush backed off from the long-term American view of the Israeli settlements as an obstacle to peace, and withdrew the demand that the 1967 borders and the right of return of Palestinian refugees should be key items on the negotiating agenda. Bush said that it would be unrealistic to ignore the "facts on the ground", namely, the settlements, and that Palestinian refugees could only hope to return to the "Palestinian state", now reduced, at best, to a group of separated bantustans, and not to Israel proper. For Sharon, who was up to his neck in allegations of corruption and the possibility of indictment, Bush's speech was a great personal victory.

While Chris McGreal assiduously reported all this, Guardian leaders became rare, and bland, describing both Israeli and Palestinian policies as "unhelpful" and advocating American intervention while ignoring its unlikelihood.[5]

After the culmination of the anti-Guardian campaign around April 2002 and the battle of Jenin that spring, there was a sharp decline both in written complaints and internet campaigns. Unlike the situation during the Lebanon war and the first intifada, the second intifada and the post 9/11 era did not bond liberal Jews and the non-Jewish left, but rather the opposite. Jews viewed with growing agitation the character of the anti-war movement over Iraq. This reflected identity rather than ideology. Many anti-war Jews could not find their place in the anti-war movement: they did not join the big anti-war rally in London in March 2003 from fear of encountering either anti-Jewish slogans or attacks on Israel which they would not be able to identify with.

The careful discourse which characterised the post-colonial left was dissolving. The traditional distinctions between terms such as "Zionist", "Israeli" "Jewish" sometimes became blurred. The Jews were not the only, nor even the predominant, victims of this "loss of language". The decline of nationalism and rise of religious and "cultural" tribalism, made words like "Arab", let alone references to Arab nationals of specific countries, almost extinct except as a synonym for Muslim. People were described as "Muslims" and the benign term "the West" was often camouflage for "the predominantly Christian world". Robert Kilroy-Silk, in his infamous defamatory attack on "Arabs" in a Sunday Express article, included non-Arab Iran in his list of "Arab" enemies, hence making clear, out of ignorance or an attempt at guilt-by-association, that he really meant Muslims.[6]

The nature of George Bush's administration, based on fundamentalist evangelistic Christian and Jewish neo-conservatism, led to a revival of the notion that "Jews are running America". Even the Israeli newspaper Ha'aretz ran a feature describing Bush's administration under the headline, A Jewish conspiracy? The New Statesman published an article accompanied by a very disturbing front-page illustration featuring a star of David standing on the union flag above the headline A kosher conspiracy.[7] The editor of the New Statesman, Peter Wilby, apologised later for the cover design and headline, which he admitted were anti-semitic, but defended the theme of the article, which described the influences of British Jewish lobbies on the media.

A cartoon by Dave Brown in the Independent on January 27, 2003, portraying Ariel Sharon eating the head of a Palestinian baby, stirred another outcry. In the cartoon, Brown made an effort to avoid "Jewish" symbols and to make a point of referring only to Sharon and his Likud party. But the association to the medieval blood libel, which claimed the Jews use the blood of Christian children to bake their Passover bread (matzoth), was all too conspicuous. Brown said quite credibly that he knew nothing of the blood libel, and the cartoon, an allusion to Goya's painting, Saturn devouring one of his sons, was merely trying to express anger at Sharon's policies. But later that year the Political Cartoon Society chose that work by Brown as political cartoon of the year: a clear indication of a prevailing feeling that accusations of anti-semitism were no more than an attempt to silence criticism of Israel, and could therefore be disregarded.

This sentiment, more and more prevalent in left and liberal circles, is reinforced by the cynical accusations actually made by the Israeli government and its supporters whenever Israel is being criticised. In March 2004, the Israeli minister of communications, Nathan Sharansky, accused the BBC reporter Orla Guerin of anti-semitism. This was because Guerin had remarked, in a report about a teenage suicide bomber who was caught, "these are the pictures the Israeli government wants you to see". Guerin's remark was perfectly legitimate. Chris McGreal in the Guardian reported immense pressure by the Israeli government on broadcasting bodies to air the pictures of the shivering teenager trying to dismantle his explosive belt, aided by directions from afar from Israel Defence Force soldiers.[8]

The Israeli government simply failed to understand that a live teenage suicide bomber is a strong enough story to enter the news bulletins without prompting, and that pressure to do it would only arouse suspicion among journalists. They were also wrong in assuming that filming the boy struggling with the explosive belt would serve them better than doing the basic humane thing and getting an IDF soldier to rescue him from his predicament. But dealing with their frustration by levelling an immediate accusation of anti-semitism turned once again into cheap coinage. Soon enough, warned Dr Brian Klug in a meeting of the Jewish Forum for Justice and Human Rights in London, people would start treating an accusation of anti-semitism as a badge of honour.[9]

In Israel, real or imagined anti-semitism has become more and more of an issue. The Israel Broadcasting Authority has a daily programme reporting on anti-semitism in the world. The belief that Europe is flooded with anti-semitism has become a truism, even in liberal Israeli circles. While trying very hard to make itself a part of the global "war against terrorism", Israel is today more isolated, segregated and paranoid than it has ever been. A fear of losing the traditional support of Europe, fed by guilt over the Holocaust, is looming. A new generation of Europeans, who have grown up knowing Israel as an occupying, brutal state rather than as a safe haven for victims, scares the Israeli establishment. A generation of immigrants from Muslim countries, many of them bitterly hostile towards Israel, some of this hatred fed on European-originated anti-semitic myths, adds to the anxiety of Jews in Europe.

Desperate to maintain the Holocaust as the biggest crime committed in history, the former Israel minister of education, Amnon Rubinstein, strove in an article in Ha'aretz to differentiate it from all other atrocities, such as the genocide that took place in Rwanda in the 1990s. [10] There was truth in much of his argument: the Holocaust was a genocide organised by the government of a highly civilised and cultured European state and with the collaboration of many other countries. But this argument also creates the impression that Jews, or at least the Jewish state, is simultaneously trying to preserve its own victimhood as unique and to capitalise on it politically, while turning a blind eye to the suffering it inflicts on others.

In its early days Israel chose to portray the lesson of the Holocaust as a nationalistic one rather than one based on internationalist humanist values. The Holocaust was seen as the justification not only of Israel's existence, but also of its belligerence and ill-treatment of the indigenous Palestinians. The pain of others is seen as incidental. Cynicism, deriving from Israel's alliance with Turkey, drove it to prohibit the commemoration of the Armenian genocide by the Armenian community in Israel. Palestinian suffering is not only ignored, it is growingly a source of satisfaction. The price was now being paid by European Jews whose grievances were met with growing impatience.

Recently, Israeli writers on the left have been warning against this phenomenon. In Ha'aretz Amira Hass wrote:

> European anti-semitism nowadays is not institutional and does not endanger the civic, economic, political and professional status of the Jews overseas [...] But that does not mean anyone should take lightly the reports of a rise in anti-semitic feelings — and in some places, with the sense of physical danger for Jews. These reports shouldn't be taken lightly, even though the Jewish and Israeli government institutions that diligently disseminate each day, use them to stain every criticism and condemnation of the Israeli occupation as "anti-semitic".[11]

Amos Noi, in the media magazine Haáin Hashviít (Seventh Eye), advised Israeli journalists who ignore blatant racist attacks against Palestinians to stop preaching at the European press, for whom "every anti-semitic incident is a front-page story".[12]

At the same time the Jewish community in Britain is becoming more politically segregated. Many Jewish critics of Israel's policies keep their views to themselves or air them only in community circles. Some feel that any criticism could be abused by people who they see as anti-semites. The Daily Mail columnist Melanie Philips believes that Jews should not speak out in criticism of Israel at all: "Many, myself included, voice their concerns in Jewish forums. I always thought that the settlements, for example, should go. But criticising Israel today only supplies weapons to anti-Jewish propaganda which demonises Israel."[13] In a meeting in London in October 2003 Jewish participants discussed the subject, Should we speak out about Israel?"[14] Jonathan Freedland was one of the participants who said that criticising Israel in public was legitimate. But there was a difference between the sharper tone on Israel in his regular Jewish Chronicle column, and his articles in the Guardian, in which he often tries to explain how things look from the perspective of Israelis. It is sometimes a thankless task; some opponents accuse him of being an apologist for Israel, despite his criticism. In October 2003, after a heavy Israeli air raid on Syria, which was, Freedland wrote, a message that

Gulliver could crush his Lilliputian neighbours whenever he chose. "That is certainly how it looks to the rest of the world," he continued, but: "[...] from inside Israel, Sunday's raid was the act of a nation driven half mad with desperation and grief. On Saturday a suicide bomber had taken 19 lives in the Maxim restaurant in Haifa, Israel's most mixed city".[15]

Freedland explains: "When I write for the Jewish Chronicle, I often set out, very polemically, to persuade those readers to be more critical of Israel's policies, but that's because that forum seems the right place to take on that job of persuasion. It's where Jewish readers feel safe. When writing in the Guardian, I don't feel there is enormous value in setting out solely to reinforce a negative opinion many Guardian readers will already have about Israel anyway. In that forum, as opposed to say the Jewish Chronicle, I often feel there's a value to explaining how Israelis feel, what drives their behaviour. I'd like to think that might also make our Jewish readership more comfortable with the paper, and maybe more likely to accept criticism of Israel, appreciating that it comes from a perspective which doesn't undermine Israel's very existence".

The issue of Israel's "right to exist" has continually arisen over the last 30 years. It is a loaded and badly phrased proposition. The phrase usually carries the implication that, yes, Israel does have the right to exist, but as a state of all its citizens where Jews and Arabs would have equal rights. But "Israel's right to exist" invokes fear in Zionist Jews and Israelis alike; for them it cloaks prospective annihilation. The total identification between Zionism as the prevailing ideology in Israel and the nation that was created in that state is understandable, if harmful. In the South African case, by comparison, the question of the state's "existence" was never raised as such. It was always the apartheid regime that was presented as illegitimate.

The liberal consensus in Europe, which was reflected in the Guardian, has been for the last three decades that while anti-semitism of any kind is strictly illicit, anti-Zionism is a legitimate political position. And while the Guardian sticks to a pro-Zionist view, which accepts the existence of a Jewish state within the 1967 borders, it has occasionally, as this book demonstrates, published articles which took a non-Zionist, anti-Zionist or post-Zionist point of view. There were always critics on the margins of the

Jewish community who depicted such views as "anti-semitic", but until recently the differentiation between anti-semitism and anti-Zionism was generally accepted. Over the past year the distinction was challenged again, and it was the Guardian that opened a renewed debate on the issue.

Under the Title "Anti-Zionism is anti-semitism", Emanuele Ottolenghi, an Israeli research fellow of St Antony's College, Oxford, propounded the formula, long desired by the Israeli establishment, which enabled him to link anti-semitism to the denunciation of Israel as a "Jewish state".

> Those who denounce Zionism sometimes explain Israel's
> policies as a product of its Jewish essence. In their view, not
> only should Israel act differently, it should cease being a Jewish
> state. Anti-Zionists are prepared to treat Jews equally and fight
> anti-semitic prejudice only if Jews give up their distinctiveness
> as a nation: Jews as a nation deserve no sympathy and no rights,
> Jews as individuals are worthy of both.[16]

The notion of denial of the "collective right to statehood" as equal to the denial of personal right, however far-fetched, caught on among Israel apologists, and is often quoted. The Times columnist Michael Gove said in an ICA discussion in March 2004 that anti-semitism always targeted the centre of Jewish existence. "When the centre was religion, Jews were attacked under religious pretext, nowadays, when the centre of Jewish existence is the Jewish state, anti-semites concentrate their attack on Israel."

Brian Klug, a philosophy fellow of St Benet's Hall, Oxford, took on Ottolenghi's arguments, and attacked them in a Guardian article a week later.

> We should unite in rejecting racism in all its forms: the
> Islamophobia that demonises Muslims, as well as the anti-
> semitic discourse that can infect anti-Zionism and poison the
> political debate. However, people of goodwill can disagree
> politically — even to the extent of arguing over Israel's future

as a Jewish state. Equating anti-Zionism with anti-semitism can also, in its own way, poison the political debate.[17]

Klug is a part of a group of liberal Jews who are deeply concerned about the closing of ranks on Israel, the silencing of critical Jews in their own communities, and the sense of segregation in the community. "If people believe they have good grounds for being opposed to Israel, and if they are labelled anti-semites for their legitimate political views, there will come a time when they start to wear that label with pride. Every time we cry wolf, we foolishly hasten that time,"[18] he said at a London meeting. "It is time for a parting of the ways. Israel needs to be taken off its mythic pedestal and to come down to earth. We needn't wave goodbye forever or cease to care. But the two identities, Israeli and Jewish, should be separated. As of now, Israel and Jewry are locked in an embrace that is distorting life for both parties. Only standing at arm's length are we in a position to offer the state the cool, careful, measured, qualified, sustained, candid criticism it needs."[19]

The Ottolenghi-Klug debate was followed by one between Max Hastings, former editor of the Daily Telegraph and the London Evening Standard, and Stephen Byers, chairman of the Parliamentary committee against anti-semitism. Hastings accused the British media of yielding to Zionist pressure groups and turning into apologists for Israel.

It is impossible to doubt that genuine anti-semitism — racial antipathy towards Jews — is resurgent in Europe and even, in some circles, becoming respectable [...] [But] many of the remarks that Jewish critics denounce as anti-semitic are, in reality, criticisms of Israel or its government [...] Attempts to equate anti-Zionism, or even criticism of Israeli policy, with anti-semitism reflect a pitiful intellectual sloth, an abandonment of reasoned attempts to justify Israeli actions in favour of moral blackmail. In the short run, such intimidation is not unsuccessful, especially in America. Yet in the long term, grave consequences may ensue. In much of the world, including Europe, a huge head of steam is building against Israeli

behaviour [...] If Israel persists with its current policies, and
Jewish lobbies around the world continue to express solidarity
with repression of the Palestinians, then genuine anti-semitism
is bound to increase.[20]

Byers repeated the theme claiming that anti-Zionism is the "new
mutation" of the "anti-semitic virus", and argued that demanding that
Jews should condemn Israel as a condition for being treated with respect
as individuals is in itself a form of anti-semitism.

> Nobody should be asked to take a loyalty and morality oath
> as a precondition for protection against racism. No citizen
> should feel that their equality before the law is dependent
> on their embrace of political views that we approve of. This
> is a totalitarian logic that undermines the very foundations
> of freedom on which our society stands. Yet present-day anti-
> semites demand precisely that of Jews [...] When it comes to
> Israel, Jews are held collectively responsible. Their sin is not
> to decide any more, nor are they accused of possessing sinister
> racial traits. In the modern world, the methods of the anti-
> semite are far more subtle. It is no longer the jack-booted Nazi;
> instead, it is anti-semitism with a social conscience, often based
> on human rights and the demand of a homeland for the
> Palestinian people. Today's Jewish "collective crime" is Israel.[21]

To an extent, the amount of space dedicated to these debates in the
Guardian, however interesting the subject may be, indicates the success
of those trying to divert the discussion from the bloody political realities
of the Middle East to the rules of discourse in Europe. It may have to do
with a post-modern era, in which words and deeds weigh the same, and
images are portrayed as more important than action. One should bear in
mind that the "new anti-semitism" — whether a real phenomenon or
merely an outburst of political rage over Israel's policies directed at those
who are conceived as its supporters — has not, fortunately, cost the life
of a single human being in Britain in the past few years. At the same

time, the death toll in Israel-Palestine is rising every day to new heights; the Israeli victims of suicide bombings are counted in the hundreds, and the Palestinian victims of air raids, "targeted assassinations", and wild shooting are counted in the thousands. The Israeli army spokesperson no longer feels the need to comment on the killing of Palestinian children, let alone to express sorrow or apologise. But during the last months of 2003 and first months of 2004, the discussion of "new anti-semitism" in the Guardian overshadowed any discussion of Israel's assassination policies, or the construction of the wall, which after long discussion is now referred to in the paper by the benign term "the separation barrier". The Palestinians call it the apartheid wall, the Israeli government named it the separation fence.

The "new anti-semitism" debate slipped not only into the Guardian's pages, but also into the paper's internal conscious.

The maverick journalist Julie Burchill, a columnist in Weekend, the Guardian's Saturday magazine, until she left for the Times, proved in November that a fig leaf is sometimes more costly than an Armani suit. In her farewell column she wrote:

> If there is one issue that has made me feel less loyal to my newspaper over the past year, it has been what I, as a non-Jew, perceive to be a quite striking bias against the state of Israel. Which, for all its faults, is the only country in that barren region that you or I, or any feminist, atheist, homosexual or trade unionist, could bear to live under. I find this hard to accept because, crucially, I don't swallow the modern liberal line that anti-Zionism is entirely different from anti-semitism; the first good, the other bad.[22]

Burchill's words gave the impression that she thought the Guardian was anti-semitic. Her column was translated into Hebrew and published by the Israeli daily Maariv. Alan Rusbridger, says: "I admire Julie immensely, without taking everything she says with complete seriousness. It was certainly news to many people that she was an authority on the Middle East, and I think it would be unwise of friends of Israel to adopt her as a great ally. Anyone who can refer in print to Arabs as 'camel-fuckers' should probably not be regarded as being in the same class as, say, Amos Oz or David Grossman."

The diplomatic editor, Ewen MacAskill, said in February 2004: "I haven't written an anti-semitic word in my life and nor has anybody in the Guardian. I find this very allegation made by lobby groups deeply offensive. But I am concerned about the rise of anti-semitism in Europe, and there is a disturbing feeling that maybe any writing about Israel could somehow contribute to it. I have kept away from Israel since the autumn of 2002, and the Iraq war supplied a good excuse for it, but soon enough the focus will return to Israel-Palestine, and I intend to go there soon."[23]

A month later MacAskill went to Israel, just in time to report on the assassination of the Hamas spiritual leader, Sheik Ahmad Yassin, and to assess its implications. He attended a conference at Tel Aviv University with foreign and local journalists and academics. He said that the atmosphere was far less hostile than he expected, but after the conference the centre-right columnist Dan Margalit of the Maariv fiercely attacked both him and the Guardian. Margalit wrote that one shouldn't waste one's time on such "Israel-haters". In Hebrew, this phrase ("sonéy Israel") doesn't refer to haters of the state of Israel, but to anti-semites.[24]

To back the allegation, Margalit quoted from a "Guardian leader column" a claim that Yassin had offered Israel a truce numerous times but was always rejected, which had, of course, never appeared in the Guardian anywhere in any form of words.

Under pressure, Margalit half-retracted, saying that the quote was from a signed article in the Guardian and that he had been misled. However, he made a point of not taking back "anything else I said about the Guardian".

Jonathan Freedland believes that the Guardian should now regard the breakdown of its relationship with the Jewish community as a problem. "Some Guardian people might wish it were otherwise, but it is a fact that the vast majority of Jews in the world today identify themselves with Israel, and see any attack on it as an attack on themselves. The result is that much of what we publish can and does offend our Jewish readers. My view is that if we are regularly offending most members of an ethnic minority, then that has to be a cause of concern [...] More widely, it's possible that there is a growing crisis between Jews and the liberal left, caught at the dead centre of which is the Guardian. If we chart a path out of it and if it is true that we are a liberal standard-setter, others may follow. Besides, the Guardian should want to solve this problem for its own reasons. First, there is a risk that Jewish dissatisfaction with the Guardian could become part of our image, not just in Britain but around the world. Second, support of Zionism is part of the Guardian's own history. This is our heritage and we cannot break from it lightly."[25]

Freedland says that the problems between the Jewish community and the Guardian are usually not over critical reporting, but over wording that "somehow suggests that the Jewish state is an illegitimate, temporary entity. An example would be the use of the word 'settler' when referring to an Israeli citizen who lives in Israel proper, not in the occupied territories. We ought to avoid items that appear casually to dispute Israel's fundamental legitimacy. Also sensitive is the insinuation that Israel is somehow responsible for all the world's problems. Such ideas are seen as a return of the old anti-semitic myth that 'the Jews are behind all the woes of humanity'. This kind of talk was prevalent in other media before and during the war on Iraq, when Israel's role in George Bush's decision-making was much exaggerated. In the Guardian, the headline, Sharon is now a danger to US troops and hopes in Iraq, looked like an example of that trait. A more subtle form of exaggeration of Israel's place in the problems of the world is over-coverage, and we may have to consider the extent of our coverage."[26]

"Most Jews," says Freedland, "do not see the Israeli-Palestinian conflict as one between the powerless Palestinians and powerful Israelis, but rather between Israel, a tiny state with 6 million citizens, surrounded by 22 hostile Arab states. This may seem ridiculous to the outside eye, which views Israel as a mighty, nuclear-armed regional power. But Israel and the wider Jewish world are, thanks to their long history and bloody experience, societies that tremble with existential fear, even, on occasion, paranoia. This must have a bearing on how we treat the subject. It requires of us a sensitivity that would doubtless be unnecessary in dealing with a nation that had only ever known power and military strength."[27]

Alan Rusbridger, editor of the Guardian, feels that the paper's approach to political violence should be seen from a wider perspective: "I'm rather proud that our paper seeks to understand the political roots of terrorism, to take the trouble to speak to people who resort to violence. It's a part of an editorial line we developed over Ireland, South Africa, Chechnya and other places, and it is not unique in respect of our treatment of the Israeli-Palestinian conflict. It's all of a part with our attempts to understand, explain and contextualise such things which are taboos to others, such as paedophilia."[28]

Freedland suggests the Guardian should adopt guidelines that might help it avoid those slips that offend Jewish readers. "It could help us to reach a better understanding of our relations with other minority groups too," he says. He stresses: "None of this should hold the Guardian back from unflinching reporting. Often that will be uncomfortable to Jewish and Israel-supporting readers. So be it. But it should be uncomfortable for reasons we can defend."[29]

Freedland's approach, albeit motivated by concern for the Jewish community and the Guardian's international image, raises problems. The underlying assumption in what he says is that a majority in the Jewish community cannot see the difference between anti-Zionism and anti-semitism, or even between criticism of Israel's regime and anti-semitism; and so the Guardian, and everybody else, should accept and act on that even though it is politically and intellectually false. His unofficial mediating role between the community and the paper puts him sometimes in the awkward position of claiming that the community's sensitivities should be indulged even when it is in the wrong.

In any case, some of the ideas Freedland attributes to "the Jews" are out-dated and bogus, not least the notion of Israel as a "tiny nation surrounded by 22 hostile Arab states". There are, of course, some in the Jewish community who still adhere to that view as, indeed, Freedland implicitly acknowledged when he addressed them in quite different terms in his Jewish Chronicle column:

Those who say the problem is not the Palestinians, but the 20-plus hostile Arab countries that encircle little Israel, should also take a hard look at the facts. Syria's army is, according to Israeli analysts, a busted flush, and the same is essentially true of its neighbours. Starved of the old Soviet aid, the Arab states cannot match Israel for hardware, training or technology. We need to kick this victimhood fetish and accept the reassurance that comes with power and the responsibility.[30]

Freedland says that because of the over-emphasis given to Israeli dissidents, "Jewish readers get the impression that we are dividing the world into good Jews and bad Jews — with the former being those who publicly detach themselves from their people." The exposure given in the Guardian to Jewish and Israeli dissidents, while sometimes obfuscating the real division of power inside Israel, is a part of the Guardian's effort to give them a platform, so isolated and scorned are their voices inside Israel. Freedland himself was among the shapers of this policy. However, the reality he reflects is strange but true: a majority in the Jewish community wants to be endorsed by the liberal media, and is willing to take a liberal stance on just about everything except Israel. They are insulted when their support for Israel is seen in the only way it could be seen in liberal eyes, especially in times of such a rightwing Israeli government — support for a violent, belligerent state which disregards human rights and international law. Freedland is optimistic in thinking that there is a way around it. Rusbridger says: "Some of our critics do value and trust the paper generally. They believe it to be truthfully edited by journalists of intelligence and integrity. To them, it is on this one issue on which the paper cannot be trusted. Doesn't it make more sense to believe that Guardian journalists come to their conclusions over Israel the same way as on every other issue rather than to conclude that they have a specific bias?" [31]

These difficulties are well reflected in the relationship between the Israeli left and Jewish liberals in Britain. Many in the Israeli left feel that the political balance of power in Israel prevents any solution from within. They seek not only a solution to the conflict with the Palestinians, but a way to stop their beloved country from going mad. They yearn for international intervention and pressure on their government, and most of them are motivated by deep patriotism. The silence of Jewish communities abroad frustrates them. "We need your help," said Varda Shiffer, former head of Amnesty's Israeli branch at a London meeting of the Jewish Forum for Justice and Human Rights. "Your silence doesn't help us. We are a society that is losing its human values. We beg you to speak your mind and put some pressure on our government."[32]

Some British Jews are shocked by this type of response. Melanie Phillips speaks with scorn and anger: "It is time for the Israeli left to wake up and smell the coffee. Their attacks on their own government give weapons to Jew-haters in Europe. They think that if only they could replace Sharon and sort out their conflict with the Palestinians everything will be fine. They refuse to understand that they are under an existential threat. They live in a paradise of fools.[33]

From the liberal wing of Zionism, Linda Grant, a novelist and a freelance writer, complained too that the Guardian, since the start of the intifada, had failed to reflect "the lives of every day Israelis and the complexity of the Israeli society." So Grant went to Tel Aviv and lived there for four months, writing a number of features, including a regular column called Tel Aviv stories. Cynics would say that she must have interviewed every available leftwinger, from women who supervise the conduct of soldiers at checkpoints, to an anti-Zionist gay theatre director, and immigrants from Russia who define themselves as "on the left" (a true rarity). The representation of right wingers and settlers existed but was conspicuously slim.

Grant obtained permission from the IDF to spend five days with soldiers who took over the roof and top floor of a Palestinian family house in occupied Nablus. Grant's heart went out to the humanity of the soldiers — one of them even used to go to Peace Now demonstrations on his free weekends — and she undertook to represent their closest hopes and predicaments in a long feature story. She reported that those soldiers who expressed racist or hostile views to Arabs belong to "the military police and border guards who accept those who fail the IQ tests - the illiterate, the damaged, the angry." They come from the ranks of "working-class immigrants from Muslim countries ... among their numbers are found some of the most rightwing and racist of all Israelis".[34]

Grant was concerned that the soldiers on the roof might be misunderstood in Europe, where some of them intended to travel after their service. At the end of the five days she left. "We shook hands on the windy street. He looked so young, years younger than when I'd seen him in uniform, and I wished I could make myself a human shield against all the hate and demonisation he would encounter from those for whom life is a collection of symbols and slogans which stamp themselves on the faces of others, obscuring their features, like a helmet."[35]

All this is perfectly legitimate journalism; and yet reflects knowingly or not a controversial category in the Israeli ethos, known in Hebrew as "shoot and weep". The genre was pioneered in *Fighters Talk*, a post-1967 book that presented soldiers' admissions of atrocities combined with a notion of "moral necessity". Yigal Alon, the chief ethnic cleanser of the 1948 war, is another example, when he talks to Alastair Hetherington (see chapter 7) of his yearning for peace. The "shoot and weep" ethos was epitomised in Golda Meir's famous observation: "We shall never forgive the Arabs for what they make us do to them." It has been argued that "shoot and weep" has been more damaging to Israel than the belligerence of the radical right because it discloses a self-righteous inability to recognise the connection between Israel's actions and its violent consequences.

On her return to London, Grant admitted that Israeli officials "urged me to publicise the Geneva accords, the reservists' protests, to keep the Israeli left alive in the eyes of the Europeans". She saw it as a subversivness on their part, but a heartbroken soldier who completes his mission despite an anguished conscience is likely to be regarded by officialdom as of far more value to Israel's international image than Sharon's professional spokespersons. And yet, whether or not Grant was taken in, her conclusions after her visit were sad and pessimistic:

> I found not a scrap of evidence that Jewish Israelis will ever
> agree to a peace deal that will result in them becoming, within a
> generation or two, a minority dependent on the goodwill of a
> Palestinian majority in a region without democracy or any real
> human rights [...] I also know what some Palestinian friends tell
> me, that the right of return is deeply embedded in the

Palestinian soul and can never be given up, that no leader can sign an agreement on their behalf which would settle it with a cheque instead [...] we might have to face the nightmare that the war between the two peoples cannot be concluded, there is no deal that can ever be signed that will not give way, almost at once, to the resumption of the struggle. No US administration, however even-handed, can settle the dispute, or even impose a settlement, over land that can neither be shared nor divided.[36]

Alan Rusbridger doesn't take kindly to the idea of giving the Jewish community special treatment based on accepting its misconceptions as a given:

The Guardian is the least monolithic of any British national newspaper, so generalisations about what the Guardian thinks always make me nervous. Israel is part of our editorial heritage. But just as newspapers change, so do countries. The Guardian's view of countries varied according to who is running them. We didn't much care for Reagan; we were attracted by much of what Clinton stood for; we strongly dislike much of what GW Bush II and the neo-cons stand for. We approved of Oslo, loved Rabin, respected Barak; and we fear and despair of Sharon. It doesn't make us anti-American or Anti-Israeli.

It is strange that celebrated reporters like Derek Brown, Suzanne Goldenberg and Chris McGreal, about whose work I never received any complaint before, are subjected to so much anger once they go to Israel. Either there's something about Israel that makes admired journalists abandon their customary professionalism, or the Israeli government and its supporters have different expectations, and habitually and deliberately criticise reporters working for influential papers which may take an editorially critical line towards a particular government.

We've made mistakes, and owned up to them, though we are seldom given much credit for doing so. We've done our fair share of agonizing publicly over the issue, perhaps too much so, and published critiques - sometimes vehement ones – of our own work within our own pages.

I don't think any other paper would have behaved in this way. That, too, is part of our history. The Guardian's coverage of the middle east is full, serious, detailed and engaged. It is not always perfectly balanced. We sometimes fail to take sufficient account of Israel's genuine security concerns. We can be reasonably criticised for not reflecting all spectrums of the debate within Israel itself. It is arguable that we carry too much coverage – though, I'd say that this is out of a genuine sense of pain and a desire to find a resolution.

But the vitriolic nature and extent of the counter-response is unparalleled, utterly disproportionate, cynical and quite ugly. I bitterly resent the frequent attempt to smear us by eliding our criticism of Israel with actual anti-semitism. I feel there has been a concerted attempt to place the Guardian beyond the pale. There has been a deliberate policy to target Israel's critics, and the more beleaguered Israel becomes – the more pronounced this tendency becomes. The prolonged assault on the Guardian has been remarkably successful in achieving a worldwide circulation of a view that the Guardian is anti-semitic. And, of course, once they've finished with the Guardian they'll move onto the Independent, or the BBC, or whoever.

British Jews are placed in an uncomfortable position. Intellectually, they often say there is very little in the Guardian that does not appear every day in the remarkably robust debate within Israel. Emotionally, they feel extremely uncomfortable about these debates taking place outside Israel, by people they believe (wrongly, in my view), to be hostile to Israel.

Many colleagues genuinely believe that this intensive pressure has had an effect and that not only that we don't single Israel out, we put kid's gloves on. I've engaged in open debate, took the trouble to find out things for myself, and did my best to be frank about our failings and sensitive to the issues. But much of the criticism we were subjected to is unacceptable.[37]

Where are the Guardian and Israel going? At the moment it seems that they are going their separate ways, at least for the near future. A newspaper with declared liberal credentials cannot but upset the representatives of a society persistently turning more and more rightwing, segregated and belligerent. There is an unbridgeable gap between the scope of the political debate conducted in Israel and the range of opinions on the Middle East in the Guardian. The most pro-Zionist staff member in the newspaper is Jonathan Freedland. In Israel he would be considered to be a radical leftwinger (though still inside the Zionist spectrum), thus representing a marginalised and powerless political group. Martin Woollacott has recently written:

> If a slice was cut to show what might be called the archaeology of European attitudes to Israel, the bottom layer, the furthest in the past, could be called 'Saving Israel from the Arabs', recalling a time when most sympathy lay with a newly independent state surrounded by enemies and when the plight of the Palestinians was hardly grasped.
>
> A second layer could be entitled 'Saving Israel from itself', representing the period when a victorious nation rejected advice to avoid expansion into the territories conquered in 1967.
>
> A third would be 'Saving the Palestinians from the Israelis', as the Palestinians forced themselves into western visibility, first by terror and then by popular resistance. The title of a fourth era, the one we have now entered, has not yet been written by history. But it is characterised by a large magnification of the potential effect on the wider world of how the conflict works out. The French thinker Dominique Moisi, for example, argued recently that 'Israelis and Palestinians are endangering much more than their lives and the lives of their children'.[38]

In an interview for this book Woollacott said: "The European media has already shifted from a line which attempts to save Israel from itself to one that calls out to save the world from Israel. This notion is likely to be found soon in the pages of the Guardian, the general UK media, and finally reach the liberal newspapers in the US."[39]

If there is no change soon in Israel towards more liberal government, and none looks likely, this will probably be the case. It might be added that the more American and British policies in Iraq are exposed for their moral and practical bankruptcy, the more Israel is likely to be criticised for its attempt to ride the neo-conservative wave and use it to increase its oppression of the Palestinians.

The Jewish community in Britain seems to follow the Israeli tune, and Jewish liberals often find themselves to the right of their Israeli counterparts. It is of little consolation to the Guardian that this group is equally alienated from the BBC and the Independent.

But there are signs of hope. A certain disillusion with Sharon's policies is starting to show in the writings of middle of the road Israeli columnists. In the British Jewish community there are little groups who feel suffocated by the pressure against speaking out, and concerned by the alienation of liberals in their community from liberals in general society. The Guardian, despite being damaged by the accusations against it, seems determined to seek ways to keep its discourse with the Jewish community going, while not abandoning its critical position.

If I may indulge a personal note in these closing lines, I was stunned by the amount of time, energy and thinking which everybody involved in Israel's coverage in the Guardian put into the task of getting it right. A hundred years of deep engagement with the subject has not been abandoned. The vociferous campaign against the paper has taken its toll. For a while, it seemed that the exhausted Guardian had decided to lay off, but not for long. The internal tension between advocates of a softer line on Israel and hardliners could be healthy, though painful, as long as they all get to participate in forging the paper's policy. The rest is in the hands of history.

In the Rubble of Jenin

Test Case

THE second intifada was rising to boiling point in the spring of 2002. On March 29, a Palestinian suicide bomber exploded himself in the midst of the traditional Passover dinner in Park hotel in Netanya, killing 16 civilians (during the next few days the death toll increased to over 20). The bombing triggered the launch of a wide pre-planned Israeli military operation in the West Bank. The declared aim of the operation, named Defensive Shield by the army, was to "destroy the terrorist infrastructure: the explosive labs, weapons and personnel".[1] During the operation the Israeli army invaded territories in the West Bank which were held by the Palestinian Authority, destroyed the civil infrastructure of the Palestinian Authority and most of its security forces, arrested thousands of people, killed hundreds, demolished buildings and exposed some laboratories in which explosive belts were manufactured.

The city of Jenin in the north of the West Bank was named "Suicide Town" by the Israeli media and earned that epithet. Twenty-eight suicide bombers who attacked Israeli civilians during the months before the operation came from Jenin refugee camp on the town's periphery. A few journalists wondered how the Israeli Defence Force would manage to enter the narrow alleys of the refugee camp without turning the soldiers into moving targets for Palestinian snipers. They would not be able to apply the surprising and cruel solution they had arrived at earlier, in Balata refugee camp near Nablus, when, instead of walking between the houses in search of weapons and wanted activists, the soldiers simply walked through the buildings, breaking walls to move from house to house without exposing themselves to the peril of the street. In Jenin, where the houses were more solidly built, this method couldn't be applied.

So the invasion of Jenin refugee camp started with a missile attack from the air and infantry activity. After the death of 13 Israeli soldiers who entered a booby-trapped alley on April 9, the army started using bulldozers and tanks, demolishing houses extensively. Journalists were kept away, as were human rights activists, medical teams and supplies. Within a few days the dreadful stench of death was rising from the ruins, engulfing the city of Jenin. Terrified refugees who escaped the camp informed journalists of the wreckage, of people who were buried under their homes, and of unarmed civilians arbitrarily shot.

In retrospect, it seems that some of the stories reflected personal perspectives of shocked, understandably dazed, people. Some of them were true, and some were not. Rumours of a terrible massacre in Jenin refugee camps spread rapidly through Israel, the West Bank and the international media. The Palestinian spokesperson Saeb Arikat claimed that the death toll in Jenin might reach 500. Israel didn't allow access to the camp until April 15, and it took a couple of weeks until it was revealed that 56 Palestinians were killed during the battle.[2] According to human right organisation reports, over 20 of them were civilians. Of the 1,800 houses in the camp, 130 were demolished.[3]

On April 19, 2002, the United Nations general assembly decided to send a fact-finding team to conduct an inquiry into the events in the camp and verify or discredit the allegations of massacre or war crimes against Israel. Israel refused to cooperate with the investigation or to admit the team. Therefore, on May 7, the general assembly asked the secretary-general, Kofi Anan, to present a report based on available sources and information. The report omitted the terms "massacre" and "war crime", which had been used by media and UN officials in the aftermath of the battle, but it did describe severe human rights violations such as the denial of medical help and supplies to the camp, IDF soldiers shooting at ambulances killing medical staff members, and the death of civilians.

Suzanne Goldenberg spent most of the days of fighting in the city of Jenin, or in the neighbouring town of Nablus. She consistently described the event as "a fierce battle", not once referring to it as a massacre. Between April 10 and April 17, Goldenberg wrote five news reports and one analysis piece about Jenin, and two reports regarding the events in Nablus. Her first report followed the death of the 13 Israeli soldiers in the camp.[4] The effort to verify facts and not be tempted by rumours is evident in all Goldenberg's texts. They include quotes from army commanders and soldiers, Israeli politicians and Palestinians in the camp. Goldenberg described the difficulties of the army in the camp, and referred to the Palestinian claims of massacre and the Israeli denial of it. She adhered to the same line of level-headed reporting throughout the week.

On April 12, Goldenberg reported on refugees fleeing from the camp with stories about Israeli abuses, including the demolition of houses with civilians still inside them, shooting combatant Palestinians after they had surrendered, the use of civilians as human shields by the IDF, and the mass burial of bodies in an attempt to conceal them. Goldenberg noted: "The stories of executions and disposal of the dead could not be verified as the Israeli army has encircled the camp with tanks, and shot at, or arrested, journalists approaching the area."[5] She added, though: "the accounts of the massive destruction of civilian homes, and of the firing on civilians, could be confirmed as they also occurred in the town of Jenin, suggesting a widespread and systematic pattern of human rights abuses that is only now beginning to emerge."[6] Indeed, later inquiries by the UN and human right organisations revealed that the first set of accusations was mostly false, and the second set true. The estimated number of Palestinian casualties, which Goldenberg quoted, was 150, the number reported at the time by the Israeli army.

The next day Goldenberg described the beginnings of body searches under the wreckage, noting that Israel was still denying journalists and aid teams access to the camp. She quoted only camp residents who could actually prove their claims, such as Issam Fashafshe, who watched his relatives' house being bombed by a tank shell. "The bodies of Ahmed Fashafshe, his wife Samira and their son Bassam were interred in the ruins until Thursday when a brief relaxation of the curfew allowed for a hurried burial. "Two other children survived," she reported.[7] Palestinian claims of "random killings" and the Israeli claim that most of the dead were gunmen were equally mentioned.[8] Goldenberg pointed out the "tremendous sensitivity" in Israel "to allegations of abuse by soldiers", and quoted a soldier saying: "Never, never do we shoot for no reason. If we shoot it's because someone is shooting from that house." Goldenberg also cited a named Palestinian resident saying: "Of course, there were fighters, but they killed many civilians as well."[9]

"The scale is almost beyond imagination: a vast expanse of rubble and mangled iron rods, surrounded by the gaping carcasses of shattered homes," wrote Goldenberg on April 16, after journalists were finally allowed to enter the camp.[10] "Palestinians accuse Israel of a massacre, and there are convincing accounts from local people of the occasional summary execution. However, there are no reliable figures for Palestinian dead and injured," she added.[11] Goldenberg described the Israeli "demolition campaign" in the camp, but explained the army's difficulties: " 'They booby-trapped every centimetre. In one metre you would find 20 small booby traps or a big balloon attached with a wire. Every metre was very dangerous,' said Dori Scheuer, who was shot in the stomach by a Palestinian gunman a week ago on Monday."[12]

On April 17, Goldenberg described the difficulties of the teams searching for bodies, and presented the scale of death toll estimates by human rights organisations and military and Palestinian sources, ranging from 40 to 500.[13] In a separate piece of analysis she looked into alleged Israeli disrespect for the Geneva Convention during Operation Defensive Shield. She wrote of the denial of medical care, food and water supplies, shooting at civilians and the conditions in which Palestinians detainees were held.[14]

> I had a strange feeling about Jenin from the beginning. You
> have to remember that journalists had been trying to get inside
> the refugee camp for days. I made it into Jenin town early on,
> but was thrown out by the Israeli army. We exhausted ourselves
> trying to get into the camp to see what was going on, and all
> the while   Palestinian officials who behaved totally irresponsibly
> – and at least one Israeli military official – were feeding the
> speculation that there had been a massacre. There was also
> enormous confusion because of the ferocity of the fighting
> around Jenin. People fled in a panic, or on foot, and their

families believing the worst, thought they were dead, although they were not.

So when I finally got into the camp, I remember feeling a sense of anti-climax. There was certainly ruin or destruction, but I did not see other evidence of the massacre people had spoken of. There was no overwhelming smell of corpses as one might have expected. I thought at the time that perhaps I was too tired to appreciate the enormity of what had happened, but as far as I could see there was no massacre, and I was not going to write that.

In the immediate aftermath – when other newspapers were using the word massacre – I felt that even more strongly. I feel now, as I did then, that by focusing on Jenin, the media missed the real story which was the destruction of the historic casbah of Nablus, and a whole systematic pattern of abuse that took part the entire length of the West Bank when the Israeli army re-occupied the territory that spring. I think that the Guardian stood out from other newspapers because we did not follow the herd in reporting Jenin as a massacre. We cover the story very well on the whole. Unfortunately, that was undermined by two things – the use of the word 'massacre' in quotation marks in a headline, and a leader comment in the Guardian. In terms of the newspaper story, the second paragraph very clearly refers to allegations of a massacre. As for the headline, the sub-editor who wrote it probably believed the use of quotation marks meant the Guardian was citing others who said what happened at Jenin was a massacre, but that convention is not widely understood outside journalism.[15]

On the same day, the Guardian carried the headline that provoked most of the indignant criticism. The story beneath, by Ian Black reporting from Brussels, and Ewen MacAskill and Nicholas Watt in the London office, covered the harsh responses in the world to the spreading news and rumours regarding Israel's actions in Jenin, and the heading read: Israel faces rage over "massacre".

On April 20, the Guardian summarised the two versions of the event, the Israeli and the Palestinian, in two pieces. Ewen MacAskill, the diplomatic correspondent, flew in from Iraq to help prime the pump, and Chris McGreal, at this point still Africa correspondent, also joined forces with Goldenberg. MacAskill conducted an interview with the IDF sergeant Israel Kaspi, who presented the Israeli account of events in Jenin, beautifully abridged by the headline: "We fight like girls and we are accused of a massacre." McGreal brought on further claims from Jenin, headed: "I saw three men shot. They surrendered but were still killed".

For the rest of April and until the end of May, the Guardian watched the attempts of the UN to send over the fact-finding team, and Israel's defiance. It also tried to work out the consequences of the operation, while still following the fast sequence of violent events in the West Bank and in Israel.

In the Guardian there is a consensus that the news coverage of Jenin was successful. "Both Suzanne and Chris were far less excitable than many other correspondents. Suzanne's coverage has always been accurate. She is a very active reporter, always on the ground, and it stood her in a very good stead in Jenin because it enabled her to assess the situation correctly," says Alan Rusbridger.[16] Ed Pilkington defines the news coverage as "very careful": "Chris's African background might have been relevant. He got to Jenin and didn't fall off his feet. He'd seen worse in Africa, but he actually continued Suzanne's line saying that it was a battle, not a massacre."[17]

Jonathan Freedland believes: "This paper distinguished itself from all the other papers, and actually excelled, even though our critics in the Jewish community didn't share that view. Suzanne Goldenberg said from the very beginning, 'this is not a massacre, it is a battle'. 'Some civilians have been killed,' she said, 'and many more who are not civilians. And actually, more people are being killed at the same time in Nablus.' The fact that she was present there all the time made her reports much more restrained than others."[18]

The pride of the Guardian's people for "getting it right" in the news coverage of the Jenin affair was upset by what most of them see as an unjust attack by their critics over the "massacre" headline. A debate developed around the question whether putting the word "massacre" in inverted commas makes it clear enough that it was referring to allegations of massacre (which were undoubtedly voiced against Israel by Palestinians and international politicians), rather than the paper itself relating to the events as a massacre.

"I think that — within the understood and universally used conventions of headline writing in this country — that it was OK to put 'massacre' in inverted commas in the headline," says Rusbridger. "The word was supported by the text — as a quote from someone described as a 'senior Palestinian'. And the story reported prominent and responsible politicians — Chris Patten and Gerald Kaufman — referring to 'alleged atrocities' and labelling Ariel Sharon a war criminal. Those were pretty heavy accusations to be flying around, and from pretty credible sources — one of them a prominent British Jewish politician. The story itself is calm in tone and gives reasonable space to an Israeli spokesperson to respond and rebut the allegations."[19]

Ed Pilkington, Brian Whitaker, McGreal, Martin Woollacott, Simon Tisdall, and MacAskill agree with the editor on that point. Freedland, on the other hand, is convinced that the headline was a big mistake. "So why are we getting such a hard time? Because we did use the word massacre once, although it was in inverted commas, in a headline. It was used because that's what people on the ground were claiming it to be, and that's what Israel was accused of. I thought inverted commas were not enough, considering the fact that we had made such an effort to be careful, to say it was not a massacre, but a battle, and because it was such a charged question," maintains Freedland.[20] Ian Katz says: "The usage of inverted commas can be dangerous because it's a very subtle thing, and sometimes the reader doesn't understand you."[21]

One of the readers who commented on the headline and was told by the readers' editor that the paper put the accusation in a "subtle form", asked how the Guardian's editors would like to read a headline such as "Guardian's editors face rage over 'rape party' ". Katz agrees that it is "a good point".[22]

Another puzzling point is why Israel's supporters directed most of their anger over the news coverage of Jenin at the Guardian, while some of the other British broadsheets used much harder language. "Israel was trying to bury the evidence in Jenin refugee camp yesterday, but it cannot bury the terrible crime it has committed," wrote Justin Huggler and Phil Reeves in the Independent.[23] The Independent also referred to the events as "a monstrous war crime" and "appalling atrocities".[24] In August, after the UN report was published, Reeves apologised for exaggerating.[25]

The Evening Standard went over the top: "We are talking here of massacre, and a cover-up of genocide," they wrote.[26] The Times used the words "carnage" and "bloodbath" in its headlines to describe the event, without using inverted commas.[27] Janine di Giovanni of the Times wrote from Jenin: "Rarely in more than a decade of war reporting from Bosnia, Chechnya, Sierra Leone, Kosovo, have I seen such deliberate destruction, such disrespect for human life."[28] "It was over the top," says Pilkington, referring to Giovanni. "We would never have written something like that in the news pages."[29]

Dozens of articles and comment pieces were published in the Guardian as the facts regarding the battle of Jenin were beginning to reveal themselves. Seumas Milne condemned the United States for not intervening.[30] Uri Avnery, the Israeli writer and peace activist, commended the spirit of the Palestinians in the camp, and claimed that due to the assault "the Palestinian nation straightened its back as never before."[31] "The terror of Jerusalem and Jenin — one delivered by a girl in a robe, the other by men in uniform — is our terror. Take it away and we would do nothing, as we have done nothing before," wrote Peter Preston.[32] Freedland explained that while the Palestinians see themselves as "victims of an aggression so brutal it has shocked even them, a people who have suffered so much", Israelis conceive themselves as acting in self-defence.[33] Ahmad Samih Khalidi, a senior associate member of St Antony's College, Oxford, and a former Palestinian peace negotiator, claimed that Sharon was leading the Israelis and Palestinians to war, after the prospect of a two-state solution had faded.[34]

Sharon Sadeh, Ha'aretz correspondent in London, wrote in the Guardian criticising the British press, including the Guardian, for using figurative language that "betrayed both bias and an attempt to elicit emotional response from the readers which could be translated into increased sales circulation".[35] Sadeh commended the Israeli and American press for their responsible coverage. Linda Grant says: "It is regrettable that Sadeh's article is the only text in the Guardian that said in so many words that what happened in Jenin was not a massacre."[36]

The Guardian's leader column dealt with the situation in Jenin both during the crisis and after it was over. One of those columns, which was subjected to heavy criticism, was published on April 17, the same day as the "massacre" headline. Headed The battle for the truth, the leader opened with the statement: "Jenin camp looks like the scene of a crime. Its concrete rubble and tortured metal evokes another horror half a world away in New York, smaller in scale but every bit as repellent in its particulars, no less distressing, and every bit as man-made."[37]

The leader called for an immediate investigation by the UN of the events in Jenin, stressing that it is in the best interest of both Israelis and Palestinians, as well as the international community: "The world needs to know what really happened in Jenin if only to be better equipped to stop it happening again. Both Israelis and Palestinians need to know, because more disinformation, more denial and lies, and yet more tragic myth-making, only feed the hatred and deepen the divide."[38]

Loyal to its line on the matter, namely that Jenin was not necessarily the only or the worst human rights violation during Operation Defensive Shield, the paper called for the scope of the inquiry to be wide. It stressed that Palestinian behaviour should be questioned too: "The EU's aid commissioner says Israel breached the 1949 Geneva Convention by blocking the delivery of humanitarian assistance in Jenin. Israel must ensure that all restrictions on aid agency and media access are lifted forthwith. These and other aspects of its behaviour in Jenin in respect of civilian rights, treatment of prisoners and the disposal of bodies must also be investigated — as should Israeli claims that Palestinian gunmen used civilians as human shields."[39]

But not many readers, it seems, went past the first paragraph. The comparison of the battle's results to the terror attack of September 11, 2001 had hit on a sensitive nerve. The repeated use of the expression "scene of a crime" did not make the column more digestible for Israel's supporters. Their disapproval is shared by quite a few of the Guardian people. "We received many emails referring to this leader," says Jonathan Freedland. "The website HonestReporting.com, which is running an organised campaign against the Guardian, spread that editorial all around the world, and that's how an image of a paper is constructed. I think there's no merit in this comparison. What does it mean anyway? When we are under the microscope all the time, we must be very careful."[40]

Woollacott says: "I think very highly of Simon [Simon Tisdall, the leader writer] but I thought this one was inappropriate. These two events, September 11 and Jenin, have nothing in common. Fifty-two casualties versus 3,000 is too vast a gap for comparison, but that's not the sole reason for it being incompatible. Jenin was an immoral act, but it wasn't an organised attack aiming to cause the biggest possible number of civilian casualties in order to achieve a political goal. It was a relatively limited military operation. There was an expectation that civilians would be killed, but it wasn't the goal. I think the comparison is like apples and oranges. There's no basis for it besides the fact that there was a lot of damage to buildings and that people were killed."[41] "I think it was a very unfortunate use of words," says Ian Katz. "What depresses me about it is that all the debate around it blurred the fact that our news coverage of the Jenin affair was so good and balanced."[42]

Brian Whitaker seems more disturbed by the inaccuracy of the comparison than with its effect on the readers: "I don't really see the merit of comparing Jenin to 9/11. Maybe saying that it had 'the smell of Sabra and Shatila' could have been more relevant, but it wouldn't have made the critics happier, would it? I commented a while ago that it takes 28 Halabjas to make one Hiroshima. I was referring to the American declaration that they might use nuclear weapons if the Iraqis use weapons of mass destruction. I was trying to say that nuclear weapons are weapons of mass destruction, whether they are in Iraqi or American hands. I think you should be careful with analogies. I thought about Hiroshima for a long time and I thought it was all right, but still there were very angry emails."[43]

Goldenberg says: "Looking back, the leader comment was a mistake – too strident in tone, although it makes a valid point that Israel should have allowed access to Jenin to clear up allegations that a crime had been committed."[44]

Chris McGreal, who was taking his first steps in the wreckage of Jenin when the article was published, didn't see it at the time: "Looking back at it you could say that it was misplaced. There's no place for this comparison because the psychology is different. If the Israelis had sent soldiers in there with the intent of killing as many people as possible, maybe the comparison would be valid, but there is no evidence that this was the case."[45]

Pilkington apologised for the leader at a public event in which Jewish community representatives and foreign editors from various newspapers participated. He bitterly regrets it. His account of the events reflects the atmosphere at the time:

> Although other British newspapers were present, everybody
> wanted to criticise coverage in the Guardian. The debate was
> very robust. People were queuing up to criticise us, and then
> someone waved this clipping at me, and said, "how dare you
> write this", and I found myself apologising. I now believe that
> I should have pointed out that the quote that was thrown at
> me was taken out of context. The events in Jenin were very
> confused and very shocking. The editorial from which the
> clipping was taken reflected the shock we all felt on that day. In
> the end, the UN report into Jenin was very severe, even though
> it was also partial. It is clear now that there wasn't an actual
> 'massacre', and that the number of civilians killed by house
> demolitions was lower than at first it seemed. Those facts have
> been fully reported in our coverage as they have emerged.[46]

Alan Rusbridger, although admitting that "the 9/11 comparison was clumsy",[47] points out that there was more to the leader than that:

> At the time, the general balance of reporting was that there was
> a possibility that a real atrocity had occurred there. The Israeli
> attitude of not allowing access to the press or to the UN

committee or to ambulances strengthened the feeling that
something terrible had happened. We were far from alone in
believing that it was in Israel's own interest to enable such access
or it might be mythologised as an appalling chapter in Palestinian
history. I think it was, and still is, a good argument. Reading the
leader again in conjunction with the news story it strikes me how
similar it was to the line being taken by the EU commissioner.
Both were calling for an investigation, both arguing that it was in
Israel's interests to allow full and open access to the area.[48]

"I don't think that the editorial is so problematic," says Ewen MacAskill.
"The fact that journalists were kept away and that Israel refused a UN
committee of inquiry raised a growing suspicion, and implied that Israel
was above international law."[49]

Simon Tisdall, who wrote the leader, defends it passionately:

In spite of the criticism, I don't take back one word of the
leader. My job is to present the paper's position, and the essence
of the article was discussed beforehand with the editor and his
assistants. The context was the whole Israeli operation in the
West Bank, and we wanted to express our deepest resentment
towards this policy. Of course I thought about it in depth, and
it seemed to me absolutely legitimate to say that in appearance
it looks like the outcome of September 11, on a smaller scale. If
people were hurt I do not apologise. The number of casualties
might have been smaller than what we thought at the time, but
at that moment we couldn't have known all the facts and the
results looks similar. The comparison shocked people and got
them to think, and I certainly don't regret that. Judging from
the force of the reaction, the leader served its purpose, which
was to get people's attention. It was an aware usage of
metaphors in order to create a dramatic impact. The UN's
inquiry and Amnesty report strengthen the feelings that things
that shouldn't have happened took place in Jenin. I know that
the editor and his assistant editor read it, and they didn't

demand a change to even a word. It's a mistake to think I wrote it off the top of my head. I was encouraged by the editors to take a hard line, and I was happy to do so. I deliberately didn't use the word massacre, which other papers have used. The only time we used the word massacre was to describe the suicide bombing in Park hotel in Netanya on Passover eve. I used this word because in my dictionary it is the word to describe the slaughter of defenceless people. I think it's very important that we stay robust. We have never let anybody have any reason to describe the Guardian as pinkish. Maybe sometimes I overstate the matter, but I'll never leave you in doubt as to what we think.[50]

After the publication of the UN report, the Guardian looked back with satisfaction at its own assessment: "As we said last April, the destruction wrought in Jenin looked and smelled like a crime. On the basis of the UN's findings, it still does."[51]

Martin Woollacott's summary of the coverage touches on subtle points: "We stayed on the right side: we didn't say it was a massacre but we did say that many civilians were killed, while noting that there was serious loss of life on both sides. I'm not sure whether in our editorial line we were clear enough in stating that the moral error was strategic rather than tactical. There was some Israeli misbehaviour in the execution of the operation but it was not at all of the order that some Palestinian accounts implied. The problem was the operation itself rather than how it was done."[52]

In the light of Rusbridger's admission that occasionally Israeli casualties were underplayed, it is valuable to examine the coverage of suicide bombings in Israel through the end of March and April 2002, the parallel period to the mayhem in Jenin.

The bombing of Park hotel in Netanya, which allegedly triggered the military operation, received the widest coverage. There were various reasons for that: the death toll was high, the attack was conducted while the innocent victims, in their best attire, were having Passover dinner, and a few of the casualties were British citizens, visiting Israel for Passover. It was also clear from the first moment that Israel was ready for vigorous retaliation. The Israeli press had been speculating about the planned military operation for some time before the attack on the hotel. On the other hand, since the operation had not yet started, more reporters were available to cover the bombing.

The bombing was reported on the Guardian website shortly after it occurred, on the night of March 27. Three stories covered the event the next day. The main one, by Suzanne Goldenberg, who was in Beirut to cover the Arab summit, was headed Israel plans unprecedented response to massacre, and began: "For days, Israel has been telegraphing its intentions to launch a sweeping new military offensive against the Palestinians [...] Last night's bloody attack on a Passover seder in Netanya provides the perfect pretext."[53] The headline, too, is interesting, because it demonstrated on one hand the problem which Ed Pilkington mentioned – anticipating the retaliation by Israelis before they bury their dead, and on the other hand Simon Tisdall's remark, that this was the only case in which the Guardian referred to a massacre. Graham Usher in Jerusalem filed the report on the attack, and Jason Keister contributed a colour story, interviewing the injured and eyewitnesses. [54]

On March 29 Usher described his visit to Netanya and the neighbouring West Bank town of Tul Karem, in a state-of-mind story. On both sides the talk is only of war, was the fitting headline.[55] In a feature article the same day the Jewish writer and stage director Michael Kustow explained why he decided not to celebrate Passover in Israel that year:

> In the end, I'm staying in London not only because I'm afraid
> of getting killed, but also because, as a diaspora Jew, I'm part of
> a conflict for which I can't avoid some responsibility. It's like
> having relatives whom you love, who won't listen to your advice
> or warnings, and who are digging their own graves.
>
> To see your blood relatives going down a blood-soaked blind
> alley hurts. To see them inflicting pain and pillage and ever-
> more ingenious humiliation on less powerful neighbours, who
> strike back with self-annihilating rage, hurts more. To realise
> that the most pitiless violence is the violence of the traumatised
> former victim, clinging to past wounds from generation unto
> generation, is the bitterest pill to swallow.[56]

The same day a teenage female suicide bomber hit a supermarket in the Jerusalem neighbourhood Kiriat Yovel, killing three. Usher reported under the heading, "At 18, bomber became martyr and murderer". His article described the event and quoted eyewitnesses, but most of it was dedicated to the story of the bomber, including interviews with her family members. Sad as this may be, it is doubtful if any professional journalist would argue that after dozens of suicide bombings, the story of a young female martyr-murderer is not of more interest than the fate of her three victims.

Operation Defensive Shield was launched after the Jerusalem bombing, and on April 10 a suicide bomber attacked bus number 960, going from Haifa to Jerusalem. Four of the eight killed were soldiers on their way to the West Bank. Peter Beaumont combined his report of the attack with interviews with soldiers who survived the assault, and soldiers who lived to tell the tale of the booby-trapped alley in Jenin, where 13 of their friends were killed a day earlier.[57] Most of the soldiers expressed hope for peace mixed with pessimism for its prospects.

On 12 April, a female suicide bomber from Jenin refugee camp hit Mahane Yehuda market in Jerusalem. Usher reported it the next day, but this time, possibly because the attack occurred on Friday afternoon, there were no interviews with the injured and relatives of the dead, most of them Chinese workers.[58]

Key Players

ISRAELIS

Ehud Barak (1942-). A daring commando leader and the most decorated soldier in the history of the Israeli army, Barak joined the Labour Party in 1995, and became leader in 1997, a year after the Likud general election victory that has shifted the balance of power in Israeli politics. Barak became prime minister in May 1999. After manoeuvring to avoid progress in negotiations with the Palestinians he attempted to impose a settlement on Yasser Arafat at the Camp David meetings of 2000, endorsed by President Bill Clinton. The supposed generosity of the offer remains a matter of controversy and the attempt led nowhere, but Barak created an Israeli consensus that the Palestinians did not want peace and remained focused on their aim of destroying Israel. His successful sabotage of Camp David and the subsequent second intifada brought about the Likud electoral victory in February 2001. Barak was forced to retire with the single tangible achievement of the Israeli withdrawal from Lebanon in 2000. Very few international observers have grasped that his main objective was to avoid serious negotiations with Syria that would have entailed a withdrawal from the Golan Heights.

Menachem Begin (1913-1992). The first non-Labour prime minister. An activist in the cause of Ze'ev Jabotinsky's Revisionist Zionism, which aspired to the entire Eretz Yisrael (Greater Israel), and as such was a prime influence on Likud. Arrived in Israel in 1942, and succeeded Yaakov Meridor as the commander in chief of the Irgun, the right wing terrorist organization. More of a political leader than a military commander, he masterminded the massacre of Dir-Yassin in 1948 and in the same year founded the Herut party which was to be united with Likud in 1973. After almost three decades as an unofficial leader of the opposition, Begin won the general elections in May 1977 and was prime minister until a nervous breakdown forced him to retire. Was instrumental in securing a peace agreement with Egypt, but was equally responsible for the invasion of Lebanon in June 1982. Died in 1992 after a long illness.

David Ben-Gurion (1886-1973). A Polish Jew who emigrated to Palestine at the age of 20, he founded the General Federation of Labour (Histadrut) in 1920 and then the Mapai (Labour) party in 1930 under the British mandate. In 1948 he became Israel's first prime minister and minister of defence. He was tenacious, single minded, and sometimes incautious to the point of foolhardiness, as during his second term as prime minister (1955-63), when he hailed the advance on the Suez Canal during the crisis of 1956 as the beginning of a new, greater Israel, and then within days had to eat his words when the the US president, Dwight D Eishenhower, forced an end to the attack on Egypt by Israel, France and Britain.

Moshe Dayan (1915-81). A native of Palestine, Dayan fought in Orde Wingate's Night Squads against Arab rebels in Palestine and lost his eye fighting with the British Army against Vichy French forces in Lebanon. Dayan was a totem to diaspora born Labour party leaders, and moved easily from military affairs to politics, never quite keeping them separate. As chief of staff (1953-1958) and defence minister (1967-1974) he led a belligerent and adventurous policy designed to drag Egypt and Syria into war with Israel. He became a national hero after leading Israel to victory in the 1967 six day war, in which he seized the moment to sweep into East Jerusalem and declare it a united city, but fell from grace after the 1973 War, in which Israel was humbled by an unforeseen attack. He deserted Labour to join the right wing Likud government in 1977, and as foreign minister in the Begin government was involved in peace negotiations with Egypt. Dayan gained some notoriety for womanising and stealing archaeological findings.

Abba Eban (1915-2003). Israel's foremost diplomat was born in South Africa and educated in England where he also taught oriental languages before serving as a liaison officer with the allies in the second world war. Eban spoke fluent Hebrew, Arabic and Persian, in addition to his excellent English, French and Spanish. Entering the political department of the Jewish Agency in 1946, Eban was instrumental in securing the UN general assembly approval in November 1947 for partitioning Palestine into Jewish and Arab states. Serving concurrently as Israel's first ambassador to the UN and the US, he was regarded as one of the most articulate and gifted envoys, and often defended in public aggressive Israeli policies, to which he was opposed privately. Settled in Israel only in 1959, foreign minister 1966-74, Eban avoided controversy and despite his doveishness enhanced the hawks' cause by calling the pre-1967 boundaries "the Auschwitz boundaries". He failed to be re-elected to the Knesset in 1988 and retired from active politics.

Levi Eshkol (1895-1969). Israel's third prime minister, and arguably the best. Immigrated to Palestine from Ukraine in 1914 and worked as an agricultural labourer. He belonged to a doveish component of Mapai, and succeeded David Ben-Gurion as prime minister in 1963. Disastrously for future policy making he succumbed to public pressure and, though remaining prime minister, he yielded the ministry of defence to Moshe Dayan on June 1, 1967, five days before the militarily successful six day war. His national unity government which led Israel into war with three of her neighbours included Likud for the first time, and when Eshkol died in harness his successor, Golda Meir, prime minister from 1969 until 1974, fought to avoid territorial concessions.

Golda Meir (1898-1978). Israeli Prime Minister 1969-1974. Her reign is remembered for the rejection of Egyptian negotiating attempts, and her fear and hatred of all Arabs, which led to the 1973 war, a national trauma for Israel because of the Arab successful surprise attack leading to huge losses of Israel troops, and one which led to her resignation after a commission of inquiry report. Notorious for pearls of wisdom like "there is no such thing as a Palestinian people", "they are not nice" (the Black Panthers, a protest movement of deprived Mizrachi Jews), and "I don't know why you use a fancy French word like detente when there's a good English phrase for it – cold war". Readers who are reminded of Margaret Thacher are not too far off. Despite tough competition, Meir was probably the worst prime minister in Israeli history.

Binyamin Netanyahu (Israel 1949-). Prime minister 1996-99. Elected Likud leader 1993. As prime minister Netanyahu led an attempt to stall the implementation of the Oslo accords signed in 1993, but was forced to withdraw from part of the city of Hebron. In 1996 he led the first Israeli attack on the occupied territories after the Oslo accords, following riots invoked by the launching of a tunnel under the western wall in occupied east Jerusalem. His tense relationship with the army prevented him from carrying on a full re-occupation of the West Bank and Gaza. A hardline radical neo-liberal, Netanyahu remains popular among settlers, Jewish US Republicans, and the Christian groups surrounding the Bush administration. Lacks the long-term planning, the ideological backbone and the military seniority (a must in Israeli politics), which characterise Ariel Sharon. Netanyahu was defeated in the 1999 general elections by Labour under Ehud Barak. As foreign minister since 2002, he is attempting a comeback by undermining Sharon among the rightwing fringe of Likud.

Shimon Peres (1923-). One of the unlikelier recipients of the Nobel peace prize, in 1994, along with Yitzhak Rabin and Yasser Arafat. Peres, born in Poland, arrived with his family in Israel in 1934 and was educated in Ben Shemen agricultural boarding school. He was one of the so-called Ben-Gurion Boys, and as the young director of the defence ministry he was one of the leading forces behind the Suez campaign of 1956, and the mastermind of Israel's nuclear strategy. Peres led the Labour party into a national unity government (1984) with Yitzhak Shamir's Likud party, and became prime minister for two years before Shamir took over. A second coalition followed the 1988 general election but fell apart in 1990. In 1992 Peres was defeated by his eternal rival, Yitzhak Rabin, for the Labour Party leadership, and bcame his foreign minister. He took over the premiership after Rabin's assassination on 1995 but was defeated in the general elections of 1996 by Binyamin Netanyahu. His international reputation as a prophet of peace suffered when he led the Labour party into Ariel Sharon's government in 2001. Into his 80s, he still leads Labour.

Yitzhak Rabin (1922-95). Israeli prime minister of Labour led coalitions in 1974-77 and 1992-95. Signed the Oslo accords in 1993, for which he received the 1994 Nobel peace prize with Shimon Peres and Yasser Arafat. He negotiated further Palestinian self-government and more Israeli withdrawals from the West Bank, and paid the ultimate price of assassination at the hands of an Israeli extremist. Rabin was born in Jerusalem, fought in the Israeli war of independence of 1948-49, spent 1954 in England at Camberley Staff College and was chief of staff during the six day war. Gained notoriety among Palestinians as minister of defence during the first intifada (1987-1992), but is remembered mainly for his shift towards negotiation. His death turned him into a symbol of peace.

Moshe Sharett (1894-1965). Born in Ukraine, Sharett (originally Shertok) came with his family to Palestine in 1906. He studied at the London School of Economics after first world war service with the Turkish rulers of Palestine. Was Chaim Weizmann's right hand man at the Jewish Agency. He became foreign minister of the new state of Israel and, from 1953 until 1955, prime minister. He was a moderate and conciliator but lost all along the line to the hawkish activists, Ben-Gurion and Dayan. Was ousted by Ben-Gurion and replaced by the hardline Golda Meir before the collusion with France and Britain in 1956.

Ariel Sharon (1928-). Prime minister since 2001 with a long track record of service in every Likud government from 1977. Sharon, Likud's leader, came from the ranks of Labour. Born in Palestine under the mandate, he joined the Hagana militia and and fought in the Arab-Israeli war in 1948-49 after the creation of the Jewish state. In the 1950s he commanded the vigilante 101 commando IDF unit conducting retaliatory raids on Palestinian villages. In 1953 the unit blew up 50 houses in the village of Qibya in Jordan, killing 69 people. Sharon rose to the rank of brigadier general and commanded a division during the 1967 six day war in which Israel captured east Jerusalem, the West Bank and the Gaza Strip. In 1971 he was in charge of ending rebellion in Gaza, an operation involving mass bulldozing of houses, indiscriminate killing, widespread arrests and the deportation of hundreds of Palestinians to the Sinai dessert. Sharon's record of political and military adventurism and his disregard of human life were to the fore when he masterminded the Israeli invasion of Lebanon in 1982. An Israeli committee of inquiry found him "indirectly responsible" for the massacre in the Palestinian refugee camps of Sabra and Shatila, conducted by Israel's allies, the Christian phalange of Lebanon. The committee declared him unfit to serve as minister of defence, a verdict which can hardly be said to have impeded his further rise. With the support of George Bush's administration, Sharon runs the most aggressive policies in the occupied territories ever entertained by an Israeli government.

Chaim Weizmann (1874-1952). First president of Israel and the key diplomat leading to its creation in 1948. Born of humble parents in Russia and educated at German and Swiss universities, he was a chemist with a growing reputation when he arrived at Manchester University in 1904, when he was already a major figure in Zionism. CP Scott met him in September 1914 and took up his cause. It was helpful that one of Weizmann's scientific discoveries was hugely important in the wartime munitions industry. Through Scott, Weizmann met Lloyd George, soon to be prime minister, and became more closely acquainted with AJ Balfour, later foreign secretary. "We had Jerusalem when London was a marsh," Weizmann told Balfour, who, in 1917, produced what quickly became known as the Balfour Declaration, committing Britain to helping to create a homeland in Palestine for the Jews. Weizmann was Ulysses to the Achilles of his arch rival, David Ben-Gurion, but though he approached the target circumspectly compared to Ben-Gurion, the principal objective were identical.

BRITISH POLITICIANS

AJ Balfour (1848-1930). From an old Scottish family, he entered Parliament in 1874 and became secretary for Scotland in 1886 and, more notoriously, chief secretary for Ireland the following year, when he became known as Bloody Balfour for his suppression of Irish home rule advocates. In 1902 he succeeded his uncle, Robert Cecil, as prime minister. In 1917 he was foreign secretary, and having met Chaim Weizmann through CP Scott and David Lloyd George, and befriended him, he wrote the Balfour Declaration promising a homeland to the Jews in Palestine.

Ernest Bevin (1881-1951). Self-educated van driver who became a dockers' union official and earned the soubriquet "the dockers' KC" when he out-argued an eminent barrister at a wages tribunal. Rose rapidly through the ranks of the Labour party to foreign secretary in the Attlee government of 1945-51. He was successful in reaching agreement on post-war problems throughout Europe and the Commonwealth, and his one high-profile failure was over Palestine. His policy, begun as early as 1945, of restricting Jewish immigration and confining illegal immigrants to camps in Palestine — husbands and wives separately — aroused bitter resentment. Press photographs of Jews incarcerated on clandestine shipping arrested by the Royal Navy off the coast of Palestine turned Bevin into a popular hate figure in both Britain and Palestine. He finally handed the whole problem over to the United Nations.

Anthony Eden (1897-1977). Foreign secretary under Neville Chamberlain, the appeasement prime minister, with whom he disagreed over policy towards Mussolini; and again under Churchill during the war. Attended the San Francisco founding conference of the United Nations. When the Tories returned to power in 1951, he was again Churchill's foreign secretary. For years the Prince Charming in waiting for the throne, he made it at last when Churchill retired in 1955. In 1956, when Britain and the US reneged on their promise to fund the Aswan High Dam, President Nasser of Egypt nationalised the Suez Canal. Convinced that he was a sinister figure in the mould of Hitler, Eden connived with

France and Israel in the disastrous invasion of Egypt. The US pulled the rug out from underneath the adventurists and a few months later Eden resigned, his career in ruins.

David Lloyd George (1863-1945). A Welsh nationalist, though born in Manchester, and a solicitor, he became a great reforming Liberal prime minister before the first world war and a great wartime prime minister during it. He was a close friend of CP Scott and so was the right man in the right place when Scott introduced him to Chaim Weizmann: Lloyd George opened doors for him in Whitehall and in the highest places in government, setting in train plans for achieving the ultimate Zionist goal of Israel.

THE GUARDIAN

Michael Adams (1920-). Born in Addis Ababa, Ethiopia. He was educated in England and took an Oxford MA in 1948 after four years as a prisoner of war in Germany. In 1956 he was appointed Manchester Guardian Middle East correspondent. He reported movingly on the plight of the Palestinians and was convinced that either the Israelis would have to give them equal partnership in the state, or it would have to drive every last Arab out; this view did not find favour with Alastair Hetherington and their disagreement ultimately brought about Adams's resignation. He became chairman of the Council for the Advancement of Arab-British Understanding (CAABU) and editor of Middle East International until he retired in 1981, and still writes for the magazine. Author of *Suez and After: Year of Crisis* (1958), *Chaos of Rebirth: the Arab Outlook* (1968), and, with Christopher Mayhew, *Cover it Not: the Middle East Cover-Up* (1975).

Ian Black (1953-). He studied history and politics at Cambridge University and London School of Economics and joined the Guardian 1980 as a sub-editor on foreign news before switching to home news reporting. Stern Fellow at Washington Post 1983. Middle East correspondent based in Jerusalem 1984-1993. Covered Iran-Iraq war, first Palestinian intifada; commended in British press awards 1988.

Diplomatic editor, based in London, 1993-99; European editor, based in Brussels, 2000-04; chief foreign leader writer, London, 2004—. Co-author of *Israel's Secret Wars* (1991).

William Percival Crozier (1879-1944). Appointed editor of the Guardian in 1932 when Ted Scott drowned three years after succeeding his father, C.P. A scholar and a humanist who kept up these interests throughout his life, he was the grandson of a miner and son of a Methodist minister from Stanhope in County Durham, and, though agnostic himself, brought the singleminded fervour of his father to encouraging the exposure of Nazism and to supporting Zionists, who mourned him when he died.

Frank Edmead (1919-2000). He joined the Guardian in 1950 after working in post-war Austria with evacuated German children and in 1956 was appointed leader writer by the new editor, Alastair Hetherington. He specialised in the Far East and the Middle East and his resignation on principle because Hetherington changed the paper's line on Vietnam and Israel within three weeks split the paper into Hetherington hawks (not many) and Edmead doves. Whereas Hetherington was a tank commander during the Normandy invasion, Edmead was a Quaker who served as an ambulanceman, once crossing a minefield to fetch a wounded German soldier. After resigning from the Guardian Edmead returned to University College, London, to do post-graduate work in conflict studies, but all along his great love had been Chinese history and culture and in his retirement he spent every other year teaching at the universities of Shanghai and Xi-an.

Jonathan Freedland (1967-). As a prominent Guardian staff columnist he has sometimes found himself in the tricky unofficial role of mediating between the Guardian and the Jewish community in Britain. He studied philosophy, politics and economics at Wadham College, Oxford, and after three years at the BBC as a radio reporter including a stint as a staff writer on the Washington Post on the Lawrence Stern Fellowhip, he joined the Guardian as Washington correspondent in 1993. He became a leader writer and columnist on the paper in 1997. His weekly piece on the Comment and Analysis pages earned him the What The Papers Say accolade as columnist of the year in 2002. He contributes to a range of US journals and appears frequently on British television and radio. His 2004 book, *Jacob's Gift*, is a family memoir exploring, among other things, the story of Zionism and Jews' attachment to Israel.

Suzanne Goldenberg (1962-). A Canadian, born in Winnipeg, joined the Guardian in 1988, working mostly as a foreign sub-editor until she was appointed South Asia correspondent, based in New Delhi, in 1995. In 2000 she went to Jerusalem as Middle East correspondent, attracting increasing hostility from the Israeli authorities, possibly because, unusually among the international press corps, she cultivated Palestinian contacts as well as Israelis. In 2002 she went as US correspondent to Washington, a prized posting that didn't prevent an Israeli press officer claiming that he had manoeuvred her removal from Israel by his complaints. Goldenberg won many accolades while she was in the Middle East: in 2001 she was named Journalist of the Year by What the Papers Say, and won the London Press Club's Edgar Wallace award and the James Cameron award. In 2002 she was again named Journalist of the Year, alongside John Kampfner of the BBC, this time by the Foreign Press Association. From January until April 2003 she was stationed in Baghdad where, in the words of Helena Kennedy QC, her "reporting of the heart of darkness in Iraq" covered the Guardian in laurels.

Linda Grant (1951-). Freelance features journalist on contract to the Guardian from 1995 to 2000 during which time her work included a column called Tel-Aviv Tales. Her novel *The Cast Iron Shore* won the David Higham First Novel Award in 1996 and was shortlisted for the Guardian Fiction Prize; in the same year she was shortlisted for features writer of the year in the national press awards. She won the Orange Prize for fiction in 2000 for *When I Lived in Modern Times*, a novel about the last years of the British mandate in Palestine. A Liverpudlian, born to Jewish immigrants from Poland and Russia, Grant read English at York University then went as a post-graduate student to Canada before returning to England in 1985 to be a journalist. Apart from the Guardian, for five years she was a columnist on the Jewish Chronicle

Alastair Hetherington (1919-1999). The dying AP Wadsworth stood down from the editorship as the Suez war broke in 1956 and Hetherington took over and opposed it throughout with unwavering moral courage. A wartime tanks officer, his great interest was defence but he also specialised in the Middle East. His occasional diktats, particularly over Israel, caused disaffection and resignations. In 1956 he worked with Richard Scott, grandson of CP Scott, in saving the Guardian from an unfavourable merger with the Times. Introduced the change from Manchester Guardian to the Guardian, the start of London printing, and finally the switch of the paper's centre of operations to London.

David Hirst (1936-). Began to report from Lebanon for the Guardian in 1963 having become fascinated by the Middle East during national service in Egypt. After Oxford University, he returned to study at the American University of Beirut, where he still lives. Joined the Guardian staff as Middle East correspondent in 1971. He has covered the evolving history of the region from the 1967 Arab-Israeli war onward. He is now a freelance and is the author of *Oil and Public Opinion in the Middle East* (1966), *Sadat* (1981), and *The Gun and the Olive Branch* (1977, 2003).

Harold Jackson (1932-). Unusually among the post-war aristocracy of the Guardian, he joined the old Fleet Street office as a messenger in 1952 after emerging from Wormwood Scrubs where he had been incarcerated for refusing on conscientious grounds to be called up for national service. This background tickled AP Wadsworth, who promoted Jackson to the editorial staff. He became the paper's indispensable "fireman", daily carrying about him a passport and a toothbrush against the likelihood that he would be dispatched at a minute's notice to cover the world's latest disaster. Among them: in 1966, Biafra; 1967, the six day war, then Jordan, Egypt; 1968, Vietnam, Egypt, Israel, Soviet invasion of Czechoslovakia; 1969, mostly Ulster; 1970, civil war in Lebanon, Nasser's funeral and aftermath, Indo-Pakistan war; 1971, Ulster again. In 1972 he covered the US election campaign and at the end of the year became features editor until 1978, when he was posted as Washington correspondent until 1985. Because of his intrepid initiation of a computer link with the Guardian he was brought home as chief systems editor. Unable to get back on the road, he resigned in 1995. Still contributes to the paper, mainly obituaries.

Chris McGreal (1960-). After education in Cornwall McGreal had a spell as a merchant seaman. He then worked for the BBC, at first in local radio and then with the World Service before going to Central America for the BBC in 1985. In 1990 he went to South Africa for the Independent On Sunday and joined the Guardian in 1992 as southern Africa correspondent, in time both for Nelson Mandela's crowning triumph in becoming president of the republic and also to cover the appalling genocide of Tutsis by Hutus that year in Rwanda. He was posted to Jerusalem in October 2002.

Peter Preston (1938-). Innovative and modernising Guardian editor who took over from Hetherington in 1975 and, like Hetherington, served for nearly 20 years but saw his core business as news, not personal involvement in diplomacy and politics. Closer to Wadsworth than to Hetherington in his grasp of the Palestinian dimension of the Middle East question, and his direction of the paper tended to be through careful appointments and constant consultation.

JMD Pringle (1912-1999). Joined the Manchester Guardian in 1935 after graduating from Lincoln College, Oxford. He served most of the second world war with the King's Own Scottish Borderers before returning to the Guardian as assistant editor to AP Wadsworth from 1944 until 1948. He wrote most of the leaders on the Middle East as the Guardian began to show awareness of the Palestinian dimension to the creation of Israel. His later career included four years as deputy editor of the Observer (1958-63) and two spells as editor of the Sydney Morning Herald.

Terence Prittie (the Hon Terence Cornelius Farmer Prittie, younger son of Lord Dunalley DSO, 1913-1985). After education at Stowe and Christ Church, Oxford, he served in the second world war with the Rifle Brigade, was mentioned in dispatches during the desperate defence of

Calais in 1940 and at the end of the war was awarded the MBE in recognition of his six escapes while a prisoner of the Germans. In 1971, following his retirement after 25 years on the Guardian, mostly in Germany, the West German government recognised his work with the Federal Cross of Merit. He was Manchester Guardian cricket correspondent for a year before he became chief correspondent in Germany from 1946 until 1963, when he became diplomatic correspondent. He left in 1970 to edit the Zionist magazine Britain and Israel following passionate disagreement with the Guardian's increasing espousement of a solution to the problem of the displaced Palestinians.

Alan Rusbridger (1953-). Took over as Guardian editor from Peter Preston in 1995 having proved himself as editor of the Weekend magazine and as features editor. Tough but imaginative, he often intervenes decisively in the daily operation but leaves most of the detail to his executives. He has made overtures to a hostile Jewish community, taking the trouble to meet them individually and as groups, explaining the Guardian's position, and inviting his critics to contribute to the paper. His top and bottom line on the current political situation of Israel is: "This newspaper has always supported the right of Israel to exist. It does not mean that we must support Ariel Sharon's government."[1]

Harry Sacher (1881-1971). On the staff of the Manchester Guardian from 1905-09 after education at University College, London, New College, Oxford, Berlin University, and the Sorbonne. From 1909 to 1915 he was with the Daily News and in 1915 he rejoined the Guardian and remained until 1919. He was a committed Zionist and during his Guardian years also edited a monthly magazine called *Palestine* and from 1927 until 1931 he was a member of the executive of the World Zionist Organisation. He was called to the bar in 1909 and practised in Palestine from 1920 until 1930. In 1905 he married Miriam, daughter of Michael Marks, of one of the founding families of Marks & Spencer. From 1932 for 30 years Sacher was a director of the company, though he continued to write leaders for the Manchester Guardian during the Crozier and Wadsworth editorships, but not on Palestine.

Charles Prestwich Scott (1846-1932). Editor at the age of 25 in 1872, when the Manchester Guardian had only been a daily from 1855, a few days after the stamp duty on newspapers ("the tax on knowledge") was abolished. By the time the white-bearded bicycling patriarch retired 57 years later, the Manchester Guardian had an international reputation and was indispensable in Britain. His most fateful meeting was with Chaim Weizmann in 1914, from which a collaboration grew which led directly to the Balfour Declaration of 1918.

Herbert Sidebotham (1872-1940). Born in Manchester and educated at Manchester Grammar School and Balliol College, Oxford, he joined the Manchester Guardian in 1895 as a military expert. He was one of a group of Zionists on the paper, with Harry Sacher and WP Crozier, who was then news editor. Sidebotham joined Sacher on *Palestine* and wrote most of the magazine's contents. From 1918 he worked for the Times and then worked as a columnist for a number of other newspapers.

Eric Silver (1935-). Born into the large Jewish community in Leeds. Joined the Guardian in 1960 as a home and then foreign news sub-editor until he emigrated to the London office as a reporter in 1964. He was diary editor following Peter Preston in 1968-72 and in 1972 he was posted as Israel correspondent, despite his own doubts about his eligibility, as a Jew, to be perceived as even-handed. In 1983 he took leave of absence to write book on Menachem Begin, and on completing that he posted in 1984 to New Delhi. In 1987 he resigned and returned to Israel to live and work as a freelance journalist.

Frederick (originally Fritz) Augustus Voigt (1892-1957). The great and fearless Manchester Guardian correspondent who covered the Hitler years. Dr Markus Huttner, a Leipzig University historian of Nazism, wrote of Voigt: "Due to his incorruptible veracity and his philosophical and theological erudition he was better able than most of his contemporaries to face the stark reality" of Europe under totalitarianism. Voigt took a first in modern languages at Birkbeck College, then served on the western front in the Royal Garrison Artillery.

Joined the Guardian in 1919. Scott sent him to Berlin in 1920, where he covered Germany and eastern Europe with high distinction. After he had reported Hitler's election it became impossible for him to remain in Germany, but when he left he immediately protested at what he clearly regarded as the inadequate work of his replacement, Alexander Werth. Crozier pulled Werth out and Voigt continued to cover Germany from Paris through his wide network of contacts. It was Werth though who wrote a historically damning phrase when, in a memo to Crozier, he reported that the Times correspondent found that "at the London end, they cut out everything that was in the least likely to offend Hitler".

Alfred Powell Wadsworth (1891-1956). Not the least of his accomplishments as editor of the Guardian was to recognise that the Balfour Declaration was deeply ambiguous and failed to address the inevitable problem in creating the state of Israel of the indigenous Palestinian population of Arabs. He had been a superb reporter and leader writer, and as editor was a workaholic who pushed up the circulation and reputation of the paper.

Martin Woollacott (1939-). Former foreign editor whose later career as a columnist was founded on extensive reporting experience around the world. He was educated at Manchester Grammar School and Merton College, Oxford, and his training in journalism from 1962-68 was at the Warrington Guardian, the Oldham Chronicle, Camera Press, and Agence France Presse. He joined the Guardian in 1968. He covered the Vietnam war and the violent break up of Pakistan when East Pakistan seceded as Bangladesh (1971), and the Indian emergency under Indira Gandhi (1971-76). Based in Cyprus from 1976-79, he was one of three Middle East correspondents (with David Hirst and Eric Silver). He covered the Iranian revolution and other stories in the Arab world, Turkey and Ethiopia. In 1979 he returned to London as assistant foreign editor and then was foreign editor from 1983-90. Returned to reporting, including the first Iraq war and the Kurdish uprising in 1991, before becoming a columnist with occasional reporting assignments abroad.

ARAB LEADERS

Yasser Arafat (1929-) Founder of the Palestinian Fatah organisation in 1959, Arafat became leader of the Palestinian Liberation Organisation (PLO) in 1968. Arafat attended King Faud University in Egypt where he received a degree in architecture and engineering in 1951. He was driven out of Jordan, where he based himself and his people in "Black September" 1971, masterminding attacks on Israeli territory and Israeli targets abroad. He fled again from his new base in Beirut to Tunis after the long siege on Beirut during the Israeli invasion of Lebanon in 1982. In September 1993 he signed the Oslo peace accords with Yitzhak Rabin, for which he was awarded the Nobel peace prize in 1994. Arafat returned to Palestine as the president of the Palestinian Authority, which came into being after the Oslo accords. After the outbreak of the second intifada of 2000 he was declared by Israel and the US a non-partner for negotiation, and was subjected to numerous attempts to undermine his authority. He is besieged in his headquarters in Ramallah, which is occasionally bombed by the Israeli army. In 2004 the Israel prime minister, Ariel Sharon, declared that he was no longer bound by his promise to President Bush to refrain from attacking Arafat physically. For the Palestinian people, despite growing criticism of his leadership, he is still an irreplaceable national symbol.

Gamal Abdel Nasser (1918-1970). President of Egypt (1954-1970). As an officer in the Egyptian army, Nasser took part in the young officers' coup against King Farouk in 1952, and in 1954 took over from the coup's leader, General Mohammed Neguib. Nasser's declared policies of pan-Arabism and third world solidarity led him to an alliance with Jawaharlal Nehru, prime minister of India, and Marshal Tito of Yugoslavia. He became a hero for Arabs all over the Middle East. In 1956, the United States and Britain retreated from their commitment to fund the building of Aswan High Dam, and Nasser retaliated by nationalising the Suez canal. Britain and France, in alliance with Israel, attacked Egypt but were forced to back down by the US. After Egypt's defeat in the six day war in

1967, Nasser rebuilt the Egyptian army. Millions of Egyptians followed his cortege in Cairo after his death from a heart attack.

Anwar Sadat (1918-1981). One of the young Egyptian officers who participated in the coup against King Farouk, Sadat took over as president after Nasser's death. He led his country, in alliance with Syria, to an unexpected and highly successful attack on Israel in October 1973. Although none of the land occupied in 1967 was regained, the war was seen in the Arab world as a triumph that redeemed previous humiliation. In 1977 Sadat visited Jerusalem and addressed the Israeli Knesset, effectively recognising the state of Israel. In 1978 he signed a peace agreement which brought him the return of Egypt's Israeli occupied lands, and a Nobel peace prize together with Israeli prime minister Menachem Begin, but subjected him to criticism in the Arab world for abandoning the Palestinian cause. Sadat was assassinated during an Egyptian military parade in 1981 by soldiers belonging to an Islamic political group.

Sheikh Ahmad Yassin (1936-2004). Spiritual leader of Hamas, was assassinated by Israel in March 2004. Born in the southern Palestinian village of Tor, Yassin was exiled with his family to Gaza during the 1948 war. An accident while playing football at 12 confined him to a wheelchair for the rest of his life. Yassin and his Hamas movement were sponsored in the early days, during the 1970s, by Israel, who wished to encourage any opposition to Arafat's nationalist PLO. It was only during the late stages of the first intifada, in 1989, that Hamas turned towards violent struggle against Israel, by attacking settlers and Israel Defence Force targets. After the Hebron massacre of Muslim worshippers by the disaffected settler Baruch Goldstein in 1994, Hamas introduced suicide bombing on civilian targets inside Israel. Yassin served time in an Israeli prison for the killing of Palestinian collaborators from 1989 until 1997, when he was released in return for two Mossad agents held in Jordan. He survived one attempt on his life in September 2003. After his killing Hamas declared that Israel has "opened the gates of hell", and threatened it with perpetual war.

OTHER PLAYERS

David Caute (1936-). Sometime academic (fellow of All Souls, Oxford), novelist, playwright, and journalist who wrote in 1984 a savage analysis of the Guardian's treatment of Sarah Tisdall, the anonymous source who was identified and imprisoned as the source after the paper handed over leaked government documents to the high court. In 1970 he wrote a three-piece series for the paper on the demonisation of the left wing in Israel.

Martha Gellhorn (1908-98). Celebrated American war reporter, including the Spanish civil war, most theatres of the second world war, and Vietnam, where she wrote a notable series for the Guardian. Her first and best collection of reporting from the front was published in 1959 as *The Face of War*.

Lewis Namier (1888-1960). Historian of Russian Jewish origin, educated Balliol College, Oxford, naturalised British 1913. As professor of history at Manchester University he created a Namier school of historical analysis of institutions, and as a key Zionist had access to top information that kept the pot boiling for WP Crozier in his Guardian campaign for a Jewish national home.

Arthur Koestler (1905-83) Born in Budapest, he worked on a kibbutz at the age of 21, became a political journalist in Germany, described his disillusionment with communism after travelling in the Soviet Union and subsequent break with the party as one of six contributors to *The God That Failed* (1950). Imprisoned and sentenced to death in Spain by the Franco insurgents during the civil war but then released (*Spanish Testament*, 1938). Escaped to England from German-occupied France; joined the British army. His experiences yielded, among many works of fiction and non-fiction, *Darkness at Noon* (1940), a political novel regarded as his masterpiece. Returned to the Middle East for the Guardian in 1948 and wrote a series attempting to predict the future of the new-born Israel. He and his wife fulfilled a mutual suicide pact in 1983 when he became terminally ill.

Notes

Chapter One: Making Righteousness Readable

1 David Ayerst, *Guardian – Biography of a Newspaper*, London, Collins, 1971, 17-19.
2 Ibid, 19-21.
3 MG, May 5, 1921, quoted in Ayerst, *Guardian – Biography of a Newspaper*, 25.
4 Ayerst, *Guardian – Biography of a Newspaper*, 23.
5 Ibid, 41.
6 Michael McNay, The First XI, Michael McNay, ed, *The Guardian Past and Present*, London, Guardian Ltd, 2002, 14.
7 Ayerst, *Guardian – Biography of a Newspaper*, 480.
8 Jean Stead, The Unclouded Face of Truth, McNay, *The Guardian Past and Present*, 46.
9 Ayerst, *Guardian – Biography of a Newspaper*, 273-274.
10 Ibid, 285.
11 The Guardian archive, 324/7.
12 See chapter 5.
13 Richard Scott, Declaration of independence, McNay, *The Guardian Past and Present*, 26.
14 Ibid.
15 Ibid.
16 Ibid.
17 Stead, The unclouded face of truth, McNay, *The Guardian Past and Present*, 49.
18 Alan Rusbridger, The Newsroom, McNay, *The Guardian Past and Present*, 3.
19 Ibid, ibid.
20 Madeleine Bunting, School for scandal, McNay, *The Guardian Past and Present*, 18.
21 Ibid, 19.
22 A liar and a cheat, Guardian, October 1, 1996.
23 Aitken to Stand Trial at Old Bailey, Guardian, December 8, 1998.
24 Mandelson, the minister and the 373,000 Loan, Guardian, December 22, 1998.
25 Bunting, School for scandal, McNay, *The Guardian Past and Present*, 19-20.
26 100 directors paid more than 1m last year, Guardian, October 5, 2002, and passim.
27 The Giving List, Guardian, November 5, 2001 and passim.
28 Bunting, School for scandal, McNay, *The Guardian Past and Present*, 20.
29 Ibid, 20-21.
30 Ibid, ibid.
31 Alan Rusbridger at a lecture in Nuffield College, Oxford, June 6, 2003.
32 Interview with Ian Mayes, readers editor, December 12, 2002.
33 Rusbridger, The Newsroom, McNay, *The Guardian Past and Present*, 3.
34 Interview with Mayes.

35 A crisis in its complexity, Guardian, January 27, 2003.

36 Interview with Mayes.

37 Personal communication, January 30, 2003.

38 Interview with Mayes.

39 Ibid.

Chapter Two: Early Days

1 Scott to Sacher, January 16, 1915. The Guardian Archive

2 Chaim Weizmann, *Trial and Error*, London, Hamish Hamilton, 1949, 190-191.

3 Weizmann to Scott, November 16, 1914. Meyer Weisgal, ed, *The Letters and Papers of Chaim Weizmann*, Oxford University Press, London, 1975, Vol. 7, 44.

4 David Ayerst, *Guardian – Biography of a Newspaper*, Collins, London, 1971, 383. Sacher and Weizmann's appointment to cover the 7th Zionist Congress, Guardian archive, A/W35/1.

5 Festival of Rosh Hashanah, MG, August 30, 1880; Jewish New Year, MG, September 1, 1880; New Year's Feast, MG, September 1, 1881; The Passover, MG, April 16, 1883; Jewish New Year, MG, September 16, 1886; Day of Atonement, MG, October 9, 1886, and many more.

6 New synagogue, MG, May 15, 1883; New Jewish school, MG, January 15, 1889; New synagogue, MG January 19, 1889.

7 Jewish Board of Guardians, MG, April 15, 1880 (And at least two references a year in the following years); Jewish Commercial Union, MG, May 14, 1886; A Yiddish newspaper, MG, September 3, 1887; Anglo-Jewish Association, MG, November 16, 1896; Chief Rabbi: proposed abolition, MG, September 19, 1911.

8 Palestine, MG, May 14, 1880. Incidentally, however symbolically, the state of Israel was announced on the same day, 68 years later.

9 Colonisation in Palestine, MG, June 22, 1891.

10 MG, August 13-20, 1900.

11 Jewish Colonial Trust, MG, September 18, 1900

12 Zionist movement: Shekel Day, MG, May 18, 1903.

13 Zionists of Africa, MG, December 9, 1904.

14 Zionist Congress Vienna, MG, August 29, 1913.

15 Colonies in Palestine, MG, September 2, 1913.

16 Weizmann to Leopold Greenberg, September 16, 1914, *The Letters and Papers of Chaim Weizmann*, vol. 7, 9-10.

17 Weizmann, *Trial and Error*, 191.

18 Ibid. 192

19 Weizmann to Scott, November 12, 1914, *The Letters and Papers of Chaim Weizmann*, Vol. 7, 38-39.

20 Weizmann, *Trial and Error*, 192.

21 Weizmann to Vera Weizmann, December 10, 1914, *The Letters and Papers of Chaim Weizmann*, Vol. 7, 77-78.

22 Weizmann, *Trial and Error*, 194.

23 Ibid, 144.

24 Ibid, 144.

25 The Jews and the War, MG, June 25, 1915.

26 Norman Rose, *Chaim Weizmann: A Biography*, London, Weidenfeld and Nicolson, 1986, 145.

27 Sidebotham to Scott, The Guardian Archive, A/S51/38a.

28 *The Letters and Papers of Chain Weizmann*, vol 7, 330-332 (notes).

29 Ibid. ibid.

30 Barnet Litvinoff, *Weizmann – Last of the Patriarchs*, Hodder and Stoughton, London, 1976, 92.

31 Trevor Wilson (ed), *The Political Diaries of C.P. Scott 1911-1928*, Collins, London, 1970, 164.

32 Ayerst, *Guardian: Biography of a Newspaper*, 384.

33 Weizmann to Scott, December 19, 1915, *The Letters and Papers of Chaim Weizmann*, vol 7, 257.

34 Tom Segev, Yemey Hakalaniot (Hebrew), Tel Aviv, Keter, 2001, 47.

35 Ayerst, *Guardian: Biography of a Newspaper*, 384

36 Scott to Weizmann, September 12, 1917, *The Letters and Papers of Chaim Weizmann*, vol 7, p509 footnote.

37 Guardian archive, A/S1/1-76

38 Weizmann, *Trial and Error*, 238-239.

39 Quoted in Margaret Macmillan, *Peacemakers: The Paris Conference of 1919 and Its Attempts to End War*, London, John Murray, 2001, 427.

40 Quoted in David Gilmour, The Unregarded Prophet: Lord Curzon and the Palestine Question, Journal of Palestine Studies, 25:3, Spring 1996.

41 Weizmann, Trial and Error, 262.

42 MG, November 9, 1917. Quoted in: Geoffrey Taylor, *Changing Faces: A history of the Guardian* 1956-88, 17.

43 One Country to Ourself, MG, August 9, 1921.
   The Future of Palestine – The Arab Point of View, MG, April 27, 1921.

44 Rose, *Chaim Weizmann, a Biography*, 143.

45 Segev, Yemey Hakalaniot, 40-43.

46 Ayerst, *Guardian: Biography of a Newspaper*, 386.

47 Scott to Weizmann, March 17, 1925, Guardian archive, A/W35/14

48 Segev, Yemey Hakalaniot, 95-96, 226.

49 Ibid, 95.

50 Ibid, 330.

51 Taylor, *Changing Faces: A history of the Guardian* 15.

Chapter Three: Waving a Zionist Flag

1 Ayerst, *Guardian – Biography of a Newspaper*, 383.

2 Werth to Crozier, February 2, 1933, quoted in *Ayerst,
Guardian – Biography of a Newspaper*, 508.

3 Crozier to Werth, February 6, 1933, quoted in Ayerst,
Guardian – Biography of a Newspaper, 508.

4 Rumours of a Terror, MG, March 13, 1933, quoted in *Ayerst,
Guardian – Biography of a Newspaper*, 508.

5 Ayerst, *Guardian – Biography of a Newspaper*, 509.

6 Voigt to Crozier, March 15, 1933, quoted in: Peter McNiven, The Guardian Archive
in the John Rylands University Library of Manchester, reprinted from Bulletin of
the John Rylands University Library of Manchester, Vol. 74, Number 2, Summer
1992, 78-79 and in Ayerst, *Guardian – Biography of a Newspaper*, 509-510.

7 Werth to Crozier, March 15, 1933, quoted in The Guardian Archive in the John
Rylands University Library of Manchester, 79.

8 Werth to Crozier, March 15, 1933, quoted in Ayerst,
Guardian – Biography of a Newspaper, 510.

9 Crozier to Werth, March 20, 1933, quoted in Ayerst,
Guardian – Biography of a Newspaper, 511.

10 Voigt to Crozier, March 15, 1933, quoted in Ayerst,
Guardian – Biography of a Newspaper, 509.

11 Anti-Semitism in Berlin, MG, March 10, 1933

12 No Planning Without Chips, Letters to the Editor, MG, March 26, 1933.

13 Persecution Very Mild, Letters to the Editor, MG, March 25, 1933.

14 MG, March 25, 1933, quoted in Ayerst, *Guardian – Biography of a Newspaper*, 513.

15 Ayerst, *Guardian – Biography of a Newspaper*, 513.

16 Ibid, 513-515.

17 Dachau Concentration Camp, MG, January 1, 1934.

18 MG, March 11, 1936.

19 What is It Worth? MG, October 1, 1938.

20 How the Jews in France Were Rounded Up, MG, September 3, 1942.

21 The German Massacre of Jews in Poland, MG, December 11, 1942.

22 MG, September 15, 1945.

23 Tom Segev, Yemey Hakalaniot (Hebrew), Jerusalem, Keter, 1999, 274-275. (Tom
Segev, *One Palestine Complete: Jews and Arabs Under the British Mandate*, London, Little
Brown, 2000).

24 A Matter of Facts, MG, April 20, 1931.

25 The Palestine Deadlock, MG, September 8, 1936.

26 More Troops in Palestine, MG, September 24, 1936.

27 Palestine Debate, MG, July 22, 1937.

28 Thinking it Over, MG, July 12, 1937

29 Ibid.

30 Letters to the Editor, The New Statesman and Nation, October 22, 1938.

31 Rose, Chaim Weizmann: A Biography, 237.

32 The Guardian Archive, 145/38/7.

33 Namier to Crozier, January 20, 1938, The Guardian Archive, 145/83/15.

34 Namier to Crozier, March 2, 1942, The Guardian Archive, 145/42/134.

35 Namier to Crozier, January 25, 1938, The Guardian Archive, 145/38/189.

36 Arab Pressure, MG, January 27, 1938.

37 A False Step, MG, March 7, 1940.

38 Palestine – The Three Zones, MG, April 8, 1940.

39 The Three Zones in Palestine, MG, April 10, 1940.

40 A Zionist Looks at Mr MacDonald's Speech, MG, March 15, 1940.

41 Namier to Crozier, September 17, 1940, The Guardian Archive, 145/40/161.

42 Namier to Crozier, March 27, 1942, The Guardian Archive, 145/42/206.

43 How to Win the War, MG, January 2, 1942.

44 Palestine Censorship and Questions to Colonial Office, MG, February 19, 1942.
   Recruiting in Palestine, MG, February 19, 1942.

45 Namier to Crozier, February 20, 1942, The Guardian Archive, 145/42/116.

46 Twenty Five Years, MG, November 2, 1942.

47 Namier to Crozier, October 29, 1943, The Guardian Archive, 145/43/35.

48 Weizmann to Crozier, December 6, 1940, The Guardian Archive, A/W35/23.
   The Refugees Come Home, MG, December 4, 1940.

49 Crozier to Weizmann, December 10, 1940, The Guardian Archive, A/W35/24.

50 Norman Rose, ed., *Baffy: The Diaries of Blanche Dugdale, 1936-1947*, London,
   Vallentine-Mitchell, 1973. 2. Victor Cazalet, aesthete and Conservative MP for
   Chippenham; Joshiah Wedgwood, Liberal MP for Newcastle-under-Lyme from
   1906 to 1919, then Labour MP for the same constituency from 1919 to 1942; Orde
   Wingate, general and leader of the Chindits, specially trained jungle fighters in
   Burma during the second world war.

Chapter Four: Delightfully Impatient with Bores

1 Avi Shlaim, *The Iron Wall*, London, Penguin, 2000, 24.

2 Ayerst, *Guardian – Biography of a Newspaper*, 562.

3 David Mckie, Keepers of the conscience, McNay, *The Guardian Past and Present*, 17-18.

4 Taylor, *Changing Faces*, 18.

5 Ayerst, *Guardian – Biography of a Newspaper*, 586.

6 Bevin's speech in the Commons, January 26, 1949, quoted in Taylor, *Changing Faces*, 18.

7 Lag Ba'omer could be seen as the Jewish equivalent to Guy Fawkes day. It
   celebrates the mutiny of Bar-Kochva against the Romans by lighting bonfires, in
   which puppets of the contemporary villain are burnt. Unfortunately for Bevin, he
   followed Hitler into the demonology.

8 Wadsworth to Cohen, Undated, The Guardian Archive, B/C164/4.

9 Wadsworth to Bentwich, Undated, The Guardian Archive, B/C164/3.

10 Segev, Yemey Hakalaniot, 386.

11 Palestine, MG, July 2, 1946.

12 MG, July 23, 1946.

13 Jewish and British attitudes, MG, July 23, 1946.

14 Crisis in Palestine, MG, July 23, 1946.

15 Time to go, MG, August 1, 1947.

16 Slight change of French opinion, MG, August 1, 1947.

17 MG, August 1, 1947.

18 Palestine, MG, December 13, 1947.

19 Shlaim, *The Iron Wall*, 25.

20 Summing Up, MG, May 15, 1948.

21 In the Wrong, MG, May 21, 1948.

22 Koestler, Israel: The Native Generation, MG, November 19, 1948.

Chapter Five: Alastair Hetherington Goes to War

1 Hetherington, *Guardian Years*, 1-2.

2 Ibid, 3.

3 Guardian, July 28, 1956, quoted in Hetherington, *Guardian Years*, 3.

4 Military Action, MG, August 2, 1956, quoted in Hetherington, *Guardian Years*, 5

5 Shlaim, *The Iron Wall*, 143-144.

6 Ibid, 144-145.

7 Ibid, 145, 162-163.

8 Ibid, 146, 149-152, 155-156, 160-162.

9 The Frontier, MG, November 5, 1955.

10 War Mongering, MG, October 4, 1955; Egypt and Blackmail, Guardian, October 21, 1955.

11 On the Border, MG, December 17, 1955.

12 Shlaim, *The Iron Wall*, 171-178.

13 Reprisals, MG, October 13, 1956.

14 Letters to the Editor, MG, 20, 25, 29, 30 October 1956.

15 Hetherington, *Guardian Years*, 7-8.

16 Guardian, September 13, 1956, quoted in Hetherington, Guardian Years, 9

17 Hetherington, *Guardian Years*, 8-9; Taylor, *Changing Faces*, 21-22.

18 To War?, MG, October 31, 1956, quoted in Hetherington, *Guardian Years*, 14

19 Ibid.

20 Taylor, *Changing Faces*, 19. More than 20 years later Harold Lever became a member of the board of directors of the Guardian and Manchester Evening News.

21 A Disaster, MG, November 1, 1956.

22 Ibid.

23 Letters to the Editor, MG, November 2, 1956.

24 Ibid.

25 Hetherington, *Guardian Years*, 13-14.

26 Taylor, *Changing Faces*, 24.

27 Hetherington, *Guardian Years*, 26-27

28 Shlaim, *The Iron Wall*, 179-183

29 Collusion, MG, November 20, 1956, paraphrased in Hetherington, *Guardian Years*, 22

30 Guardian, November 27, 1956, quoted in Taylor, *Changing Faces*, 23-24

Chapter Six: Watershed

1   A cooling breeze in Cairo, Guardian, January 18, 1964.

2   Jordan water and Arab refugees, Guardian, January 8, 1964.

3   Taylor, *Changing Faces*, 111.

4   Jordan waters, Guardian, January 27, 1964.

5   Ibid.

6   Prittie to Hetherington, Guardian archive, C1/P8/22/1.

7   Hetherington to Prittie, Guardian archive, C1/P8/23/2.

8   Hetherington to Prittie, Guardian Archive, C1/P8/31.

9   Hetherington to John Cole, Guardian Archive, C1/P8/40.

10 Hetherington's papers, Guardian Archive, C1/P8/43.

11 Taylor, *Changing Faces*, 111.

12 Shlaim, *The Iron Wall*, 238.

13 Ibid, 245.

14 Ibid, 244-245.

15 Hetherington, *Guardian Years*, 240.

16 Two UN forces or one?, Guardian, May 18, 1967.

17 No cause for killing UNEF, Guardian, May 19, 1967.

18 Deadlock over the Straits, Guardian, May 29, 1965.

19 Guardian, May 29, 1967.

20 Taylor, *Changing Faces*, 113.

21 Pledge for Mr Eshkol, Guardian, May 30, 1967.

22 A war to be stopped, Guardian, June 6, 1967.

23 Taylor, *Changing Faces*, 113-114; Hetherington, *Guardian Years*, 241-242.

24 Ibid.

25 Letters to the editor, Guardian, June 12, 1967.

26 Letters to the editor, Guardian, June 23, 1967.

27 Letters to the editor, Guardian, June 28, 1967.

28 Letters to the editor, Guardian, June 23, 1967.

29 Letters to the editor, Guardian, June 12, 1967.

30 Revenge or peace: the choice, Guardian, June 12, 1967.

31 Guardian, June 12, 1967.

32 Taylor, *Changing Faces*, 242.

33 Is it peace?, Guardian, September 11, 1967.

34 Taylor, *Changing Faces*, 59.

35 Ibid.

36 The Times, May 10, 1967.

37 Taylor, *Changing Faces*, 110.

38 Hetherington, *Guardian Years*, 242.

39 Taylor, *Changing Faces*, 116.

40 Casualties and propaganda, Guardian, July 24, 1967.

41 Why the refugees ran, Guardian, July 25, 1967.

42 Ibid.

43 Ibid.

44 The foundations of peace, Guardian, June 15, 1967.

45 Guardian, January 25, 1968.

46 Guardian, February 19, 1968.

47 Adams to Taylor, February 6, 1968, Michael Adams's personal archive.

48 Adams to Hetherington, February 12, 1968, Michael Adams's personal archive.

49 Hetherington to Adams, March 10, 1968, Michael Adams's personal archive.

50 Adams to Hetherington, March 12, 1968, Michael Adams's personal archive.

51 Hetherington, *Guardian Years*, 42. The alleged letter from Lord Marks failed to emerge later, in the libel suit discussed on above.

52 Interview with Michael Adams, Exeter, August 7, 2003.

53 Vanished villages, Guardian, June 5, 1968.

54 Michael Adams, CAABU and the Guardian, 1967-68, undated, Michael Adams's personal archive.

55 Interview with Michael Adams, Exeter, August 7, 2003.

56 Interview with Martin Woollacott.

57 Deposition by Michael Adams in the High Court of Justice, 1971 G. No, 3319, Guardian Newspapers Unlimited v. British Broadcasting Corporation and Richard Ingrams, Michael Adams's private archive.

58 Ibid.

59 Statement in open court, October 16, 1072, 1971 G. No, 3319, Guardian Newspapers Unlimited v. British Broadcasting Corporation and Richard Ingrams, Michael Adams's private archive.

60 Libel apology to the Guardian, Guardian, October 17, 1972.

61 David Hirst, *The Gun and the Olive Branch*, Faber, 2003

62 Hetherington to Adams, May 2, 1968, Michael Adams's private archive.

63 Adams to Hetherington, May 4, 1968, Michael Adams's private archive.

64 Survival of the fittest, Ha'aretz (English internet edition), January 8, 2004.

Chapter Seven: Shock and awe

1   Shlaim, *The Iron Wall*, 295-296.
2   Ibid, 309-318.
3   Avi Shlaim, Interview with Abba Eban, March 11, 1976, Israel Studies, volume 8, Number 1, Spring 2003.
4   No Man's Land, Guardian, January 25, 1970.
5   The Razor's Edge, Guardian, January 26, 1970.
6   Little Europe in the Sands, Guardian, January 27, 1970.
7   Hetherington, *Guardian Years*, 250.
8   What 'home' for the refugees? Guardian, February 19, 1970.
9   Hetherington, *Guardian Years*, 243.
10 Ibid, 244.
11 Ibid, ibid.
12 Hetherington's notes, the Guardian archives, C5/418/3.
13 To Mr Allon and Mr Eban, Guardian, February 27, 1970.
14 Hetherington, *Guardian Years*, 245.
15 Abba Eban, *An Autobiography*, London, Random House, 1977, 199.
16 Avi Shlaim, Interview with Abba Eban, March 11, 1976, Israel Studies, volume 8, Number 1, Spring 2003.
17 Ibid.
18 Hetherington's notes of a meeting with Eban, March 19, 1970, the Guardian archives, C5/423/1.
19 Hetherington, *Guardian Years*, 244.
20 Hetherington's notes of a meeting with Eban, March 19, 1970, the Guardian archives, C5/423/1.
21 Segev, Yemey Hakalaniot, 315, 349.
22 Benny Morris, *The Birth of the Palestinian Refugee Problem 1947-1949*, Cambridge, Cambridge University Press, 1987, 101-104, 121-123, 207-208, 210-211, 234-235.
23 Hetherington, *Guardian Years*, 245-6.
24 Hetherington's notes of a meeting with Allon, March 14, 1970, the Guardian Archive, C5/417/1.
25 Hetherington, *Guardian Years*, 246.
26 Hetherington's notes of a meeting with Allon, March 14, 1970, the Guardian Archive, C5/417/1.
27 Ibid.
28 Hetherington, *Guardian Years*, 245-246.
29 Ibid, 246.
30 Ibid.
31 Bulldozing through Arab History, Guardian, April 27, 1972.
32 Peter Jenkins, Guardian, May 5, 1971; Prittie to Hetherington, the Guardian archive, C1/P8/59/1.
33 The worst – and the best – of both worlds, Guardian, May 9, 1972; Prittie to

Hetherington, the Guardian archive, C1/P8/66.

34 Sadat turns to war, Guardian, October 8, 1973.

35 Two in the Wilderness, Guardian, October 27, 1973.

36 Taylor, *Changing Faces*, 169-170.

37 Ibid; Hetherington, *Guardian Years*, 42-43.

38 Hetherington, *Guardian Years*, 43, 44.

39 A Dialogue Worth Pursuing, Guardian, April 6, 1974.

40 Moshe Shemesh, The Palestinian Entity 1959-1974, Arab Politics and the PLO, London, Cass, 1988, 314-315.

41 Costs of living under arms, Guardian, November 14, 1974.

42 Gill to Hetherington, January 30, 1973, the guardian archive, C3/Z8/1.

43 See chapter 6.

44 Hetherington to Gill, 5 February 1973, the Guardian archive, C3/Z8/3.

45 Gill to Hetherington, August 15, 1974, the Guardian archive, C3/Z8/4.

46 Hetherington to Gill, September 4, 1974, the Guardian archive, C3/Z8/7.

47 A wild swipe at Israel, Guardian, November 12, 1975.

Chapter Eight: Sour Grapes

1 Israel voters pull away the peace rug. Menachem Begin elected Prime Minister, Guardian, May 19, 1977.

2 Interview with Martin Woollacott, London, October 21, 2003.

3 Interview with Peter Preston, Guardian editor 1975-1995, London, November 13, 2003.

4 Ibid

5 The Palestine Report (advertisement), Guardian, May 15, 1967.

6 Ma'alot: on May 15, 1974 a group of the Popular Front for the Liberation of Palestine took over a school in Ma'alot, north Israel, taking 90 children hostages. 27 were killed during the Israeli army's attempt to rescue the hostages by force. Munich: On September 5, 1972, during the Olympic Games in Munich, Germany, members of the Palestinian Black September group entered the Olympic Village and took 11 members of the Israeli delegation hostages. A failed attack by German forces led to a firefight. Nine hostages, five terrorists and one policeman were killed.

7 The Palestinians' next step, Guardian, May 15, 1976.

8 A brave man and a brave gamble, Guardian, November 17, 1977.

9 Ibid.

10 Can Israel follow through?, Guardian, September 22, 1978.

11 Now Mr Begin must move, Guardian, December 7, 1977; Nobody can forget the PLO, Guardian, December 17, 1977; Everything rests on the West Bank, Guardian, September 5, 1978; The peace of the open mouth, Guardian, September 22, 1978.

12 Israel plays it honourably, Guardian, May 4, 1978.

13 Interview with Martin Woollacott, London, October 21, 2003.

14 A Land which waits in Vain for Reinforcement, Guardian, May 28, 1979.

15 A Desert that blooms with machines, Guardian, May 29, 1979.

16 The tunnel vision of endless wars, Guardian, May 30, 1979.

17 Israel's West Bank burden, Guardian, May 31, 1979.

18 Ibid.

19 Ibid.

20 Letters to the Editor, Guardian, June 8, 1979.

21 Redefining the Role of Zionism, Guardian, June 11, 1979.

22 Ibid.

23 Ibid.

24 Ibid.

25 Hebron and the threat to peace, Guardian, February 15, 1980.

26 What they have they hold, Guardian, August 1, 1980.

27 Mr Peres and the West Bank, Guardian, December 22, 1980.

28 Ibid.

29 Jerusalem Post, August 3, 1982, quoted in Avi Shlaim, The Iron Wall, 411.

30 Avi Shlaim, The Iron Wall, 411.

31 The shooting of Mr Argov, Guardian, June 5, 1982.

32 New frontiers won't bring peace, Guardian, June 7, 1982.

33 Interview with Eric Silver, Jerusalem, May 22, 2003.

34 Ibid.

35 Interview with Martin Woollacott, London, October 21, 2003.

36 Interview with Eric Silver, Jerusalem, May 22, 2003.

37 Ibid.

38 A symbol of safety for Galilee, Guardian, June 8, 1982.

39 Israeli invaders get a Christian welcome, Guardian, June 23, 1982.

40 Israel's tough solution to Lebanon's crisis, Guardian, June 9, 1982.

41 Stopping at the one-way checkpoints of Beirut, Guardian, July 7, 1982.

It's easier to flatten Beirut than the PLO, Guardian, July 13, 1982.

42 The Israeli onslaught that raises the ghosts of peace, Guardian, July 5, 1982.

43 Israel and the massacre, Guardian, September 20, 1982.

44 Interview with Melanie Phillips, former Guardian columnist and leader writer, columnist for the Daily Mail, March 4, 2004.

45 We did not know what was going on, Guardian, September 20, 1982.

46 Letters to the Editor, Guardian, September 23, 1982. The claim about ignorance of religious practices apparently referred to the fact that in the cartoon Sharon wears a paper hat and his tank is decorated with balloons: the massacre took place during the Jewish new year (Rosh Hashanna), and paper hats and balloons are not a part of traditional celebrations.

47 Why Israel's moral blackmail has backfired, Guardian, September 20, 1982.

48 The verdict of Kahan, and the context, Guardian, February 9, 1982.

49 The Times, August 23, 1982; The Times, August 7, 1982.

50 The Times goes to war, Melvin J. Lasky, Encounter, September-October 1982; British media under fire, Hyam Corney, The Jerusalem Post, May 20, 1983.

51 The Times, August 13, 1982.

52 The Times, May 18, 1983.

53 Interview with Martin Woollacott, London, October 21, 2003.

54 Interview with Eric Silver, Jerusalem, May 22, 2003.

55 Interview with Peter Preston, London, November 13, 2003.

Chapter Nine: Raining Stones

1　Interview with Eric Silver.

2　Interview with Ian Black.

3　Ibid.

4　Ibid.

5　Violence takes over a West Bank town, Guardian, December 12, 1987.

6　Ibid.

7　West Bank escalation, Guardian, December 16, 1987.

8　Ratz's main agenda concerned a struggle against "religious coercion" and for citizens' rights. It did not have a socialist agenda, but was doveish in its attitude towards peace. Most of its voters were identified with the non-parliamentary movement Peace Now. Before the general elections of 1992 it united with two other Zionist dovish parties, socialist Mapam and Liberal free-market oriented Shinui, to form Meretz. The formation of Meretz reflected a feeling among Israeli liberals that peace has precedence over social agenda.

9　Plumping for Peres, Guardian, October 25, 1988.

10 No Can Likud, Guardian, December 1, 1988.

11 Doing time in Israel, Guardian, October 14, 1988. Morris gained some notoriety recently, when he publicly justified the policies of ethnic cleansing against Palestinians during the 1948 war, about which he made a significant contribution as a historian to its exposure. In an interview to Ha'aretz (Survival of the fittest, January 9, 2004.) he described Palestinians as "barbarians", who should be locked in "something like a cage". His old prison diaries show that in 1988 Morris thought that "what we are doing in the territories is a crime". His bigoted and condescending ideas were directed to fellow Jews of Mizrachi (Arab) origin. In his Guardian prison diary he wrote: "The sergeant, Shaul, from a development town in the south of Moroccan parentage, had a typical Sephardi (oriental Jewish) rightwing gut response to the situation"; "That a Jew, even in the heat of argument, and even if Sephardi, and perhaps only vaguely familiar with the Holocaust, can speak blithely of mass murder …".

12 Plucking the fruit of the intifada, Guardian, October 14, 1988.

It's a Battlefield. Guardian, 19 October 1988.

13 Young Arab Rambo lives on borrowed time, Guardian, December 1, 1989.

14 Guardians of intifada mete out bloody justice to suspected collaborators, Guardian, June 28, 1989.

15 Hard thinking in exile, Guardian, December 30, 1987.

16 Ibid.

17 The Losers in a contest no one can win, Guardian, December 24, 1987. In the same article, Israel was again compared to South Africa, with the justification: "It doesn't need a British newspaper to draw the parallel, however inexact, because the Israeli press has already done so."

18 Israeli Troops at the sharp end of provocation, Guardian, December 19, 1987.

19 Three more die in Gaza strip 'uprising', Guardian, December 19, 1987.

20 Ibid.

21 Time to redraw the Israeli maps of Gaza, Guardian, December 21, 1987.

22 Eyeless in Gaza, Guardian, January 28, 1989.

23 Ibid.

24 The Palestinian declaration of independence, Guardian, November 17, 1988.

25 A crunch for Israel, Guardian, November 22, 1988.

26 Arafat rides a winning streak, Guardian, December 7, 1988.

27 Arafat calls on Israel to make peace, Guardian, December 14, 1988; Israel denounces Geneva speech as 'deception', Guardian, December 14, 1988.

28 Defiant Israel builds settlements in West Bank, Guardian, December 16, 1988.

29 Gabby on Gaza, Guardian, January 18, 1989.

30 Silicon Gaza, Guardian, March 10, 1989.

31 The West Bank spiral, Guardian, May 2, 1989.

32 A sham of a plan, Guardian, July 7, 1989.

33 Israeli vent rage over bus deaths, Guardian, July 8, 1989.

34 Curfew for Palestinians as Israelis honour the dead, Guardian, May 10, 1989.

35 So successful was Israel's bargaining chips concept, that Obeid ended up being released only in 2004, together with his kidnapped colleague Mustafa Dirany, another 429 Arab and Palestinian prisoners, and the bodies of 60 Hizbullah militants. Israel received in return the dubious businessman Elhannan Tennenbaum, kidnapped by Hizbullah in 2002, and the bodies of three IDF Soldiers.

36 A killing with cause and effect, Guardian, August 1, 1989.

37 Damn Israel – and you damn the Jews everywhere?, Guardian, March 17, 1988.

38 Rabin must hit the ground running, Guardian, June 24, 1992.

39 Waiting for justice to be done, Guardian, January 25, 1993.

40 Now Israel itself is trapped in between. Guardian, January 29, 1993.

41 Signing up for a long hard road to peace, Guardian, September 11, 1993.

42 After the slaughter Israel must search its soul, Guardian, March 16 1994.

43 The peace process in paramount, Guardian, January 23, 1995.

44 Apartheid is not the answer, Guardian, January 28, 1995

Chapter Ten: Under Fire

1 Interview with Simon Tisdall, London, December 9, 2002.
2 Israel at the crossroads – Likud's election will be bad news for peace, Guardian, May 31, 1996.
3 Israeli elections: foreign leaders force smiles, Guardian, May 31, 1996.
4 Israel's opportunity: if Barak cannot deliver, who can? Guardian, May 19, 1999.
5 Barak on the brink, Guardian, July 10, 2000.
6 The price of failure, Guardian, October 3, 2000.
7 Standing up for peace, Guardian, October 24, 2000.
8 Interview with Jonathan Freedland, December 9, 2002.
9 Interview with Suzanne Goldenberg, January 16, 2004.
10 Ibid.
11 Interview with Ed Pilkington, London, December 9, 2002.
12 Interview with Alan Rusbridger, London, November 26, 2002.
13 Interview with Seumas Milne, London, March 3, 2004.
14 Interview with Alan Rusbridger, London, February 21, 2003.
15 Alan Rusbridger, Separate and Equal, The Spectator, June 2, 2001.
16 Interview with Linda Grant, London, Febtuary 21, 2003. Amira Hass covered the occupied territories for Ha'aretz. She used to live in Gaza and later in Ramallah. She often reports on the hardship of Palestinians day to day life, and states of mind in Palestinian society.
17 A mission to murder: inside the minds of the suicide bomber, Guardian, June 11, 2002; The men behind the suicide bombers, Guardian, June 12, 2002.
18 Interview with Alan Rusbridger, London, November 26, 2002.
19 Interview with Ed Pilkington, London, December 9, 2002.
20 City under curfew reaches boiling point, Guardian, October 5, 2002.
21 Interview with Chris McGreal, January 24, 2003.
22 The buisness of death, Guardian, July 12, 2000; Swiss toll, Guardian, July 13, 2000.
23 An enemy of the people, Guardian, July 14, 2000.
24 Interview with Ian Katz, London, January 14, 2003.
25 Tell the truth about Israel, Guardian, November 1, 2000.
26 Fair comment, Guardian, November 11, 2000.
27 Interview with Seumas Milne, London, February 3, 2004.
28 Israel simply has no right to exist, Guardian, January 3, 2001.
29 Thinking the unthinkable about Israel, Guardian, January 5, 2001.
30 Interview with Alan Rusbridger, London, November 26, 2002.
31 Between heaven and hell, Guardian, May 21, 2001.
32 Ibid.
33 Letters, Guardian, May 22, 2001.
34 Prophet of hope, Guardian, August 27, 2002.
35 Israel set on tragic path, says chief rabbi, Guardian, August 30, 2002.

36 Now every Jew must decide, Guardian, August 30, 2002.
37 Courage to speak out, Guardian, August 29, 2002.
38 Chief rabbi recants on religious tolerance, Guardian, September 27, 2002.
39 No dignity in denial, Guardian, January 6, 2003.
40 Interview with Jonathan Freedland.
41 See chapter 11.
42 Interview with Seumas Milne, London, February 3, 2004.
43 Interview with Ian Katz, London, January 14, 2003.
44 Interview with Ed Pilkington, London, December 9, 2002.
45 Interview with Alan Rusbridger, London, February 21, 2003.
46 Interview with Jonathan Freedland, London, December 9, 2003.
47 Interview with Ian Katz, London, January 14, 2003.
48 Secret peace talks in Britain, Guardian, June 1, 2002.
49 Interview with Jonathan Freedland, London, December 9, 2003.
50 Interview with Ewen MacAskill, London, December 9, 2002.
51 Interview with Ed Pilkington, London, December 9, 2002.
52 About us, www.honestreporting.com
53 Tips for writing good letters, www.honestreporting.com
54 Readers editor correspondence, courtesy of Ian Mayes.
55 Who's watching the Guardian, www.honestreporting.com, February 19, 2001.
56 Israel bus stop killer was on medication, Guardian, February 16, 2001.
57 Media manipulation, Guardian, February 22, 2002.
58 Ibid.
59 The Guardian's selective memory, www.honestreporting.com, August 15, 2002.
60 Ibid.
61 Interview with Alan Rusbridger.
62 Interview with Ed Pilkington.
63 Ibid.
64 Interview with Brian Whitaker, London, January 14, 2003.
65 Interview with Ewen MacAskill, December 9, 2002.
66 Interview with Simon Tisdall, December 9, 2002.
67 Interview with Chris McGreal, January 24, 2003.
68 Interview with Martin Woollacott, London, February 7, 2003.
69 Interview with Chris McGreal, January 24, 2003.
70 Interview with Alan Rusbrisger, London, 21 February 2003.
71 Interview with Ian Katz, London, January 14, 2003.
72 Interview with Jonathan Freedland, London, December 9, 2002.
73 Ibid.
74 Interview with Ian Katz, London, January 14, 2003.
75 Interview with Ian Mayes, London, December 12, 2002.
76 Interview with Brian Whitaker, London, January 14, 2003.
77 Interview with Chris McGreal, London, January 24, 2003.
78 Interview with Simon Tisdal, London, December 9, 2002.

79 Interview with Linda Grant, London, February 21 2003.

80 Interview with Ian Black, February 19, 2003.

81 War and pieces, Guardian, May 18, 2002.

82 The right to be heard, Guardian, June 3, 2002.

83 Interview with Ian Mayes, London, December 12, 2002.

84 Readers'editor correspondence.

85 Interview with Danny Seaman, Kol Ha'ir, October 11, 2002.

86 Letter from Alan Rusbridger to Danny Seaman, October 2002

87 Editors dismiss Israeli press chief's allegation of bias, www.Thestar.com, October 18, 2002.

88 Letter from Daniel Seaman to Alan Rusbridger, October 17, 2002, Alan Rusbridger's personal archive.

89 Seaman lets it slip, Guardian, October 17, 2002.

90 Interview with Simon Tisdall, London, December 9, 2002.

91 Richard Allan Green, Coverage of Mideast violence is unfair to Israel, JTA, March 18, 2001.

92 Interview with Yonatan Peled, Israeli foreign office spokesman, Jerusalem, May 20, 2003.

93 Interview with Alan Rusbridger.

94 Interview with Martin Woollacott.

95 Interview with Ian Katz.

96 Interview with Brian Whitaker, London, January 11, 2003.

97 Interview with Alan Rusbridger, London, February 21, 2003.

98 Interview with Alan Rusbridger, London, February 21, 2003.

99 About us, www.honestreporting.com.

Chapter Eleven: Aftermath

1 Dangerous liaisons, Guardian, April 16, 2004.

2 Sharon's triumph is Blair's defeat, Guardian, April 16, 2004.

3 Losing Falluja, Guardian, April 16, 2004.

4 Who will speak out, Guardian, April 17, 2004.

5 Israel was mentioned in the Guardian 2,471 times in 2002 and 2,111 times in 2003.

6 Robert Kilroy-Silk, We owe Arabs nothing, Sunday Express, January 4, 2004.

7 New Statesman, January 14, 2004.

8 BBC accused of bias against Israel, Guardian, April 1, 2004.

9 Anti-semitism and the Middle East conflict: fresh perspectives, with Varda Shiffer, Brian Klug, Anthony Lerman, London, February 9, 2004.

10 The essential difference of the Holocaust, Ha'aretz (Hebrew Edition), April 18, 2004.

11 Breaking an iron rule, Ha'aretz, April 21, 2004.

12 Haain Hashviit, vol.49, March 2004.

13 Interview with Melanie Philips, March 4, 2004.

14 Should we speak out?, the Israel Diaspora Trust, London, October 21, 2003. Participants: Jonathan Freedland, Ned Temko, Rabbi Sidney Brichto, Daniel Finkelstein.

15 Impotence of power, Guardian, October 8, 2003.

16 Anti-Zionism is anti-semitism, Guardian, November 29, 2003.

17 No, Anti-Zionism is not anti-semitism, Guardian, December 3, 2003.

18 Anti-semitism and the Middle East conflict: fresh perspectives, with Varda Shiffer, Brian Klug, Anthony Lerman, London, February 9, 2004.

19 Ibid.

20 A grotesque choice, Guardian, March 11, 2004.

21 Anti-semitism is a virus and it mutates, Guardian, March 15, 2004.

22 Good, bad and ugly, Guardian, November 29, 2003.

23 Interview with Ewen MacAskill, &&.

24 The Guardian as an example, Ma'ariv, March 26, 2004.

25 Interview with Jonathan Freedland, London, December 2, 2004.

26 Ibid.

27 Ibid.

28 Interview with Alan Rusbridger, London, February 11, 2004.

29 Interview with Jonathan Freedland, London, December 2, 2004.

30 Jonathan Freedland, Let's venture beyond confines of the club, Jewish Chronicle, November 7, 2003.

31 Interview with Alan Rusbridger, London. February 11, 2004.

32 Anti-semitism and the Middle East conflict: fresh perspectives, with Varda Shiffer, Brian Klug, Anthony Lerman, London, February 9, 2004.

33 Interview with Melanie Phillips, March 4, 2004.

34 What the war does to us, Guardian, November 29, 2003.

36 Ibid.

36 Inside the bubble, April 8, 2004

37 Interview with Alan Rusbridger, February 11, 2004.

38 Now Europeans see Israel as a threat to their existence, Guardian, November 7, 2003.

39 Interview with Martin Woollacott, London, October 21, 2003.

Appendix: In the Rubble of Jenin

1 Lt-Col Adir Haruvi, Jenin: the operational considerations, Hirsh Goodman and Jonathan Cummings, eds., The Battle of Jenin: A Case Study in Israel's Communications strategy, Tel Aviv University, Tel Aviv, 2003, p15.

2 Lior Yavne, Human rights and Jenin, The Battle of Jenin, p20.

3 Ze'ev Schiff, Facts, illusion and strategy, The Battle of Jenin, p18.

4 Toll of the bloody battle of Jenin, Guardian, April 10, 2002.

5 Refugees flee camp with reports of Israeli abuse, Guardian, April 12, 2002.

6 Ibid.

7 Bodies search begins in rubble, Guardian, April 13, 2002.

8 Ibid.

9 Ibid.

10 The lunar landscape that was Jenin refugee camp, Guardian, April 16, 2000.

11 Ibid.

12 Ibid.

13 Disaster zone hides final death toll, Guardian, April 17, 2002.

14 Evidence of Israeli contempt for Geneva Convention, Guardian, April 17, 2002.

15 Interview with Susanne Goldenberg, January 16, 2004.

16 Interview with Alan Rusbridger, 21 February 2003.

17 Interview with Ed Pilkington, 9 December 2002.

18 Interview with Jonathan Freedland, 9 December 2002.

19 Interview with Alan Rusbridger, 21 February 2003.

20 Interview with Jonathan Freedland, 9 December 2002.

21 Interview with Ian Katz, 14 January 2003. 22 Ibid.

23 Israel buries the bodies but cannot hide the evidence, Independent, April 13, 2002.

24 From the ruins of Jenin, the truth about an atrocity, Independent, April 20, 2002.

25 Even journalists have to admit they're wrong sometimes, Independent, August 3, 2002.

26 The Evening Standard, April 15, 2002

27 Bloodbath kept from the eyes of the world, Times, April 10, 2002; Jenin carnage makes Powell's job even tougher, Times, April 10, 2002.

28 Inside the camp of the dead, Times, April 16, 2002.

29 Interview with Ed Pilkington.

30 Our friends in Jenin, Guardian, April 11, 2002.

31 Immortal heroes of Jenin, Guardian, April 16, 2002.

32 Tongue-tied in Arafat's shattered bunker, Guardian, April 15, 2002.

33 Parallel universes, Guardian, April 17, 2002.

34 Sharon is taking us back to 1948, Guardian, April 30, 2002.

35 How Jenin battle became a 'massacre', Guardian, May 6, 2002.

36 Interview with Linda Grant.

37 The battle of the truth, Guardian, April 17, 2002.

38 Ibid.

39 Ibid.

40 Interview with Jonathan Freedland, 9 December 2002.

41 Interview with Martin Woollacott, 7 February 2003.

42 Interview with Ian Katz, 14 January 2003.

43 Interview with Brian Whitaker, 14 January 2003.

44 Interview with Suzanne Goldenberg, January 16, 2004.

45 Interview with Chris McGreal, 24 January 2003.

46 Interview with Ed Pilkington, 9 December 2002.

47 Interview with Alan Rusbridger, 21 February 2003.

48 Ibid.

49 Interview with Ewen MacAskill, 9 December 2002.
50 Interview with Simon Tisdall, 9 December 2002.
51 Truth-Seeking in Jenin, Guardian, 2 August 2002.
52 Interview with Martin Woollacott, 7 February 2003.
53 Israel plans unprecedented response to massacre, Guardian, March 28, 2002.
54 I felt shock waves and blacked out, Guardian, March 28, 2002.
55 On both sides the talk is only of war, Guardian, March 29, 2002.
56 How can I celebrate Passover when this is happening? Guardian, March 29, 2002.
57 As suicide bomber strikes again, Israeli soldiers see no hope for peace, Guardian, April 11, 2002.
58 Six killed by Jenin camp girl bomber, Guardian, April 13, 2002.

Biographies

1 Interview with Alan Rusbridger, London, November 26, 2002.

Index